hoopla

ARSENAL
PULP PRESS

VANCOUVER

hoopla

the art of
unexpected
embroidery

Leanne Prain

PHOTOGRAPHY BY JEFF CHRISTENSON

HOOPLA
Copyright © 2011 by Leanne Prain
Photographs copyright © 2011 by Jeff Christenson

ARSENAL PULP PRESS
Suite 101, 211 East Georgia St.
Vancouver, BC
Canada V6A 1Z6
arsenalpulp.com

The publisher gratefully acknowledges the support of the Government of
Canada (through the Canada Book Fund) and the Government of British
Columbia (through the Book Publishing Tax Credit Program) for its publishing
activities.

All photographs by Jeffrey Christenson unless otherwise noted.

Book design by Diane (Yee) Robertson, Electra Design Group
Cover photograph: *Hippo* by Tumim & Prendergast. Photo by Olivia Tumim.

Printed and bound in Hong Kong

LIBRARY AND ARCHIVES CANADA CATALOGUING IN PUBLICATION

Prain, Leanne, 1976–
    Hoopla : the art of unexpected embroidery / Leanne Prain.
Includes bibliographical references and index.
Issued also in electronic format.
ISBN 978-1-55152-406-1

    1. Embroidery. 2. Embroidery—21st century. 3. Embroidery
in art. I. Title.

TT770.P73 2011   746.44   C2011-900778-9

This book is dedicated to those who embroider
and to those who wish to learn.

Doilies embroidered by Eva Margaret Black,
my great-grandmother, in the 1950s.

Contents

Foreword

BETSY GREER

Embroidery. What I like most about it is how it can be, as the title of this book says, unexpected. It can be teeny tiny or massive and still catch you unawares. Having done various types of needlecraft, I especially love the intimacy of embroidery—the fairytale essence of using a needle and a thread, the idea that creation can mend as well as better.

After spending several years focused on knitting, I've moved on to cross-stitch. In 2005, I began a series of cross-stitch pieces based on international war graffiti. I felt so helpless in the face of the vast and visceral reality of war and horrified by how we have become so used to it—that it turns into backdrop instead of news. Sometimes, just walking down the street, I'd be humbled by the fact that thousands upon thousands of people can't walk down the street themselves because of war. Looking online, I saw anti-war graffiti pieces created by people around the world whose voices aren't being heard, and it was heart-breaking. Turning those rough, real images, painted on brick walls, into soft pieces of cross-stitch was a way of marking the presence of the pieces, a way of affirming what someone anonymous scribbled on a building thousands of miles away. And all those thousands and thousands of stitches ended up helping me find my own calm center amidst my anger and frustration at my government's foreign policy. Similar sentiments seem to echo in the work of many contributors in this book, as we find embroidery allows us to find that place within ourselves that is alive, meditative, strong, connected, and safe.

In giving us the chance to fully concentrate on what's happening with our hands and hoops, either by offering a meditative calm or a necessary respite from the chaos of the everyday, embroidery allows us to be silent but not subservient. This trademark silence can put things back in perspective, mend our thoughts, calm our confusion, energize us. The work leaves behind the mark of human hands, and as it grows toward its completion, it reminds us that there is perfection in the imperfection, both in our own lives and in our work. Like our individual lives, our work is malleable, in transition, a figment of our imaginations made real by needle, thread, and time.

The work in this book is proof that even the tiniest of movements (a single stitch) can change our attitudes, our minds, our days. Not only can embroidery fortify the maker, it can also fortify those who view it. It lets us know we're not alone, that there is power in making, that there is infinite beauty embedded in the smallest of acts and items. Whether we're stitching on playing cards, canvas, dolls, or a bed sheet, we're all saying, "We were here. This moment, this image matters." We're reclaiming, strengthening, and sharing our own voices, and in doing "so, hopefully helping others to do the same, to explore, play, create, and love with each and every stitch, just as with each and every breath.

Betsy Greer is the author of *Knitting for Good! A Guide to Creating Personal, Social, and Political Change, Stitch by Stitch* and runs the website **craftivism.com**.

International War Graffiti. Cross-stitch Series #3, Newcastle, 2008, floss on fabric, 6 × 10 in (15.24 × 25.4 cm)

Annie Coggan Crawford, *Marie Antoinette's Garden: Le Petit Trianon*,
2008, embroidery, fabric, bench, 34 (ht) × 40 (length) × 20 (depth) in
(86.36 × 101.6 × 50.8 cm). Photo: Jennifer Hudson

Acknowledgments

This book would not have been possible without the contributions, enthusiasm, and support of the following people:

I'd like to thank Jeff Christenson for everything he does. Thanks Jeff for the days (and nights) of hard work, the downtime, and everything in between.

Special thanks to Diane Farnsworth, Laura Farina, Angela Ready, Kat Siddle, and Susannah M. Smith for making the long journey of writing bright, and to my parents Connie and Dan Prain for setting me on a crafty path early on in life.

I sincerely appreciate the very photogenic crowd of friends who were willing to model projects: Erin Ashenhurst, Adam Farnsworth, Andrew Luketic, Mandy Moore, Julia Monks, Julie Morris, Angie Ready, Kat Siddle, Paul Skrudland, and Audrey Wang.

I'd like to acknowledge Cathy Christenson, Maryanne Chu, Emily Carr University of Art and Design, Otis Records, Christie Paterson, Shelley Prain, Angie Ready, Jim Sawada, and Kat Siddle for lending props and letting us take photographs in your homes and businesses.

Thanks to Diane Yee of Electra Design for creating another beautiful book. You are a pleasure to work with.

Thanks to Shyla Seller for championing the idea for this book, and to Robert Ballantyne, Cynara Geissler, Brian Lam, and Susan Safyan for allowing me the opportunity to bring some more textile mayhem to Arsenal Pulp Press. I feel honored to be able to work with such great people.

This book would not exist without the participation of the many artists, photographers, and designers who took the time to tell me about their lives, send files, and create original patterns. A huge and heart-felt thank you to the contributors who trusted me with their work and their stories: Amy Adoyzie, Cate Anevski, Joanne Arnett, Heather Bain, Jennifer Baker, Amanda Bowles, Malarie Burgess, Jason Cawood, Jamie Chalmers, Annie Coggan Crawford, Kirsten Chursinoff, Caleb Crawford, Jacque Lynn Davis, Natalie Draz, Jessica Dreker, Andrea Drawjewizc, Angela Duggan, Sarah Edwards, Ulrika Erdes, Karyn Fraser, Brette Gabel, Alyssa Glass, Betsy Greer, Jenny Hart, Sarah Haxby, Eliot M. Henning, Sarah Hernandez, The Hopeso Group, Marie Horstead, Jennifer Hudson, Takashi Iwasaki, Nicola Jarvis, Lynn Kearns, Abby Krause, Liz Kueneke, Siobhan Long, Aubrey Longley-Cook, Rosa Martyn, Ray Materson, Laura McMillian, Krista Muir, Johnny Murder, Rebekah Nathan, Penny Nickels, Esther Oh, Iviva Olenick, Andrew J. Phares, Claire Platt, Christopher Prendergast, Jo Safferton, Richard Saja, Ellen Schinderman, Kat Siddle, Laura Splan, Erin Stanton, Sarah Terry, Matilda Tumin, Olivia Tumim, Allison Tunnis, Barbara Randall, Alexandra Walters, Jenny Webb, Sasha Webb, and Sherri Lynn Wood.

Richard Saja, *Just This Once*, 2009, embroidery floss, toile, 23 in (58.42 cm) diameter. Photo: Richard Saja

CHAPTER 1

The Evolution
of Embroidery

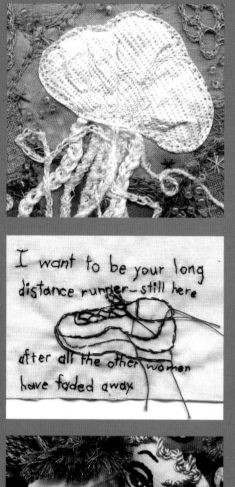

I want to be your long
distance runner—still here

after all the other women
have faded away

Taking Stitching Seriously

Like many of the things that have been cast aside with our society's love affair with technology, embroidery is a practice often relegated to nostalgic hobbyists. Akin to activities such as sign painting or cobbling, hand stitching is rarely acknowledged in our contemporary culture. Not only have we built industrial factories to replicate embroidery, we can clone animal DNA, use mobile devices to manage our schedules, and unlock doors with a retinal scan. We seem to have little in common with those who stitched through the centuries for reasons of economic or marital security. So, why is hand embroidery important now?

Find slowness in our fast paced world! Stitch and create something beautiful. —SASHA WEBB

Unlike our ancestors, who were often indentured servants of the needle and thread, we have the opportunity to revive embroidery as a contemporary art form. While our faces often glow in the light of laptops, many of us still have the urge to express ourselves through the use of tactile materials, and embroidery offers a wonderful, slow-paced way to do so. The aim of this book is to encourage you to pick up a needle and thread with the intention of exploring stitching as a creative medium.

Embroidery has such scope; it can be so low-brow, common, pre-fab as well as highbrow, uncommon, and unique. —SARAH HAXBY

When embroidering, the person stitching is often seen bent over a hoop in quiet repose. This posture is often associated with silence, which can be confused with subservience. Do not be fooled! The unconventional embroiderers profiled in this book include conceptual artists, guerrilla stitchers, manbroiderers, a horror-movie fiend, a beatbox celebrity, young feminists, abstractionists, an attendee of the Royal School of Needlework, and even an anarchists or two. Whether a long-time gallery artist or an embroidery newbie, each contributor has

Jenny Webb, *Klaatu Barada Nicto*, 2009, Aida cloth, embroidery thread, lace, cloth, 12 × 10 in (30.48 × 25.4 cm). Photo: Jenny Webb. "I love cult movies and movie quotes. So, I decided to mix two of my favorite things and make quote-themed cross-stitch pieces. They look like something you would find in your grandma's powder room, but on closer inspection, you find they have one of your favorite lines from *Raising Arizona* or *Dune*."

(FACING PAGE) Kirsten Chursinoff, *Jellyfish*, 2010, floss, thread, beads, thread fabric, 4 × 4 in (10.16 × 10.16 cm). Photo: Ernst Schneider

Iviva Olenick, *Still Here*, 2009, embroidery on fabric, 3.75 × 2 in (9.53 × 5.08 cm). From the collection of Emily Levin. Photo: Iviva Olenick

Jacque Lynn Davis, *Silly Little Dolls*, 2009, dolls made from upholstery fabric samples and other notions from the St. Louis Teacher's Recycle Center, filled with recycled bags, each approx. 12 in (30.48 cm) tall. Photo: Jacque Lynn Davis

Sherri Lynn Wood, based on tattoo designs by Kate Hellenbrand, detail of *Sailor FeeBee*. Photo: Sherri Lynn Wood

a strong viewpoint on their art, technique, and place within this long-practiced discipline. While it is impossible to cover the entire contemporary embroidery movement within one book, these pages investigate the practices of a handful of those who really know how to work a needle and thread—and they have a lot to say about it!

The Slow Stitch

Like all other forms of human expression, embroidery is a means of communication. The stitches, like handwriting or drawing, make marks. A stitch can form a mark of love, a mark of hate, or simply indicate "I was here."

My hand makes imperfect letters and imperfect stitches. But I know my handwriting from anyone else's and I love it—just like I love the exact color of my eyes—because it's mine. My artwork is marked with my hands, too. It's as personal to me as my fingerprints. My heavy, clumsy hands have been all over it. A thousand stitchers with a thousand embroidery kits couldn't make what I made, because it's mine. It comes from my very personal hands.
—ALEXANDRA WALTERS

The care and attention that embroidery requires demands that you give it the world's most valued commodity: time. The slow art of embroidery is time—time spent, time wasted, or time valued. It serves to mark an occasion when the embroiderer was fully present in their craft.

Both [Craft and the Slow Movement] think through where things are made and by whom and engage in ideas of provenance, of being immersed…in a rich narrative of human experience. They ask us to slow down, perhaps not literally, but certainly philosophically, and to reflect on other and perhaps more thoughtful ways of doing things. —HELEN CARNAC, *Taking Time: Craft and the Slow Revolution*

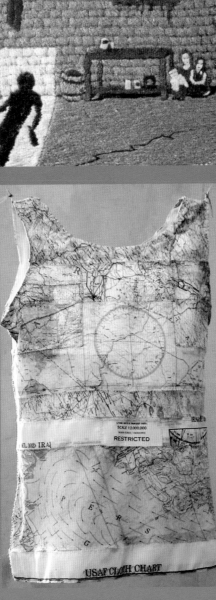

(FACING PAGE) Jenny Webb, *You Can't Really Dust for Vomit*, 2009, Aida cloth, embroidery thread, lace, cloth, 8 × 6 × 1.5 in (20.32 × 15.24 × 3.81 cm). Photo: Jenny Webb. Inspired by a quote from the movie *This Is Spinal Tap*.

(THIS PAGE) Tumim & Prendergast, detail of *Fall Fig Leaves, Farewell to a Flimsy Disguise*. Photo: Olivia Tumim

Ray Materson, *untitled*.

Ulrika Erdes, *Public Embroidery: Crossstitched Seat*, 2007, embroidery floss on upholstery, 7 × 7 in (17.78 × 17.78 cm). Photo: Ulrika Erdes

Annie Coggan Crawford, detail of *Vicksburg Chair*, 2010, from Civil War Furniture, embroidery on upholstery, chair, 34 (ht) × 40 (length) × 20 (depth) in (86.36 × 101.6 × 50.8 cm). Photo: Caleb Crawford

Liz Kueneke, detail of *Ribbons and War Machines*, 2001, a baby's dress made from a double-sided cloth military map of Iraq and Afghanistan, 10 × 19.5 × 4 in (25.4 × 49.53 × 10.16 cm). Photo: Liz Kueneke

TATTOOED BABY DOLLS:
An Interview with Sherri Lynn Wood

San Francisco-based artist Sherri Lynn Wood has used embroidery as a central motif in several works. Her Tattoo Baby Doll Project *brought together the diverse social communities of embroidery art fans and tattoo enthusiasts.*

Q: **How did the *Tattoo Baby Doll Project* come about?**

A: In 1998, I attended a three-month residency at the Headlands Center for the Arts outside of Sausalito, California. While I was there, I read Rozsika Parker's *The Subversive Stitch*, which shows how embroidery was both oppressive and empowering to women throughout history. Embroidery provided a sense of community and solidarity for women to express themselves in subversive ways. I drove across country for the residency and, along the way, stopped at thrift shops, where I picked up a lot of cloth-bodied baby dolls.

Headlands Center is not far from San Francisco, so I would go there a lot. There was a huge renaissance in tattooing going on, and I saw a lot of tattoos on women. I started to notice that some looked like the traditional embroidery images that I saw in *The Subversive Stitch*. I started thinking about the relationship of images to women; back then, women

embroidered images on cloth, but now they're getting those images on their own bodies to express themselves.

After I left the residency, I started looking up female tattoo artists to ask them if they wanted to participate. I sent them the cloth-bodied dolls and asked them to do whatever they wanted: to name the doll and write a statement or tell a story about the doll and draw the tattoos. When they sent the dolls back to me, I interpreted their drawings with embroidery. I worked with about sixteen different artists; a lot of these women were forerunners in tattoo art in the 1990s.

Q: **How does narrative play into this work?**

A: The stories that the tattoo artists told were very interesting. Kate Hellenbrand's *Sailor FeeBee* was covered in old sailor tattoos. The story was about her struggle to become a tattoo artist and her struggle to have a choice about what tattoos

Tattoo Baby Doll Project show by Sherri Lynn Wood
at Lump Gallery, Raleigh, North Carolina, 2000.
Photo: Sherri Lynn Wood

Sherri Lynn Wood, based on tattoo design
by Laura Sadaati, *Good Time Girl,* 2001
found doll, embroidery floss, 26 × 16 × 13 in
(66.04 × 40.64 × 33.02 cm). Photo: Sherri
Lynn Wood

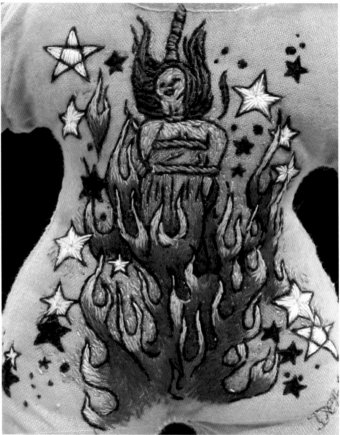

Sherri Lynn Wood, based on tattoo designs by Sarah Peacock, *Lydia the Protégé*, 2000, baby doll, embroidery floss, 26 × 16 × 13 in (66.04 × 40.64 × 33.02 cm). Photo: Sherri Lynn Wood

Sherri Lynn Wood, based on tattoo designs by Debbie the Illustrator, detail of *Destiny*, year unknown, found doll, embroidery floss, paint, 26 × 16 × 13 in (66.04 × 40.64 × 33.02 cm). Photo: Sherri Lynn Wood

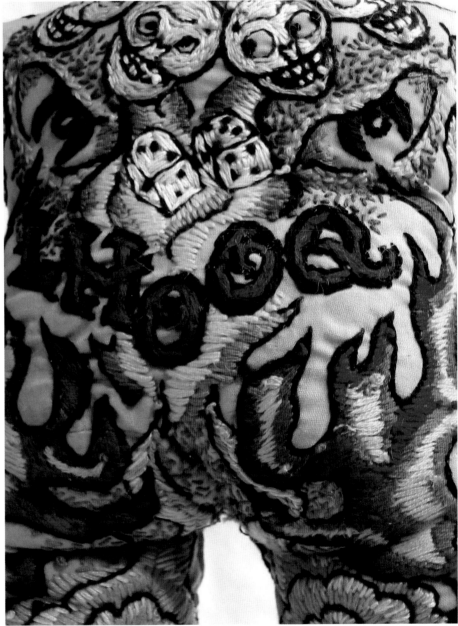

Sherri Lynn Wood, based on tattoo designs by Denise de la Cerde, *Hot Ass Baby*, 2000, found doll, embroidery floss, 26 × 16 × 13 in (66.04 × 40.64 × 33.02 cm). Photo: Sherri Lynn Wood

Sherri Lynn Wood, based on tattoo designs by Denise de la Cerde, Detail of *Hot Ass Baby*. Photo: Sherri Lynn Wood

she wanted to have on her own body. She would go to a tattoo parlor, and if she wanted an anchor or a sailboat or something, the men in the shop would suggest a bird or a flower or a heart. The doll said a lot about her struggles to becoming a leader in the field. She was one of the very first women to have her own shop.

I read Rozsika Parker's *The Subversive Stitch*, which shows how embroidery was both oppressive and empowering to women throughout history. Embroidery provided a sense of community and solidarity for women to express themselves in subversive ways.

Some of those dolls have 100 hours of embroidery in them, and I did all of it myself. One thing I discovered in talking to the tattoo artists is that it takes about the same time to hand-embroider an image on a doll as it does to tattoo a body suit onto a person.

The dolls are a snapshot of women in tattooing at that particular moment. If I did the project again, with women or with men, I would get a completely different range of both images and stories. They became a historical record of the culture and the ideas and beliefs at that moment in time.

(ABOVE) Sherri Lynn Wood, *repent*, 2003–2007, found blanket, clothing scraps, wood, string, safety pins, 72 × 70 in (182.88 × 177.8 cm). A communal mourning project concerning the war in Iraq. The names of approximately 1,500 American and Allied soldiers and Iraqi civilians who have died in the war are hand-stitched on coffin-shaped fragments of red clothing and appliquéd onto a blue blanket to spell the word repent. Photo: Sherri Lynn Wood

(FACING PAGE) Sherri Lynn Wood, based on tattoo design by Kim Reed, *Forever in My Heart*, 1999, found doll, embroidery floss, 26 × 16 × 13 in (66.04 × 40.64 × 33.02 cm). Photo: Sherri Lynn Wood

Q: **What are you working on now that the *Tattoo Baby Doll Project* has come to an end?**

A: I have an ongoing embroidery project around the war in Iraq. The *prayer banners* (*mercy* and *repent*) are a communal bereavement project inspired by Elizabeth Roseberry Mitchell's Graveyard Quilt from the 1840s.

In 2003, the war in Iraq began, and my mom passed away on Christmas Eve. In my feelings of anger and sadness, I thought a lot about families dealing with death around the holidays, especially those who lost loved ones in the war.

At the time I began the *prayer banner* project, 240 American soldiers had died in the war, so I thought, why don't I sew the names of the soldiers onto these coffins and put them on this blanket? For me, the actual stitching of the name of the soldier was an act of prayer or a meditation that connected my loss to the loss of others. I began to realize, however, that I wasn't going to stitch all the names myself. It was more meaningful to stitch with other people, so I began holding sewing circles.

The coffins are sewn onto the blankets to spell out different words. On the very first blanket, *repent*, the coffins actually spell out the word. It's very subtle. The second blanket spells out the word "mercy," and the third blanket will spell out the word "glory."

I think what people connect to [with these projects] is the intense amount of time [that went into them]. Each name easily represents thirty to forty-five minutes of stitching. Most people have lost someone. They often pick the name they want to stitch by choosing one that they connect to in some way; it might be their age, a location, or a family name.

I remember somebody saying to me that they thought about all of the time it took to stitch the names and of all of the lives lost—the wasted time and wasted lives, lives that should never have been wasted. The war can be overwhelming. A lot of times, people can't talk about it. Stitching the name of the dead is a simple activity that allows people to connect to their sense of communal loss, and it allows people who wouldn't normally do this sort of activity to interact with each other.

Find Sherri online at **daintytime.net**, **mantratrailer.com**, and **passagequilts .com**.

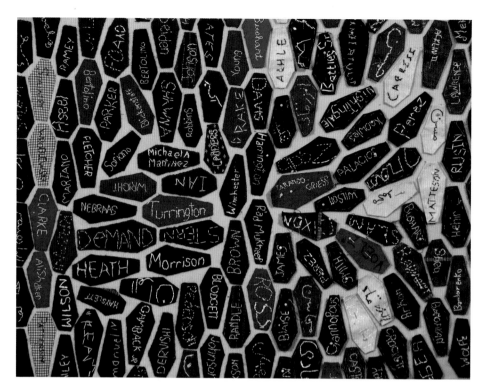

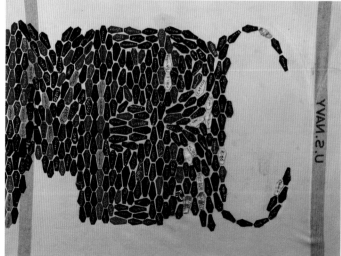

Sherri Lynn Wood, detail of *mercy*. Photo: Sherri Lynn Wood

Sherri Lynn Wood, *mercy*, 2008, cotton, thread, recycled materials, 6 × 8 ft (1.8 × 2.4 m). A prayer banner in progress; the names of 350 American and Allied soldiers and Iraqi civilians who died in the war were stitched by volunteers. Photo: Sherri Lynn Wood

Sherri Lynn Wood and her baby doll project. Photo: Sherri Lynn Wood

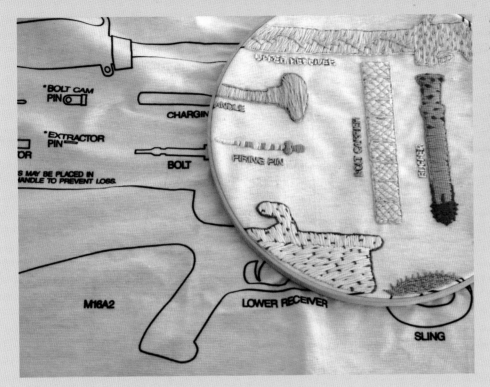

Andrew J. Phares, detail of *At Needle Point*, 2000, military drop cloth, embroidery floss, 20 × 32 in (50.8 × 81.28 cm). According to Andrew, "It's a US Army-issue drop cloth used by soldiers to keep track of all the parts of their M16 assault rifles when they are disassembled for cleaning. I was given this drop cloth by someone who was retired from the military. When I first saw the cloth, I thought it looked so much like a store-bought pre-printed embroidery pattern that I just put a hoop on it and stitched everything within the hoop in a fleshy color to complement the phallic shapes of the gun parts. I left it in the hoop with a threaded needle stuck through it as if Grandmother had just set down her work for a moment."
Photo: Andrew J. Phares

Early embroideries were stitched to tell religious and social histories, and they depicted scenes not only of peaceful domestic life, but also the horrors of conquest.

A Brief and Incomplete History of Embroidery

If you've ever picked up a needle and thread, chances are that you've pricked your fingers once or twice. While sticking yourself with a needle can seem contrary to a craft that often conjures up imagery of lovely florals and doves, embroidery has often mixed pleasant imagery with uncomfortable circumstances. Early embroideries were stitched to tell religious and social histories, and they depicted scenes not only of peaceful domestic life, but also the horrors of conquest. Embroidered cloth has been a consistent element in ceremonies throughout the world, and it retains a presence in the birth, death, and marriage rituals of many cultures. Embroidery has accompanied the human race at our finest and our darkest moments.

Embroidered cloth has been found in Egyptian tombs and on Indian appliqués from as early as 2000 BCE. In the Middle East, needlework had matured by the fifth century BCE, and by the fourth century BCE, stitchers in China were creating elaborate embroideries on the fine surfaces of silk and gauze. In the fifth century, Chinese embroidery spread to Korea and Japan, and the Moors carried their embroidery techniques into Western Europe. In many cultures, stitchers were taught to embroider through oral instruction, and this knowledge passed from one person to another so that the design sensibilities of embroidery expanded as each culture widened its sphere of influence.

Embroidery has evolved under the influences of religious migrations and technological advancement. In first-century Egypt, Christianized Egyptians created detailed textiles with Christian themes using straight stitches and satin stitches. The spread of Islam from the Middle East to

Jacque Lynn Davis, *Toile with Attitude*, 2010, cotton toile and embroidery thread, 11 × 13 in (27.94 × 33.02 cm). Photo: Jacque Lynn Davis

North Africa influenced designs in North Africa by discouraging imagery of humans and animals. In Central Asia, nomadic peoples adapted embroidery motifs to adorn their costumes, yurts, and animal traps to ward off danger, and to identify their cultural identities as they moved from one region to another.

> A woman who had nimble fingers for embroidery symbolized all the desirable attributes of a wife: obedience, silence, and a willingness to follow instructions.

While the earliest extant needleworks existed in the Maya, Inca, and Aztec cultures and pieces dating from 900–400 BCE have been found, the nature of stitching changed in South America as the peoples of this continent had contact with conquerors from Spain and Portugal. Visiting missionaries encouraged cultural changes, such as wearing clothes, which were often adorned with embroidery.

While wool embroidery remnants have been found from the first century, it was the Bayeux Tapestry, created in 1077 to capture the Norman Conquest and the Battle of Hastings, that most resembles what we think of as embroidery today. The Tapestry, stitched in ten colors of wool, featured many kinds of embroidery stitches, including cross-stitch, buttonhole stitch, satin stitch, and running stitch. It also has a running narrative that viewers can follow scene by scene, and has been referred to as the world's "first comic book."

Until the medieval era in Europe, embroidery was not viewed as a gendered craft but as an art form. Embroidery was created in guilds, monasteries, nunneries, and schools and was considered an equal art form to that of painting or sculpture by the clergy. Both men and women contributed equally in telling ecclesiastical stories through their stitching. But, as author Rozsika Parker wrote in her excellent history of embroidery, *The Subversive Stitch*, "to know the history of embroidery is to know the history of women." In many cultures, stitching was used to demonstrate not only women's skills but their place in society. Embroidery was used to mark milestones in their lives, to signal changes in their marital status, or to commemorate the births and deaths of their children.

In the fifteenth and sixteenth centuries, most young women in the western world didn't attend schools, but spent hours learning skills such as embroidery. They often stitched letters that they themselves could not read. A woman's worth was not measured by her knowledge of educational subjects but by the quality of her embroidery—stitched embellishments were often counted among the household valuables, after livestock holdings and grain. A woman who had nimble fingers for embroidery symbolized all the desirable attributes of a wife: obedience, silence, and a willingness to follow instructions.

While oral cultures and craft teaching have remained strong in many parts of the world, in Western countries, the development of the printed pattern affected embroidery's cultural value in Europe and colonized North America. During the seventeenth to nineteenth centuries, young girls between the ages of six and fifteen were taught to stitch samplers. The first extant sampler was from England and then, as commercial samplers proliferated, the craft spread to North America and other parts

I tried to reconnect with an old Lover. I thought there might be a shared space to return to, or something left unfinished. I missed his thick, dark hair and long body. After a few emails, I remembered why it didn't work out. He would get inside my skin, open me up completely, stomp around my apartment naked, sleep curled up beside me, then leave abruptly the next morning, muttering about an appointment. His kisses, however gentle, did not placate me. It's like he was saying, I'll give this much but no more.

(THIS PAGE) Iviva Olenick, *How I Left My Phantom Lover*, 2007, embroidery on fabric, 5 × 9.25 in (12.7 × 23.50 cm). Photo: Iviva Olenick

Liz Kueneke, detail of *The Urban Fabric—El Tejido Urbano* (*Barcelona, Spain*), 2008. Embroidered map on cloth sheet, threads, needles, foldable embroidery table, 3.25 × 6.5 ft (0.99 × 1.98 m). Photo: Liz Kueneke

Andrew J. Phares, detail of *Cover Your Shame*. Photo: Andrew J. Phares

Jenny Hart, *Dirty Face, Crowning Glory*, 2003, hand-embroidery on cotton panel, 17 × 18 in (43.18 × 45.72 cm). Collection of Dan Ferarra. Photo: Jenny Hart

(NEXT PAGE) Eliot M. Henning, *Embroidoid 1, detail*, 2010, yarn on canvas with spraypaint and marker, 19.5 × 16 in (49.53 × 40.64 cm). Photo: Eliot M. Henning

(THIS PAGE) Mr X Stitch, *Bill Hicks*, 2009, variegated floss on black Aida cloth, 5 in (12.7 cm) in diameter. Photo: Jamie Chalmers

Sarah Haxby, *Free Trade Agreement, 2009*, embroidery thread and vintage wool on canvas, 17 × 17 in (43.18 × 43.18 cm).

Penny Nickels, *Clearly You Haven't Earned Them Yet*, 2009, hand embroidery with hand-spun silk on hand-dyed silk, pheasant wing, 14 in (35.56 cm) in diameter. Photo: The Hopeso Group

of the world. It was particularly popular among settler communities in Canada and the US.

The sampler (the word derives from "examplar," an example to be followed), often consisted of alphabets and numbers that aided in the teaching of basic literacy and mathematics to girls. Samplers displayed the skills of the embroiderer and served as a reference for different stitches and patterns. A completed sampler included the dates when the stitching began and ended, the maker's name and, often, her birthday. The sampler was hung in a place of pride in the home, showing that a young girl was being raised correctly by her family—and was developing into suitable marriage material. Not all girls enjoyed creating samplers, though. One of the most famous samplers, dated from around the eighteenth century, exhibited its maker's disgruntled feelings towards her craft. It was signed: "Patty Poke did this and she hated every stitch she did in it. She loves to read much more."

In the Victorian era, samplers began to slip out of fashion when new commercial patterns came into vogue. During the Industrial Revolution, literacy grew among women from the lower classes, who also lost their work as embroiders, work which was increasingly done by machines. While these hand skills were no longer required of working-class women, middle- and upper-class ladies of leisure began to take up embroidery for entertainment. This abrupt cultural change altered the perception of embroidery, inherently linking it to the notion of an idle pastime for the well-heeled. Some feminist historians suggest, however, that embroidery was a medium that brought women together to socialize, to express their personalities through stitching, and to allow them the rare luxury of interacting with each other without having to attend to the men in their lives.

I love how portable embroidery is, and I have always used handiwork to soothe myself during family gatherings or stressful times. —SASHA WEBB

Embroidery guilds were established in Europe and North America in the nineteenth century. The most famous of these were at the Glasgow School of Art (founded 1845) and the Royal School of Needlework in Britain (founded 1872). While the embroidery world changed with the advent of printed patterns for the masses, the development of guilds formalized the training, teaching, and preservation of professional embroiderers in the Western world.

In the late nineteenth century, the British Suffragette Movement used embroidery as a tool of communication and power, associating an emblem of femininity with women's strength. The suffragettes modified and subverted the union banners and political petitions of their day by embroidering signatures on handkerchiefs while imprisoned or on hunger strikes, and embellished parasols—the ultimate symbols of weak femininity—with suffrage-group initials and colors. Large silk parade banners were stitched with the names of local professional associations or accomplished women who served as role models to the feminist cause, among them poet Elizabeth Barrett Browning, Queen Victoria, and scientist Marie Curie.

Between the 1880s and the 1930s, the Arts and Crafts Movement, led by socialist William Morris, sought to elevate needlework as a craft and an art both technically masterful and creatively original. Morris declared, "Have nothing in your houses that you do not know to be useful or believe to be beautiful," and he envisioned a time when the gender divide between the domestic and fine arts would be eliminated. However, after picking apart some crewel work, Morris appointed his

daughter May to run his firm's embroidery workshop where women workers executed and crafted his designs.

One of the most unexpected uses of embroidery was within the Dada art movement (ca. 1916–22). Taught to stitch by artist Sophie Taeuber-Arp, the painter Jean (Hans) Arp also began to make embroideries utilizing natural and geometric forms, considering them "unburdened by tradition." Hannah Hoch, the only woman in the Berlin Dada school, mixed embroidery and lace with domestic mottos in order to create gendered commentary on the sexism of her society and many of her contemporaries.

In the 1940s and '50s, pattern companies such as Vogart, Aunt Martha's, and Workbasket released popular commercial designs to be stitched onto pillowcases, baby clothes, and table linens. Mostly available at convenience stores (known "five-and-dimes"), their motifs included days of the week, "gay kittens and puppies," "frisky lambs," and "Mr & Mrs" monograms. These designs were highly popular with the post-war generation and are coveted by collectors today.

A needlework revival occurred in North America and Europe in the

late 1960s and early 1970s, which popularized denim embroidered with groovy, psychedelic images such as butterflies, rainbows, and abstract patterns. Stitching once again became a popular pastime associated with anti-materialism and the back-to-the-land movement.

In 1973, former Los Angeles Rams and New York Giants football player Rosey Grier created a beginner needlepoint book for men and boys: *Rosie Grier's Needlepoint for Men*. Introducing the skill by stating, "If Rosey's massive hands can create lovely designs on canvas, then so can just about anyone's," the book was introduced as "unique because it is masculine" and included patterns such as gangsters holding bombs, golf-club covers, Japanese warriors, directors' chairs, and manly monograms.

Making or designing something for a special lady in your life can be better than sending her roses or wining and dining her in some classy joint. —ROSEY GRIER

In the late 1970s, embroidery was once again used by the feminist movement. In 1979, artist Judy Chicago debuted an art installation piece titled *The Dinner Party*. Created when the accomplishments of women were still not broadly acknowledged in the fields of publishing or academia, Chicago designed a table that held an embroidered place-setting for thirty-nine notable or illustrious female guests. The goal of Chicago's project was to "end the ongoing cycle of omission in which women were written out of the historical record." Using "thread as brush stroke," Chicago followed *Dinner Party* with other works that employed needlepoint and embroidery to create controversial high-brow art that asserted the strength and power of women. Notably, she produced *The Birth Project,* which included dozens of needlepoint images of the female experience of labor, a subject largely ignored by art history.

During the 1980s and early 1990s, hand-embroidered designs began to be rapidly commercialized. Canvas prints of ready-made patterns were created and distributed through hobby shops and craft superstores. Ducks in bonnets, cartoon characters, Americana, and kitten patterns proliferated.

The main thing I love about stitching is that it combines creativity with a simple, repetitive process that enables your brain to enter a somewhat meditative state. It's extremely relaxing, and the rewards when you complete a piece and share it with someone are priceless. —JAMIE CHALMERS, MR X STITCH

While embroidery became increasingly associated with kitchsy consumer designs, the DIY movement of the 1990s and early 2000s sparked an uprising in unconventional craft projects. In 2001, Austin, Texas, crafter Jenny Hart developed her company Sublime Stitching, which specialized in embroidery kits of retro-cool patterns. In 2003, Julie Jackson launched Subversive Cross-stitch, a series of cross-stitch pattern kits featuring cutting phrases such as "Bite Me" and "#@%$!!"

¡Lucre Libre! a Sublime Stitching pattern. One 8.5 × 11 in (21.59 × 27.94 cm) sheet of a multi-imprinting, iron-on embroidery pattern. Photo: Jenny Hart

Rites of Passage: Embroidery Traditions

- In Romania, a piece of embroidery was hung outside the home to indicate that a girl was eligible for marriage.

- In Turkey, a man who died in battle was buried in his most elaborately embroidered clothes.

- Young girls in the village of Csokoly, Hungary, embroidered linens with red thread for their own funeral beds. If they lived to the age of forty, the linens were re-worked in yellow thread.

- In many parts of Sweden and Norway, a richly embroidered cloth was used to cover a coffin before burial.

- New mothers in Uzbekistan asked other women who had recently given birth to healthy children to embroider a skullcap for their own newborns, thereby passing on good health.

THE POETIC STITCH:
An Interview with Tumim & Prendergast

Christopher Prendergast and Matilda Tumim are a husband-and-wife team from Stromness in the Orkney Islands of Scotland. Primarily research-led artists, their conceptually challenging embroideries are the result of careful planning and execution. They often focus on the subject of loss, replicating ephemera such as candy wrappers and hand-written notes to pay respect to what is discarded by society and to show how such objects can be used as symbols of storytelling and of collective loss.

Q. **What inspired your project *Fall*?**

A: **Matilda:** The theme for this work was loosely based on J.J. Cale's song "Travelin' Light" which has the line "one-way ticket to ecstasy." We were responding to a call for artwork that focused on the journeys regularly undertaken by young London-based libertines and merchants of the sixteenth and seventeenth centuries, taking their silks and spices abroad or simply coming of age and journeying in search of carnal delights, reputed to be in abundance in Venice, then known as the Pleasure Capital of Europe. The artworks followed the same trading route—from the canals of East London to the open sea, before eventually arriving at the waterways of Venice.

It was an opportunity for us to explore the ideas of censorship, too, as represented in the fig leaf, and to research biblical themes. We refined our metaphors until eventually we arrived at the word "fall," which stood for the fall of Adam and Eve, the fall of Rome, the American term for the fall of leaves in autumn, and even the recent collapse of the world economy. We worked with silk threads, which seemed apt for the silk trading routes of the sixteenth century, and colors that referred to the natural decay of leaves and seemed to match our ideas about Shakespearian clothing.

Q: **Then how did *Extasie* come about?**

A: **Matilda:** While working on *Fall*, we read pre-Enlightenment poetry, which led us to John Donne. We were fascinated by the concept of metaphysics ("the science of things transcending what is physical or natural") and had the idea to create our own metaphysical conceits using embroidery, a "conceit" being a concept that marries two discordant or incompatible subjects.

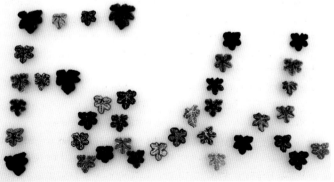

(ABOVE) Tumim & Prendergast, *Fall Fig Leaves, Farewell to a Flimsy Disguise*, 2009, embroidery silk on linen, 9 × 12 × 1 in (22.86 × 30.48 × 2.54 cm). Photo: Olivia Tumim

(RIGHT) Tumim & Prendergast, detail of *Fall Fig Leaves, Farewell to a Flimsy Disguise*. Photo: Olivia Tumim

(ABOVE) Tumim & Prendergast, *Extasie*, 2009–10, silk embroidery threads on cloth mounted on panel pins, 12 × 59 × 1.6 in (30.48 × 149.86 × 4.06 cm). Taking the John Donne poem "The Extasie" as their inspiration, Tumim & Prendergast have used embroidery to replicate sixty-four life-size candy wrappers, which are arranged to form the word "Extasie." Photo: Olivia Tumim

(FACING PAGE) Tumim & Prendergast, detail of *Extasie*. Photo: Olivia Tumim

Tumim & Prendergast, detail of *Orkney Seagull's Eggs* label on *Extasie*. Photo: Olivia Tumim

Tumim & Prendergast, detail of *Fritt wrapper* from *Extasie*. Photo: Olivia Tumim

(FACING PAGE) Tumim & Prendergast, dog detail from *Travellers, A Work In Progress*. Photo: Olivia Tumim

(ABOVE) Tumim & Prendergast, hippo detail from *Travellers, A Work In Progress*, 2007–08, embroidery thread and buttons on soft toys, 39 × 63 in (99.06 × 160.02 cm). Photo: Olivia Tumim

Sweetie [candy] wrappers emerged as our subject because they are factory-made, and to replicate them in the labor-intensive form of embroidery was so unlikely. It also tied in with the other longer term strand of our work, which is concerned with items deemed to be "throwaway," and took our metaphorical referencing into a whole exciting new arena.

Q: **What do you hope that your work says to the world?**

A: **Matilda:** We enjoy giving the viewer the opportunity to take their own journey. It is important that, at first glance, our work is visually beguiling and as beautifully crafted as we can manage—and that our hard work is apparent and enjoyed. We aim to provoke enquiry and hope to do this by communicating our own excitement, but not to provide finality or solutions in our work. We view all of our artworks as stopping points on a journey or as works-in-progress.

Chris: Our work is primarily concerned with loss: both items that have been lost or discarded and lost loved ones, but also people who lose their way (including us, sometimes), the loss of dignity (the *Art of Rejection* for example), lost youth (*Travellers*, our embroidered and buttoned soft toys), and the loss of innocence (*Fall*). We are currently making an installation called *73 Leaves*, which is a tribute to Matilda's late mother, who died at the age of seventy-three. We are embroidering replica leaves of different species of trees, each representing a year of her life.

Q: **Can you tell me about *Winifred's Last Checklist*?**

A: **Matilda:** When my mother died unexpectedly, I found myself trying to piece together her final days. In the process of clearing up her house, I found a list stuck on the inside of her front door. When I left her house for the last time, I took it with me and copied it using embroidery, and it has now become part of our project *Clues*, comprised of many embroidered post-its of all shapes and sizes. In many ways, we feel that by embroidering something seemingly ordinary, we are paying homage to the person who wrote it.

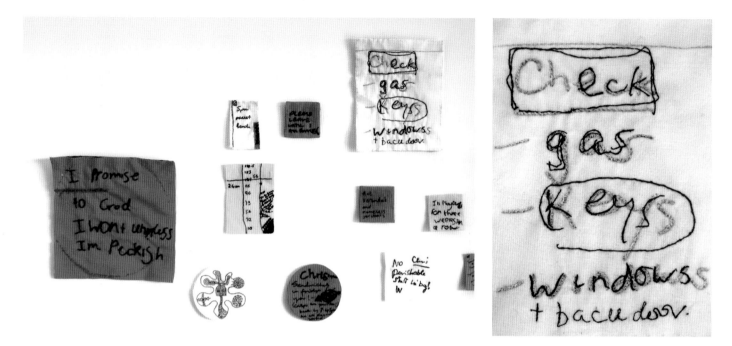

To see more of Tumim & Prendergast's work, visit **axisweb.org/artist/ tumimandprendergast**.

(ABOVE) Tumim & Prendergast, *Clues*, 2009–10, embroidery silk thread on felt, 8 × 8 in (20.32 × 20.32 cm). *Clues* is an ongoing wall-based artwork in which Tumim & Prendergast embroider the ephemera of everyday life. By copying and enlarging these items with embroidery, their work serves as both archive and homage to the people who owned these scraps of paper. Photo: Matilda Tumim

(ABOVE RIGHT) Tumim & Prendergast, *Winifred's Final Checklist*, 2010, embroidery thread on muslin, 8 × 5 in (20.32 × 12.7 cm). An embroidered replica of a checklist found stuck on the inside of Tumim's late mother's front door. "The discarded fragments that are left when someone leaves their world behind unexpectedly are very poignant —an endless source of inspiration and fascination." Photo: Matilda Tumim

(LEFT) Tumim & Prendergast play John and Yoko and embroider in bed. Photo: Erlend Prendergast

(FACING PAGE) Tumim & Prendergast, *The Consequence Family From No. 5*, 2007 embroidery silk thread, fabric, embroidery hoops, embroidered figures on tapestry frames, 37 × 37 in (93.98 × 93.98 cm). Images taken from a family game of Consequence played in 2006. Photo: Matilda Tumim

I don't think that my gender has influenced my attraction to needlework, as it is a simple pleasure that should transcend social and gender constructs. However, there's no denying that there is a great novelty in my position as an overt manbroiderer. The mainstream market is skewed toward women, for better or worse, and I think this makes it difficult for men to engage with embroidery in the first place and more of a challenge for those who stitch patterns bought from mainstream craft stores. There's little content designed for the twenty-first-century man. If the use of the term "manbroiderer" enables us to promote embroidery and overcome some of the historical gender bias, then it's worth a go. However, a manbroiderer is still an embroiderer, just maybe with more facial hair.
—JAMIE CHAMBERS, MR X STITCH

Embroidery Today

With the proliferation of the DIY movement, many artists and crafters have rediscovered embroidery. They often congregate online, gathering inspiration from embroidery blogs such as Mr X Stitch or Feeling Stitchy. Some learn stitching from their crafty acquaintances; others rely on YouTube to learn new stitches. Embroiderers participate in curated art shows, in traditional galleries, and in public installations. Some needlepoint artists sell their wares through the online market-place Etsy.com and some are entrepreneurs, publishing their own designs for others to make and enjoy.

Modern embroiderers stitch a wide gamut of subjects, including live animations, political alliances, porn, celebrity-fan portraits, pop culture iconography, technological motifs, and diarized confessions. They might mix machine embroidery with hand-stitching. Some research embroidery in other cultures in order to broaden their understanding of the craft, while others are happy to create work that is reflective of their personal experience. Embroidery is now a medium open to reinterpretation and reinvention.

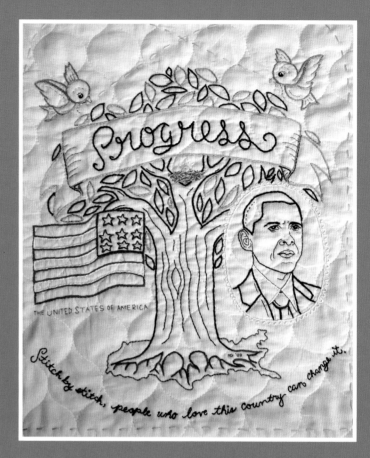

Alyssa Glass, *Obama Manifest Hope Campaign*, 2008, thread, cotton, 15.5 × 12.5 in (39.37 × 31.75 cm). Glass wrote: "I created this piece as an entry for the Manifest Hope art contest during the 2008 US presidential election. I used embroidery as my medium because the slow, deliberate process of stitching each line suited my wish to make my own contribution to the Obama campaign, and I wanted to create something to represent the idea of individuals each playing their own small part in effecting change on a large scale." Photo: Alyssa Glass

When you look up information on the Internet, there is a Eurocentric idea about where embroidery comes from. But once you really start digging for information, you can see it from a world view—and it's fascinating. —PENNY NICKELS

MANBROIDERY:
An Interview with Johnny Murder

Johnny Murder hails from Texas but currently lives in Portland, Oregon. A musician, cartoonist, and artist, he coined the term "manbroidery" and runs the Manbroidery Flickr Pool, which encourages men around the world to share images of their embroidered work.

Q: **What is manbroidery?**

A: Manbroidery is a blanket term for fiber art done by guys. Once I started doing embroidery, I noticed that there were a bunch of very talented men working in the medium, but they seemed to lack a voice in the field, which is generally dominated by female artists. I wanted to give the guys a sense of empowerment and a venue to showcase their work. I basically felt that we needed an identity that would motivate us to keep on stitching.

Q: **How did you learn to do embroidery?**

A: My wife, Penny Nickels, had started embroidering and told me that I needed a "bed hobby"—something artistic that I could do while in bed watching TV. Once I started, I realized that adapting versions of my comics and strange characters to the embroidery medium was a natural. The needlework format really brings out a new dimension in the work.

Q: **Do you think that being male is an advantage or disadvantage in the embroidery world?**

A: I don't think it makes a huge difference, at least not to me. I tend to judge art on its own merits, and who the artist is usually is a secondary thing. However, I believe that by embracing the "manbroidery" label, it gives male artists a sense of inclusion. It is not just a gender thing; manbroidery is as much about style as it is about gender.

Q: **Why did you start the manbroidery Flickr group?**

A: The Flickr group is a place for male needleworkers to post photos of their work and make connections with other manbroiderers and fans. It feels nice to have a place to show your work and get positive feedback and support. It is a place to run your work up the flagpole and see if anybody salutes.

Johnny Murder, *Smurfly Delights* (year unknown), embroidery thread, cotton, 8 in (20.32 cm) in diameter. Photo: The Hopeso Group

(NEXT PAGE) Johnny Murder, *Pro Life* (year unknown), embroidery thread, cotton, 8 in (20.32 cm) in diameter. Photo: The Hopeso Group

Johnny Murder, *Cardinal Richelieu*, 2010, embroidery thread, cotton, 10 in (25.4 cm) in diameter. The first part of a triptych based on Ken Russell's film *The Devils*. Photo: The Hopeso Group

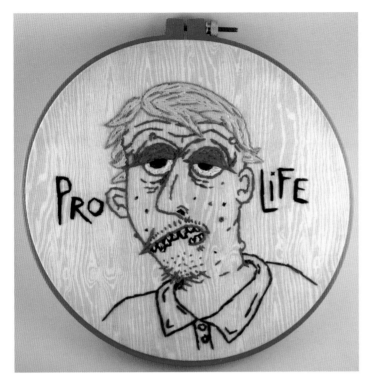

Q: **What types of subject matter do you use in your embroidered work?**

A: I usually do portraits of what are generally considered "ugly" people. Sometimes I add words, phrases, or speech balloons with random (and usually offensive) dialogue—obviously a holdover from my comics. I try to bring out the beauty that lies beneath the ugliness of the average Joe. "Beauty" is boring. "Ugly" is interesting.

Q: **Why embroidery?**

A: I have a deep need to create—whether it's music, prose, or visual art. I have a lot of things inside my warped brain that need to be released or else I think I would probably be a serial killer or something. I believe that all true artists have that same aching need to create. That's why the best art gives you an immediate emotional response; it is a shared feeling between artist and viewer.

Find more of Johnny Murder's work at: **manbroidery.blogspot .com.**

I believe that all true artists have that same aching need to create. That's why the best art gives you an immediate emotional response; it is a shared feeling between artist and viewer.

Johnny Murder, *Ralph Speaks* (year unknown), embroidery thread, cotton, 8 in (20.32 cm) in diameter. Photo: The Hopeso Group

Johnny Murder, *Pussy Magnet*, 2009, embroidery thread, cotton, 8 in (20.32 cm) in diameter. Photo: The Hopeso Group

It Takes All Kinds:
Types of Embroidery

At the most basic level, the term "embroidery" defines a design created with a needle and thread, but there are many different types of stitchwork that are housed under this general label. Here are some of the most popular types.

COUNTED NEEDLEPOINT or counted thread embroidery is any sort of embroidery in which the stitches are counted by the embroiderer. This type of work is usually made using even-weave fabric, as the warp and weft of the fabric is evenly spaced, and this helps to guide the stitching for the embroiderer.

FREE EMBROIDERY is the exact opposite of counted embroidery. In free embroidery, fabric is embellished with a needle and thread and may also include other materials such as beads, sequins, or ribbon. While an embroiderer may still follow a design to create free embroidery, the number of stitches required to achieve an effect are not exact and will differ from one person to another.

MACHINE EMBROIDERY means that the stitching is done with a sewing machine. Stitches that echo the look of hand-embroidered stitches, such as satin stitch or chain stitch, are often employed in machine embroidery.

BLACKWORK (A.K.A. HOLBEIN WORK) is one of the oldest styles of embroidery—it originated in North Africa, spread to southern Spain and then the British Isles, and was mentioned by Chaucer in *The Canterbury Tales*. Usually composed entirely in one color of thread (black is traditional), blackwork stitches are counted straight stitches used to create geometric lines and patterns.

CREWEL is a type of embroidery created with wool thread, often on linen or wool fabric; it has been around for more than 1,000 years. Crewel wool is very strong and textured, and this freeform embroidery often has a very lavish, raised look. A crewel needle has a large eye in which to hold the woolen thread.

CROSS-STITCH is created with a series of counted stitches that make uniformly sized crosses (or xs). In cross-stitch, each stitch contributes to the larger picture—the crosses work together, much like a tile mosaic, to create an image. Cross-stitch is nearly always created on an even-weave fabric such as Aida cloth (see p. 107).

WHITEWORK is the name given to embroidery in which the thread color matches the color of the foundation fabric. Traditionally this has been white thread stitched onto white linen, but any monochromatic piece can claim this definition.

GOLDWORK is embroidery stitched with metallic threads. Although it's called "gold" work, the metal threads may be made of silver, copper, or imitation gold. Real gold is rarely used. Developed in Asia and adopted by European embroiderers in the Middle Ages, the oldest extant goldwork is more than 2,000 years old.

This book features freeform embroidery with a few counted cross-stitch and needlepoint patterns, but don't let this stop you from experimenting with other techniques. You never know what new ideas you may discover! Embroidery is an easy activity to start, but mastering it, as with any craft, can take a lifetime. The trick is to find the stitching techniques that work best for you.

Jenny Hart, *Oh Unicorn*, 2005, artist's own hair embroidered onto soft leather, 9 × 9 in (22.86 × 22.86 cm). Photo: Jenny Hart

Embroidering ... with hair?

Not all stitchers worked with thread or floss. Chinese women in the Tang Dynasty (ca. 618–907 CE) often used human hair to embroider on silk. Referred to as *moxiu*, which means black ink or black hair, these works were often used as pious offerings in Buddhist worship. In North America and Europe during the Georgian and Victorian eras, the hair of loved ones who had died was sometimes woven into bracelets or stitched into pictures to become mementos of remembrance. The art was revived in the 1970s, and hair embroidery is still practiced today in China, though the craft has widened to use all colors of human hair. One of the most notable practitioners of modern hair embroidery is Professor Wei Jingxian, who practices "hair embroidery diplomatism," having created thirty-four life-like portraits of monarchs, philosophers, and American presidents, which have been gifted from China to countries around the world.

EMBROIDERY AS ART:
An Interview with Jenny Hart

If there is one person to thank for the dearth of bonneted ducks and cutesy kittens in modern embroidery, it is Jenny Hart. Her embroidery design company, Sublime Stitching, has encouraged embroiderers to tackle subject matter as varied as scooter babes, prescription pills, zombies, sexy librarians, robots, and Mexican wrestlers. In addition to her commercial work, Jenny Hart is also a fine artist and has stitched a wide variety of pieces, including celebrity portraits. From creating original patterns to authoring her own line of embroidery technique books, Jenny Hart is a sublime force in the stitching world.

Q: **How did you get into embroidery?**

A: When I was finishing college, around 1994, I started taking an interest in hand-embroidery. There was something simple but also mysterious about it. It caught my eye, but I had no idea how to start.

During my teenage years in the 1980s, crafting was really démodé. During that decade people were getting their first home computers and VCRs, and there was a proliferation of shopping malls. The idea of doing something by hand was systematically plucked from my childhood.

Q: **You come from an art school background. Was this the main influence for your work?**

A: My dad had an eye for fine art, illustration, and comic art. One of my brothers was also a complete comic nut. In the 1970s and '80s, my brother had a treasure trove of the greatest independent comics in the United States. I was always sneaking them out of his room and reading them. [In] my fine art background, [there is] a chasm between commercial art and fine art, which is how I feel about fine art and embroidery. It is analogous, creatively.

Jenny Hart (embroidery) and Dame Darcy (illustration), *Blue Lass*, 2004, hand-embroidery on cotton panel, 18 × 24 in (45.72 × 60.96 cm). Photo: Jenny Hart

When I was finishing college, around 1994, I started taking an interest in hand-embroidery. There was something simple but also mysterious about it.

Q: **So, how did you move from being interested in embroidery to actually trying it?**

A: I was always spending inordinate amounts of time in hospitals with my parents. My dad had been really sick and then my mother-in-law passed away, unexpectedly, from brain cancer. A year later, my mother got breast cancer, and I had a hard time coping with it all.

In the summer of 2000, I was at my parents' house watching TV with my dad. And I thought, this would be a good time to get my mom to teach me how to embroider. I'm kind of bored. All the supplies are in the next room in her sewing basket. I'm now confronted by her mortality—I had better learn. If she won't teach me, who will?

So I sketched out her portrait from a photo that had been taken of her in 1952. My mother had to show me how to put the fabric on the hoop and how to insert my needle. I didn't know if I was going to like it or if I was going to have the patience for it, but once I got going, it was so relaxing and so

engrossing that I embroidered every day for the next five years.

Q: **You create embroidery projects for Sublime Stitching, and you create large portraits that have been used both as illustrations and collected by art devotees. What is the difference between these two practices?**

A: Sublime Stitching is about contemporary embroidery design and accessible instructions. I sell embroidery patterns and kits and offer resources for embroidery techniques. When I started the company, there was no alternative to the traditional re-threaded and reworked embroidery designs, which was a big reason why embroidery didn't appeal to me when I was growing up.

I was my own first customer. I wanted to see vintage tattoo embroidery patterns rather than ducks on my pillowcases. I drew flaming martinis and daggers. I was fascinated with learning embroidery techniques and pattern making.

I wondered if it would be too shocking for the traditional embroidery industry, but people have been overwhelmingly supportive, particularly the most traditional needleworkers. They think that it's great that Sublime Stitching gets people interested in embroidery again.

(FACING PAGE) Jenny Hart, *Iggy Pop*, 2004, hand-embroidery and black sequins on cotton panel, 16 × 24 in (40.64 × 60.96 cm), public collection, Arkansas Arts Center and Museum, Little Rock, Arkansas. In response to an open assignment from *Nylon* magazine to create an illustration of a dream concert, Jenny Hart stitched Iggy Pop performing with the Staple Singers in the hospital where she was born, on her birth date. Photo: Jenny Hart

(ABOVE) *Tattoo Your Towels*, a Sublime Stitching pattern. One 8.5 × 11 in (21.59 × 27.94 cm) sheet of a multi-imprinting, iron-on embroidery pattern. Photo: Jenny Hart

Jenny Hart, *Dirty Face, Crowning Glory*, 2003, hand-embroidery on cotton panel, 17 × 18 in (43.18 × 45.72 cm). Collection of Dan Ferarra. Photo: Jenny Hart

My company and my personal work are very different. My day job is running a design company. My personal work is play, which I don't have a lot of time for. I embroider personal projects when I'm winding down in the evenings.

Q: **You've described embroidery as the "frosting of needle arts" and have said that, in your work, it is more important to embellish an embroidery as a standalone piece rather than using embroidery to enhance an object.**

A: I view embroidery as an embellishment of a drawing. I love pencil drawings, which are drawings in their pure form, but by the time I get to stitch a project, it is the fourth generation of the original drawing. It has changed while being transferred to the fabric with carbon and imprinted on the fabric—it looks different from the actual project.

Traditionally, embroidery is secondary to the functional objects it decorates. [Embroidery is found] on tea cozies, sheets, or towels. I wanted to use that sort of American craft type of embroidery on something that had no function but to be fine art. As an artist, my challenge was to make something so fantastic in embroidery that no one would think of it as anything else.

Q: **You've recently done several collaborations with comic artists such as Gary Baseman. What sort of artistic return do you get from those collaborations, when you're working with art that has already been drawn?**

A: [I work with these artists] because I love their work and I love embroidery. So I double-love their work in embroidery! I recently created a piece with performance artist Dame Darcy whose aesthetic, vision, and drawing style I love. I wrote to her and asked specifically for a drawing for a collaboration. Within twenty-four hours, she had drawn a wonderful shipwrecked lass on a rock. I was inspired and added ocean waves and birds, and words coming out of her mouth.

As an artist, my challenge was to make something so fantastic in embroidery that no one would think of it as anything else.

Jenny Hart, *All the Girls Wept Tears of Pure Love / St. John the Baptist* (Jordan Lee), 2007, hand-embroidery and sequins on cotton panel, 18 × 20 in (45.72 × 50.8 cm). Photo: Jenny Hart

Jenny Hart, *Girl with Japanese Clouds*, 2006, hand-embroidery on denim, 12 × 12 in (30.48 × 30.48 cm).
Photo: Jenny Hart

My favorite collaborations have been with Jim Woodring. He's excited about the hand-embroidery and let me publish his drawings as patterns. I get a goofy thrill getting to work with artists that I'm a huge fan of. *Frank* [cartoon] readers will know about the jeweled tops called Jivas that float around and get implicated in his storylines here and there. I wanted to stitch the Jivas so bad! Most of the *Frank* books are in black and white. The collaboration with Jim gave me an opportunity to interpret his characters in the colors that I had envisioned.

Q: **Is there anything else you'd like to tell me about yourself?**

A: When you are an artist and you want to do something, you have to work with what is available or have things custom-made. It's not always easy, if you've got a strong idea of what it is that you'd like to create. I think that's the hardest thing. Nine times out of ten, it doesn't look like what you expect it to be. You've got to decide whether you love that child or not. Can you love the thing that you made, even if it's not what you had in mind?

For more on Jenny Hart, see **embroideryasart.com**, **jennyhart.net**, and **sublimestitching.com**.

CHAPTER 2

Charting Unknown Territory

The artists profiled in this chapter chart unknown territories—whether through the act of participatory embroidery, careful self-instruction, or following the lines of their hearts through stitched confessionals. Using a needle and thread, they record actions, ideas, and sentiments. Their findings range from the observational to the personal to the imagined.

(FACING PAGE) Annie Coggan Crawford, detail of *Mr Faulkner's Homestead*, 2009, embroidery, fabric, chair, 34 (ht) × 29 (depth) in (86.36 × 73.66 cm). Photo: Jennifer Hudson

(TOP TO BOTTOM, LEFT TO RIGHT) Iviva Olenick, *He Wears His Heart on His Sweater*, 2008, embroidery on fabric, 5 × 8.25 in (12.7 × 20.96 cm). Photo: Iviva Olenick

Liz Kueneke, *The Urban Fabric—El Tejido Urbano* (Quito, Ecuador). Photo: Liz Kueneke

Abby Krause, details of Allsort candy from *Black Licorice*, from the series *Food My Husband Doesn't Eat*. Photo: Angela Duggan

Ray Materson, *Once a Young Man*, 1996, embroidery on cotton, 2.25 × 2.75 in (5.72 × 6.99 cm). Photo: Ray Materson

PARTICIPATORY EMBROIDERY:
An Interview with Liz Kueneke

Liz Kueneke is an American artist living in Barcelona, Spain. In her art practice, she investigates the relationships between people and their environment through the use of mapping, installations, and public interventions. Liz has created her participatory stitching projects in cities around the world, including Barcelona, Manhattan, Los Angeles, Bangalore, Quito, and Fez. She explores citizen interaction and community-building through the use of embroidery and public dialogue.

Q: **Tell me about your embroidered maps.**

A: I use embroidery in my participatory mapping activities and installations. I embroider maps of different cities or neighborhoods onto cloth, and then I take those maps into different public spaces. I stretch the work out onto a foldable embroidery table. Then I sit and wait for passersby, who I ask to respond to a series of questions about their public space. I ask them about their use of the city: itineraries, routes, and their opinions and memories about their environment.

Participants respond to these questions by embroidering symbols onto the map. They might mark where they live or where they think the heart of the city is or a positive place for the community or a place that needs to be changed.

People often find neighbors that they've never met. They both start embroidering the same little building with the same symbol and then start talking. Sometimes a person will be embroidering one place with a positive symbol, and someone else will want to mark it as a problematic place. That starts discussions as to why that place is problematic or why it's good, or how it needs to be fixed.

Q: **Are there cultural differences in the cities that you work in? I imagine that most people in Manhattan, for example, would probably feel more comfortable holding a ballpoint pen than an embroidery needle.**

A: In each country, people have had a different relationship with embroidery. In New York, most people were surprised [by the project], but I found quite an openness to doing new things there. In Ecuador, the men tend to avoid doing embroidery, though most of them were taught it in school. It was a matter

Liz Kueneke, *The Urban Fabric—El Tejido Urbano*
(Quito, Ecuador), 2010. Embroidered map on cloth sheet,
thread, needles, foldable embroidery table, 3 × 6.5 ft
(0.91 × 1.98 m). A public intervention where citizens
participate by marking significant places into a hand-
embroidered map of their city. Photo: Liz Kueneke

Liz Kueneke, *The Urban Fabric—El Tejido Urbano*
(Quito, Ecuador). Photo: Liz Kueneke

Liz Kueneke, *The Urban Fabric—El Tejido Urbano*
(Quito, Ecuador). Photo: Liz Kueneke

(RIGHT) Liz Kueneke, detail of *The Urban Fabric—El Tejido Urbano* (Bangalore, India). Photo: Liz Kueneke

(BOTTOM) Liz Kueneke, detail of *The Urban Fabric—El Tejido Urbano* (Bangalore, India), 2009. Embroidered map on cloth sheet, thread, needles, foldable embroidery table, 3.25 × 6.5 ft (0.99 × 1.98 m). Photo: Liz Kueneke

I'm trying to foster dialogue about the city with this project. I spend about 100 hours embroidering each map, and it's my gift to the city.

of convincing them. In India, it's the men who are the tailors, so there was absolutely no taboo for them with embroidery. I would start setting up my table and there would be twenty to thirty men waiting to embroider. It was difficult getting women to participate in India, because they seem to be a little shy in the public space.

Q: **What attracted you to mapping?**

A: I began to be interested in mapping when I moved to Barcelona eight years ago. As a visitor, I had my own experiences, memories, and opinions. |I wanted to get to know the place better from a local's perspective.

Liz Kueneke, detail of *The Urban Fabric—El Tejido Urbano* (Barcelona, Spain). Photo: Liz Kueneke

Liz Kueneke in collaboration with Margarita Pineda, *Household Routes*, 2006, 2009, cloth, thread, suitcases, embroidered maps, dimensions variable. Photo: Liz Kueneke

Q: **Why embroidery?**

A: One reason is that I simply enjoy it; it's a meditative act for me. Second, I wanted to have participants embroider because it requires them to sit longer around the table, and I'm trying to foster dialogue about the city with this project. I spend about 100 hours embroidering each map, and it's my gift to the city. I hope that if people see how much I've put into the work, they won't mind giving a few minutes of their time.

Q: **You've also used embroidery for other projects. Tell me about *Household Routes*.**

A: Columbian artist Margarita Pineda and I both embroidered a series of maps of different scales of both Mexico City and Figueres in Spain. We created a city map, a country map, and a world map. We asked people different questions about their feelings about these places. We had a couple of suitcases, and in each suitcase we built rooms of a house with miniature pieces of fabric furniture. Each piece had a different meaning attached to it; for example, a refrigerator was a place to be preserved or a bed was a place that you are transported to in dreams. If a person wanted to be transported to Southern Mexico in their dreams, they would connect their piece of thread from the miniature bed all the way to Southern Mexico in the embroidered map.

Q: **You've also used stitching on your piece *Ribbons and War Machines*.**

A: When Bush was first threatening to invade Iraq, I happened to find some old blueprints of military vehicles and machine gun parts at a school where I was teaching. I was really angry about the whole political situation, and I started to use thread, ribbons, and old scraps of fabric to modify these blueprints. I wanted to make them symbolically useless, so I stitched them until they were unreadable.

Q: **What is the message you hope your work sends out into the world?**

A: One thing that I really enjoy about the project is that people are rubbing elbows and talking with people they never would have spoken to otherwise. In India, there is a rigid caste system, and I would have homeless boys embroidering alongside very posh ladies. I hope that it encourages people to keep talking with people they don't know and find out what they have in common. Underneath it all, everyone is pretty similar and wants the same things.

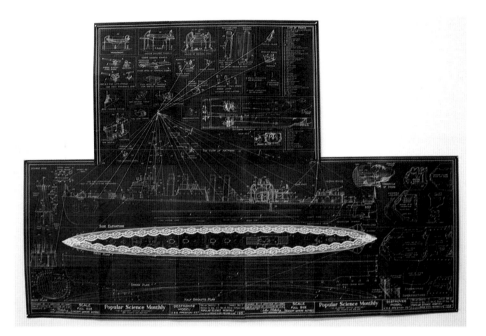

Liz Kueneke, *Ribbons and War Machines*, 2001, lace, thread, blueprint, 39.25 × 27.5 in (99.69 × 69.85 cm). Photo: Liz Kueneke

Liz Kueneke. Photo: Carmen Espinosa

For more information, visit Liz Kueneke's website: **lizkueneke.com.**

DIARIZED EATING HABITS:
Abby Krause

Abby Krause is a wife and mother from Denver, Colorado. She works at the Colorado Historical Society where she creates exhibit materials by soldering, welding, matting, and framing. She also wields a mean embroidery needle. In 2009, she created a series of embroidered placemats entitled Food My Husband Doesn't Eat.

Q: **Why did you use embroidery as an art medium for this project?**

A: I only use embroidery as an embellishment to a surface. I set up a still life of banana chips on my desk, did a pencil sketch, sketched it onto my fabric, and then "drew" it with the thread. I really enjoy the results of combining three different colors of thread in one stitch. It's the whole process of "letting go" but taking control of the medium at the same time. I like that I can't entirely predict where the different colors of thread will end up on the surface, yet I control the beginning and end point into the fabric.

Q: **How does your creative process work?**

A: I start drawing in my sketchbook, and then I need the discipline to sit down and craft something based on an initial sketch. I like gathering materials too. A lot of my ideas come to me when I have my materials around me.

Q: **Do you have a favorite piece among the series?**

A: The *Banana Chips* placemat. It's the first one that I did in the series, and when you create a series of work, the second, third, and fourth pieces try to achieve the success of the first piece, but you never quite accomplish that.

This *placemat* series makes me smile when I look at them. The pumpkin pie makes me hungry for autumn, and I can smell the licorice when I see the allsorts. It reminds me to enjoy the food and things that my husband doesn't.

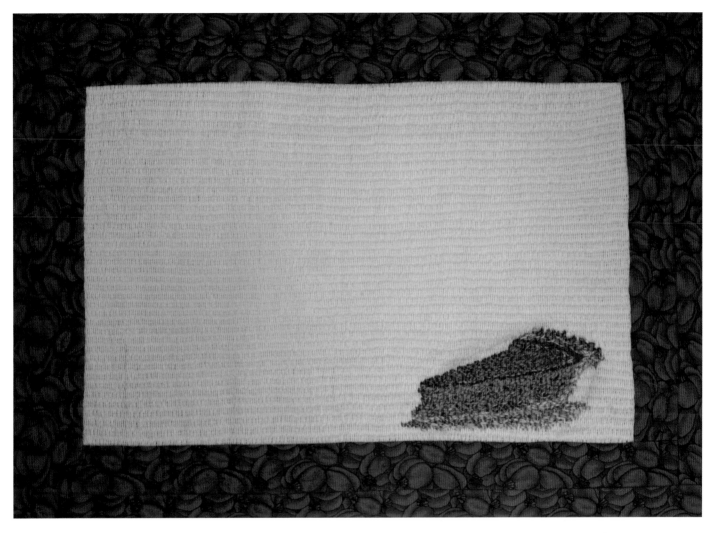

(FACING PAGE) Abby Krause, detail of *Banana Chips*, from the series *Food My Husband Doesn't Eat*, 2006, embroidery thread, placemat, 13.5 × 20 in (34.29 × 50.8 cm). Photo: Angela Duggan

(ABOVE) Abby Krause, *Pumpkin Pie*, from the series *Food My Husband Doesn't Eat*, 2006, embroidery thread, placemat, 13.5 × 20 in (34.29 × 50.8 cm). Photo: Angela Duggan

(RIGHT) Abby Krause, detail of *Flan*, from the series *Food My Husband Doesn't Eat*, 2006, embroidery thread, placemat, 13.5 × 20 in (34.29 × 50.8 cm). Photo: Angela Duggan

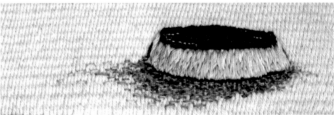

EMBROIDERED PLACE-MAKING:
An Interview with Annie Coggan Crawford

Annie Coggan Crawford is a designer, artist, and assistant professor who teaches furniture design, construction classes, and interior design at Mississippi State University. Originally trained as an architect, Annie stitches compelling maps and plans onto furniture upholstery. Her upholstery projects have included embroideries of Marie Antoinette's garden plot, a floor plan of William Faulkner's cottage, and the military movements of General Ulysses S. Grant.

Q: **As a designer who reworks wooden furniture, what led you to embroidering upholstery?**

A: I wanted a way to work that did not require me to be in a shop all of the time. I can work [on embroidery] at home with my daughter while homework is being done or while watching a movie with her. I returned to stitching in the last three years, and I have pretty much taught myself.

Q: **What sort of techniques do you use in your work?**

A: I am "Queen of the Backstitch." I use it as if I am drawing a line on paper. I use very thin single-strand thread for most lines, and double the thread or retrace a line in order to make it pop. I use the same visual rules that one uses for drawing. Often I use machine stitches for lines that I want to be delicate. I experiment with the landscape of the subject matter. I look for stitches that might be swamps or rivers or mountains. I suppose I am building a library of marks.

Q: **How do garden plans, floor plans, and military maps represent historical figures?**

A: I read a lot, and all of my work involves some deep research into a character that I admire. The maps and floor plans are all efforts to bring meaning to the upholstered pieces of furniture. Maps and floor plans can tell a person's story or their journey.

Q: **Tell me about the *Flora and Fauna* chair.**

A: Southern writer Eudora Welty uses characters who work in the garden as a way of getting through dramatic issues. I wanted to make a chair that talked about the idea of a garden taking you away to solve a problem.

Annie Coggan Crawford, detail of
*Marie Antoinette's Garden:
Le Petit Trianon.* Photo: Jennifer Hudson

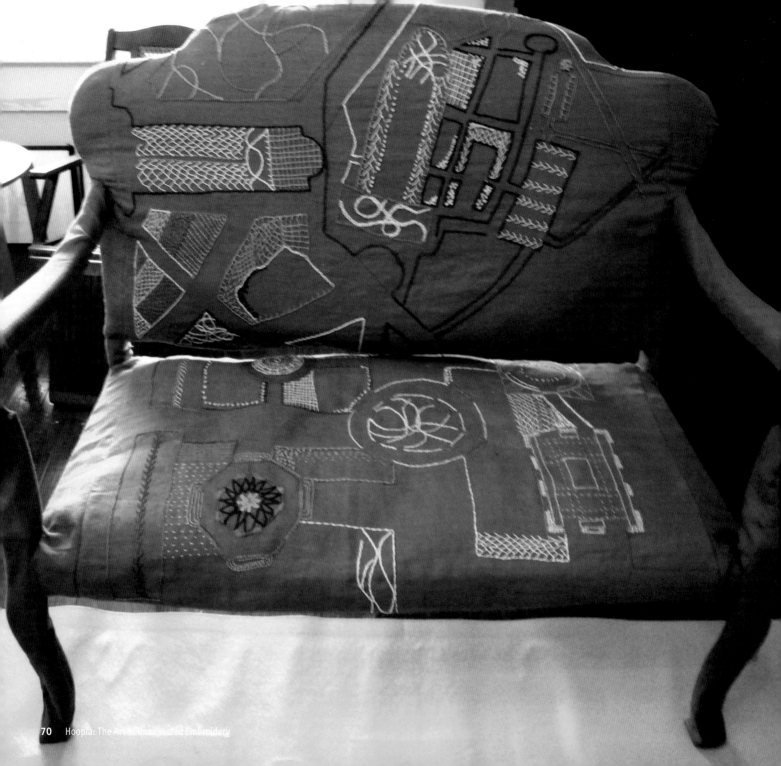

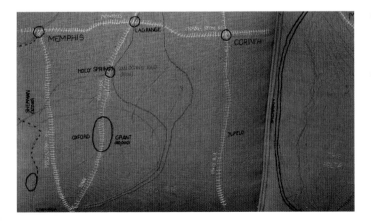

Annie Coggan Crawford, *Mississippi Campaign Loveseat*, 2010, from *Civil War Furniture*, embroidery on upholstery, love seat, 34 (ht) × 40 (length) × 20 (depth) in (86.36 × 101.6 × 50.8 cm). This piece maps General Grant's movements through Mississippi during the American Civil War. Photo: Caleb Crawford

Annie Coggan Crawford, *Vicksburg Chair*. Photo: Caleb Crawford

(LEFT) Annie Coggan Crawford, detail of *Mississippi Campaign Loveseat*. Photo: Caleb Crawford

Q: Who are your next embroidery subjects?

A: Varina Davis (US President Jefferson Davis's wife) and Julia Dent-Grant (General Ulysses S. Grant's wife). Both women were devoted spouses to husbands who were important figures in the American Civil War. I am making maps of all the places they lived during the war. They were both nomadic, yet both were matriarchs of their families.

Q: Do you believe that your gender or social class has any bearing on your attraction and involvement with needlework?

A: Functionally, it's a medium that I can participate in while being with my family. I feel that I belong to a tradition of communicating through needlework. It's a social way to work; one can stack functions while stitching.

Q: If you were trying to convince someone else to take up embroidery or another of the needle-arts, what would you say to convince them?

A: It's a safe way for an artist to explore— there is a privacy at the beginning. You can quietly work by yourself and then bring the work forward when you are ready.

For more about Annie Coggan Crawford, visit: **chairsandbuildings.blogspot.com**.

(FACING PAGE) Annie Coggan Crawford, *Miss Welty's Garden*, 2009, embroidery, fabric, chair, 34 (ht) × 29 (depth) in (86.36 × 73.66 cm). Photo: Jennifer Hudson

Annie Coggan Crawford, detail of *Miss Welty's Garden*, 2009, embroidery, fabric, chair. Photo: Jennifer Hudson

Annie Coggan Crawford, detail of *Miss Welty's Garden* 2009, embroidery, fabric, chair. Photo: Jennifer Hudson

I feel that I belong to a tradition of communicating through needlework. It's a social way to work; one can stack functions while stitching.

Krista Muir is a producer, songwriter, performer, and costume designer based in Montreal, Quebec. She collaborated with Shane Watt, a cartographer of semi-fictional maps, to embroider *Moderato*. The project is a map of a city of Shane's imagining where every color, stitch, and contour holds a meaning. Shane regularly creates thematic maps featuring pieces of actual cities, people, symbols, and objects in order to create a story.

(FACING PAGE) Krista Muir and Shane Watt, *Moderato*, a work in progress, 2010, muslin cloth, ink, embroidery thread, 8.5 × 8.5 in (21.59 × 21.59 cm). Stitched while traveling between Montreal (Quebec), Kingston (Ontario), London (Ontario), Charlotte (Michigan), Northville (Michigan), Southfield (Michigan), Brooklyn (New York), and Hollywood Beach (Florida). Photo: Krista Muir.

Krista Muir:
THE TRAVELING MAP MAKER

"The more I travel, the faster [my embroidery] gets done. I only work on it when I'm in transit—bus, train, car, or plane."

WERE I SO BESOTTED:
An Interview with Iviva Olenick

A textile artist based in Brooklyn, New York, Iviva Olenick embroiders diarized confessions of her dating life. Through her stitching, she explores her hopes, disappointments, and observations as a single woman looking for her soul-mate. When not creating her "besotted" embroideries, she works as a textile designer of men's fashion and as a teacher at the Pratt Center for Continuing and Professional Studies, at the 3rd Ward in Brooklyn, New York, and at the Center for Book Arts. Ivivia Olenick is represented by the Muriel Guepin Gallery in Brooklyn.

Q: **How did you learn to do embroidery?**

A: About eight years ago, I became interested in using embroidery as an art-making tool, and I taught myself stitches from books. In 2003, I also took a three-hour quilt-making class at the Brooklyn Museum. This class, along with the Gee's Bend Quilt exhibit at the Whitney Museum, compelled me to adapt stitching as my primary art form.

Q: **You create narratives with your embroidery, often recounting your experiences with dating. What inspired you to start creating work on this subject?**

A: In my late twenties and early thirties, I was adamant about finding a lasting love relationship. I dated with a near

religious fervor: meeting men through dating websites, at art openings and parties, and through friends. The contrast between my actual dating experiences and the intimate relationship I sought inspired my embroidery series *Were I So Besotted*.

Q: **Your work seems personal and confessional. Do your pieces serve as a diary or do you consider them works of fiction?**

A: I think of the series as a hand-embroidered blog, so the work is primarily autobiographical. I edit my choice of language and images very carefully, however, so I would stress that the work is consciously constructed.

Iviva Olenick, *Play*, 2007, embroidery and colored pencil on fabric 5 × 8.5 in (12.7 × 20.96 cm). Photo: Iviva Olenick

Iviva Olenick, *Here to Stay*, 2009, embroidery on fabric, 5 × 8.25 in (12.7 × 20.96 cm). Photo: Iviva Olenick

I am every-thing he ever wanted, as well as some things he could not have imagined. We're about to have our third kid, and he still hasn't removed his internet dating profile!

Q: **Why use embroidery for this project?**

A: Embroidery requires thought, care, and commitment, which are qualities that make relationships lasting and meaningful. I find the act of embroidering soothing, and I like the quality of line that I can achieve with thread and a combination of stitches. I think there is something intimate about the process and the resulting artwork, which feels like a good match for my content.

Q: **You have used a variety of different materials to stitch on, such as plastic bags or recycled fabric. Do the materials you use have a relevance to the subject matter?**

A: Sometimes my choices of surface material are practical: I used plastic bags to withstand rain when I knew I was installing my work outside. I installed a series of maps and hand-stitched messages onto plastic bags along my Brooklyn running route. My goal was to share the emotional and psychological insights, thoughts, and experiences that happen as I run.

As far as fabric goes, I love hand-me-downs and antiques. Each piece tells its own story. At this point, I rarely buy fabric. I have many wonderful friends who give me all kinds of fabric to work with. Sometimes the fabric inspires an idea for a piece or adds another layer of meaning to my work.

Q: **Can you explain the FiberGraf project?**

A: FiberGraf is a collaboration with graffiti artist Jon Baker. We merge street art with fiber art. I translate Jon's "tags,"

(FACING PAGE) Iviva Olenick, *Everything He Ever Wanted*, 2008, embroidery on fabric. 5 × 8.5 in (12.7 × 20.96 cm). Photo: Iviva Olenick

Iviva Olenick, *Rose Hens*, 2010, embroidery on fabric (ink jet print of graffiti, done with markers on paper, by Jon Baker), part of FiberGraf series, 9.75 × 7.5 in (24.77 × 19.05 cm). Photo: Iviva Olenick

Iviva Olenick, *Hens with French Knots*, 2009, embroidery on fabric (ink jet print of digital graffiti by Jon Baker), part of FiberGraf series, 8.5 × 11 in (21.59 × 27.94 cm). Photo: Iviva Olenick

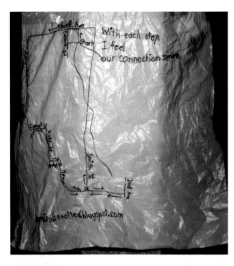

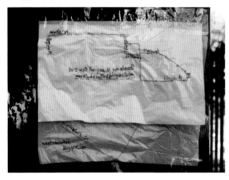

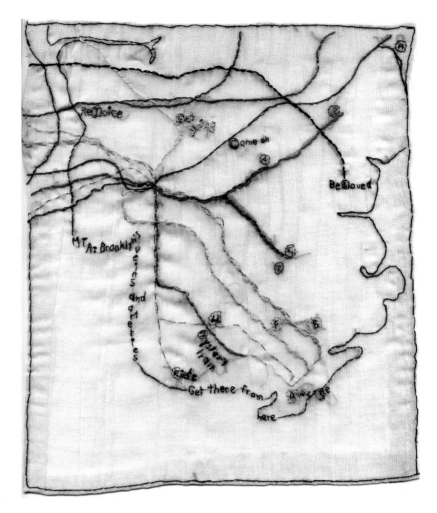

Iviva Olenick, *Mapping My Run*, 1, 2010, embroidery on plastic bag, 6 × 8 in (15 × 20.32 cm). Installed in Boerum Hill, Brooklyn, 2010. Photo: Iviva Olenick

Iviva Olenick, *Mapping My Run*, 2, 2010, embroidery on plastic bag, 7 × 4 in (17.78 × 10.16 cm). Installed in Boerum Hill, Brooklyn, 2010. Photo: Iviva Olenick

Iviva Olenick, *Brooklyn's Veins and Arteries*, 2010, embroidery on fabric, 7.75 × 9.5 in (19.69 × 24.13 cm). Photo: Iviva Olenick

Iviva Olenick, *Chastity Bracelet*, 2007, embroidery on trim with button, 6.5 × 1.5 × 0.5 in (16.51 × 3.81 × 1.27 cm). Photo: Iviva Olenick

Iviva Olenick. Photo: Marci Senders

designs, "throw-ups," and "pieces," which are created digitally and with markers and pen on paper, into embroideries. I exploit the graphic nature of Jon's work while using fabric and fiber techniques to soften the aggressiveness typically associated with graffiti.

Q: **Many of your works refer to the Internet—some of your diarized entries mention Internet dating profiles, emails, and Adobe Photoshop. What role does the digital world play in your embroidered works?**

A: We have become reliant on the digital world to guide our communications and relationships. Twitter, Facebook, text messaging, and instant messaging are primary ways in which we connect.

Rarely do we call each other on the phone or send letters. Plans are made, changed, and broken at a moment's notice because of the ease of getting in touch through technology.

In dating relationships, courtship no longer exists in an old-fashioned sense. The boundaries between friendship, dating, and casual sex have collapsed. There are no guidelines for how to navigate romantically. Speed and accessibility of communication and contact outweigh depth and commitment.

I embroider as an antidote to the heightened pace and fleeting nature of contemporary dating and modes of communication. I long for a different pace. I long for a return to romantic courtship. I long for permanence and a sense of comfort and commitment.

Find more about Iviva at **wereisobesotted.blogspot.com**, **IvivaOlenick.neoimages.net**, or **IvivaOlenick.com**.

SINS AND NEEDLES:
An Interview with Ray Materson

An internationally renowned embroidery artist, Ray Materson taught himself to stitch while incarcerated. Inspired by a pair of socks, he now creates miniature masterpieces that hold 1,200 stitches per square inch. As a speaker and author, Ray shares his life story of incarceration, embroidery, and redemption by needle and thread as a means of offering hope to troubled youth.

Q: How did you learn to do embroidery?

A: It was largely out of boredom. I'd been incarcerated for a year. One day I asked God to help me find a way out of the hell-hole that I'd gotten myself into. Instead of a host of angels to set me free, I recalled how my grandmother would sit for hours embroidering on our front porch. She seemed totally absorbed in the task and was very peaceful when creating images. I recalled the embroidered patches on my scout uniform and baseball hat. There was something very appealing about those little emblems.

At the same time, I recalled how I enjoyed going to football games at the University of Michigan. The maize-and-blue banners and clothing were all over the city and heavily represented in the stadium—known, ironically, as the Big House!

Anyway, while thinking all these things, a prisoner in the next cell was hanging out some socks and underwear to dry on his cell bars. Amidst my neighbor's wash was a pair of white tube socks with maize-and-blue stripes. I bartered a pack of cigarettes for them and set about to make myself a University of Michigan emblem to celebrate my favorite college team, the Michigan Wolverines.

I made a sewing hoop out of a round Rubbermaid dish and drew a pattern on a piece of bed sheet. I learned to unravel socks to get the colored thread, and from there it was a matter of securing a sewing needle. Fortunately, the guards kept those handy in the event that a button came off a shirt. When I imagined embroidering, it seemed that it would be quite easy, but it took me considerable time to master it.

Ray Materson, *Anywhere Next Exit, #1*, 1991, embroidery on
cotton, 2.25 × 2.75 in (5.72 × 6.99 cm). Photo: Ray Materson

Ray Materson, *Little Green Bags*, 1991, embroidery on cotton,
2.25 × 2.75 in (5.72 × 6.99 cm). Photo: Ray Materson

My fingertips were pricked so many times that I developed calluses! Ultimately, I completed my U of M patch and wore it proudly on a hat that I made.

Since hats with logos were not permitted in prison, my creation drew considerable attention, mostly from other prisoners who decided they would like an embroidered image for themselves. A business was literally born overnight.

Q: **How did the other inmates react to your embroidery? Was it difficult to get the proper materials to stitch with in prison?**

A: Except for a few, the other inmates embraced my artwork. I did dozens of sports logos, flags, Harley Davidson patches, and hearts-and-flower images for my fellow inmates. And all of them, save for one slacker, paid me for my work—cartons of cigarettes and bags of coffee! I was, in the local parlance, "living large."

Besides the works I made for my fellows, I was often asked about images that I was creating. Because Shakespeare was one of my themes, I often had to explain dramas to men with typically little education. I enjoyed that, and the other prisoners respected my work. To gain respect in prison is extremely important. Prisoners are respected for being tough. I was respected because I

Ray Materson, *Still in Saigon*, 1992, embroidery on cotton, 2.25 × 2.75 in (5.72 × 6.99 cm). Photo: Ray Materson

(FACING PAGE, LEFT TO RIGHT) Ray Materson, *The Kid with the Works*, 1994, embroidery on cotton, 2.25 × 2.75 in (5.72 × 6.99 cm). Photo: Ray Materson

Ray Materson, *Shower Scene*, 1997, embroidery on cotton, 2.25 × 2.75 in (5.72 × 6.99 cm). Photo: Ray Materson

had mastered what is largely thought of as a womanly art form. Go figure!

As for getting materials to work with, I used thread from socks—still do. If someone came to me with a request for a piece of work, I would ask him to supply me with the colors that I needed. I also asked friends on the outside to send me colored socks and white boxer shorts. I discovered that the polyester-and-cotton blend of the boxers worked well as a base material. Sometimes, I received gifts of sewing needles and spools of thread from prisoners who had heard of my work and wanted to support my efforts.

Q: You've written a memoir about your time in prison and your embroidery called *Sins and Needles*. Tell me about the book.

A: The book tells the story of how I started out as a successful and law-abiding youngster. I wrote plays and I was involved in sports—I was even voted class president during my sixth grade year! But there were problems at home. My dad was a heavy drinker and could be quite abusive. Then there were geographical changes that uprooted the family repeatedly. Ultimately, I ended up with groups of unsavory characters, left school, and began using drugs.

The book relates this, using images that I created to complement the stories. There are about fifty color pictures in the book. One story is about a crime spree that I was involved in to support my addiction to heroin and cocaine. I ended up in prison serving a fifteen-year sentence for armed robbery and drug-related offenses, as well as escape from custody. I hasten to point out that all of my crimes were committed using toy guns. I'm not trying to justify robbery, but I didn't physically hurt anyone and, in fact, could not have.

The book goes on to share the story of my redemption within the confines of prison, and how I became involved with a woman who helped promote my artwork. The book is about sinking to the social depths and then rising up out of those depths. It's a hopeful story, and most people think it quite inspiring.

Q: What sort of embroidery work do you do now?

A: Each image I create—measuring roughly two by three inches—takes between fifty and sixty hours to complete. That does not include design time and sketches.

Q: In interviews, you've mentioned that embroidery teaches people about patience. Why is patience important?

Ray Materson, *The House on York Road*, 1995, embroidery on cotton, 2.25 × 2.75 in (5.72 × 6.99 cm). Photo: Ray Materson

Ray Materson, *The Prisoner*, 1991, embroidery on cotton, 2.25 × 2.75 in (5.72 × 6.99 cm). Photo: Ray Materson

Ray Materson, *The Good Boy*, 1991 embroidery on cotton, 2.25 × 2.75 in (5.72 × 6.99 cm). Photo: Ray Materson

A: My grandmother often said, "Patience is a virtue." As a youngster, I never gave the notion much credence. In fact, my life was largely a study in impatience. I wanted something, and I wanted it "now." I don't think I could have sat and embroidered for hours on end in those days.

Prison slowed me down, way down. I tried to keep to myself, and any bravado or wildness I may have portrayed on the street no longer existed in me. Still, I had a need to do something with my pent-up energy. When the embroidery came along, I found an art form that allowed for amazing creative versatility but at the same time was very labor-intensive. After completing my first couple of pieces, and being pleased with the outcome, I began the slow process of learning that rewards come slowly sometimes.

I would have a completed art piece already in my mind, but to bring it to life took time. I used that time to examine my own life, to consider the importance of "the moment." I don't know that I'm virtuous, but I have learned that good things come to those who wait.

Q: **Do you have a favorite piece from among your works?**

A: They are all my favorites! Although I am fond of the baseball images I've created. I have a wonderful grouping of the New

York Yankees from their [World Series] 2009 championship season. I think it is some of the best work I've done.

Q: **You've been trying to bring an embroidery program into the American prison system much like the Fine Cell Work program in the UK. Why it is important for prisons to have embroidery programs?**

A: I have developed a proposal that could easily and inexpensively be incorporated into existing prisoner art or education programs in the US. I have forwarded copies of my proposal to education officers and programmers at prisons in New York, Connecticut, California, and the Federal Corrections Department. To date, I have heard nothing back from any of these agencies.

Promoting programs for prisoners isn't a warm, fuzzy kind of labor. Of all the issues that our society is currently dealing with, arts programs for prisoners is probably not on anyone's list of priority items. It's a shame, because people fail to realize often enough that eighty-five percent or more of current prison inmates are going to be released some day, many sooner than society would prefer. So, the question is: Would you rather have a person released into society who has an art skill and maybe even some education? Or would you prefer a convict who has done nothing in their time away besides grow in muscular bulk and anger?

There is a huge body of research that supports the idea that arts and education programs in prisons are good, that they help prevent recidivism and promote a healthy transition into regular society. Would an embroidery program in US prisons be a good thing? Yes.

Q: **What sort of message do you hope that your work sends into the world?**

A: I've had very positive feedback from a wide variety of individuals. Michael Kimmelman, the senior art reviewer for the *New York Times,* talked about my work in his book *The Accidental Masterpiece: On the Art of Life and Vice Versa.* He stated that my portraits were of "amazing delicacy." Holland

There is a huge body of research that supports the idea that arts and education programs in prisons are good, that they help prevent recidivism and promote a healthy transition into regular society.

(FACING PAGE) Ray Materson, *Mickey Mantle*, 1993, embroidery on cotton, 2.25 × 2 in (5.72 × 6.99 cm). Photo: Ray Materson

(LEFT) Ray Materson, *Derek Jeter*, 2009, embroidery on cotton, 2.25 × 2.75 in (5.72 × 6.99 cm). Photo: Ray Materson

(RIGHT) Ray Materson, *Hideki Matsui*, 2009, embroidery on cotton, 2.25 × 2.75 in (5.72 × 6.99 cm). Photo: Ray Materson

An excerpt from Ray Materson's memoir *Sins and Needles*

Standing in line for lunch one day, I found myself between two arguing gang members. Whatever the fundamental subject at issue might have been, it was quickly lost as the tension and anger escalated. Taunts between the two men soon turned into threats of violence, and one of them pushed me aside to get in the other's face. The next thing I knew, a fist was thrown. Like ripples on a dismal pond, the ugly energy in the surrounding space began to spread out. I don't want to be in the middle of this, I thought to myself. Then, quite out of nowhere, Miguel—the Puerto Rican guy who had given me my first embroidery commission—stepped right into the center of the escalating violence.

Spouting a few commands in Spanish, he grabbed one of the brawling men by the collar. "Yo, this man here"—he pointed directly at me—"he did work for me!" As the combatants directed their attention toward me, Miguel explained in a threatening tone, "I don't want anything to happen to this guy. Comprende?"

The fight was over as quickly as it had begun. I breathed a sigh of relief and whispered a prayer of thanksgiving. Embroidery had some far-reaching benefits, I mused to myself as I returned to my place in the chow line.

Ray Materson, *Opening Day*, 1999, embroidery on cotton 2.25 × 2.75 in (5.72 × 6.99 cm). Photo: Ray Materson

Cotter of the *New York Times* said that my work and that of a few other "outsider artists" matched the quality of work hanging in the Met. I have had prison inmates, guys that have been incarcerated for decades, tell me that they'd seen a lot of different artwork in the prisons but had never seen anything like my embroidered tapestries.

When one of the first news articles about my work was published nationally, I received dozens of letters from people who were moved by the art and the story behind it. One note, from a woman in Ohio, sticks out in my mind. She said, "I just saw your pictures and read the story about you in the newspaper. You give us hope."

I cried when I read that note. To give someone hope is no small thing. I pray that my work will continue to give people hope.

Ray Materson, *(Give 'Em Hell, Bo!) Legendary Michigan Football Coach Bo Schembechler*, 1998, embroidery on cotton, 2.25 × 2.75 in (5.72 × 6.99 cm). Photo: Ray Materson

To see more of Ray Materson's work, visit **raymaterson.com**.

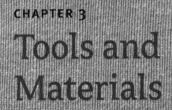

CHAPTER 3

Tools and Materials

W hile crafters rarely have trouble amassing materials, embroidery projects generally require very little equipment. One of the pleasures of an embroidery project is that you only need the most basic tools to get started: some fabric, a needle, some floss, a hoop, and a pair of scissors. However, if you are the type to collect a lot of craft materials, it is likely that many additional embroidery odds and ends will have a way of finding you.

Spend a long time at the craft store, falling in love with all the options. Buy something to play with and then set aside some time to work. Stop hesitating, just do it, and don't be afraid to mess up. Accidents sometimes make the best pieces. – ABBY KRAUSE

In embroidery, as with most arts and crafts, great tools can help, but ultimately it is your imagination that will create a successful end product. If you can dream it up, you can stitch it!

Stitch Like You Mean It

The place that you choose to embroider will affect how much you enjoy working on your project. Be sure to find a comfortable chair—you may be sitting there for hours. As you work, keep your most-used tools within arm's reach.

While you try not to prick your fingers, there are other ways you can take care of yourself. Work near a sunny window or set up a task lamp to save your eyes. And don't forget to get up and stretch from time to time. Tension in your body will affect how you pull your thread, resulting in inconsistent stitches.

Crafts are also mood-dependent; don't try to work when you are tired, angry, or distracted. Don't let a terrible mood tangle up a long-term project—set your work aside until you are feeling better.

(FACING PAGE) Sarah Haxby on Bowen Island.

Kitted Out

Filling your embroidery basket does not have to be expensive. You should be able to purchase new floss, needles, and fabric for under fifteen dollars. It can also be rewarding to re-purpose unused supplies. Look for materials at thrift stores and garage sales or talk to relatives and friends to see if they have spare materials. As you ask for their cast-offs, you are likely hear some stories about their stitch-work, and you might even be able to pick up a stitching lesson or two.

You will also need a container to hold your supplies. While fabric-lined baskets have traditionally been used to hold embroidery, there are all sorts of vessels that you can use. If you live in a child- and pet-free space, use something decorative and beautiful like an open bowl. If you have young children and pets, a container such as a lunchbox or a food-safe tub may serve your needs better. Recycled glassware, such as wide-mouthed Mason jars, are an inexpensive but pretty way to hold your work. Artist Sarah Haxby (facing page) uses a recycled plastic case that was originally a package for a duvet cover. The case has handles for easy carrying, a zipper enclosure, a waterproof exterior, and is transparent so that she can be inspired by the materials that she carries inside. Find the container that works best for you!

One of the pleasures of an embroidery project is that you only need the most basic tools to get started: some fabric, a needle, some floss, a hoop, and scissors.

Here is a photo of artist Jacque Davis's favorite embroidery supplies:

- deep basket with a sturdy handle that I can carry out to the porch

- a 6-in (15.24-cm) embroidery hoop because 7-in hoops are too large for my hands

- a fabric tube that I made with magnets in each end to hold needles and the blunt-nose Gingher scissors!

- a DMC #18 chenille needle. It has a good sharp point, and the eye is large enough that I can easily use craft thread or all six strands of embroidery floss.

- Read more about Jacque on p. 142.

Needle Me

There are many types of needles used for stitch work—most commonly, crewel, chenille, and tapestry needles. For embroidery, crewel needles, which are short and sharp, in a size between #5 and #7, are most commonly used. Blunt-ended tapestry needles are preferred for cross-stitch, as they will poke through the holes in even-weave fabric without piecing the fabric itself.

Embroidery needles are numbered for their gauge or thickness. The higher the number, the finer the needle will be. The thickness of the needles will dictate the thickness of the thread. When choosing a needle, ensure that the eye is slightly thicker than the strand of thread, and that the thread can pass through the eye of the needle with ease. The needle should also pass through the fabric evenly when threaded with floss. If you are using a fabric that has a tight weave, choose a thinner needle. For thick fabrics, use a thicker needle. If you are unsure of what needle to choose for a piece of fabric, try slipping several sizes through an inconspicuous part of your fabric to see what slips through easily.

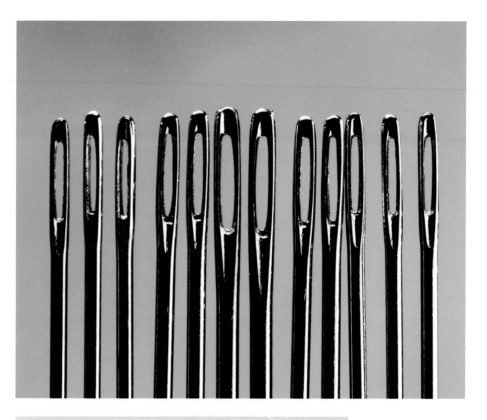

Quirky Containers

Perhaps one of these unusual containers may suit your personality:

- An old eyeglass case
- 1950's ceramic planter
- Typewriter case

- A tackle box
- A coffee or tea tin
- A cigar box

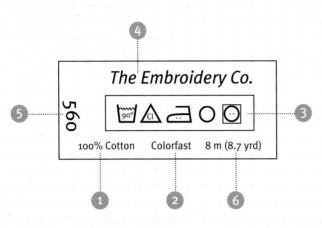

The Embroidery Co.

560

100% Cotton   Colorfast   8 m (8.7 yrd)

A Fine Thread

Embroidery floss generally comes wrapped in a paper label that can provide a lot of information about the floss, such as:

1 FIBER COMPOSITION. Typically six-strand floss is made with 100-percent mercerized cotton, which has been treated by a chemical process to be strong, smooth, and shiny. But floss isn't always cotton; it can also be made up of other sorts of fibers, so you will want to check your skein wrapper when purchasing materials.

2 COLORFASTNESS. When using vintage floss, test a small bit on scrap fabric by dabbing it with a damp paper towel to see if the color bleeds.

3 WASHING INSTRUCTIONS. Remember that these washing instructions only apply to the floss, and that you will also need to determine the fiber composition of your foundation piece when cleaning your work.

4 THE MANUFACTURER. You may want to ensure that all of the floss in a piece comes from the same product line so that the threads respond consistently to cleaning.

5 THE COLOR CODE. Each floss company has their own color matching system. If you require more of a particular color from a company, you'll want to ensure that you know the color number. When purchasing a large amount of floss, it can be helpful to snip a tiny end off and scotch tape it down in a little notebook with your floss wrapper so that you can remember how to locate the shade again.

6 THE LENGTH AND YARDAGE of the strand contained within the skein of floss. For example, the floss company DMC often packages their mercerized cotton flosses in 8.7 yd (8 m) skeins. If you are creating a project that requires 17.4 yds (16 m) of floss, you will need to purchase two of their skeins.

Stop licking your embroidery thread!

Many sewers were taught to moisten thread by licking it before threading their needles. Unfortunately, this is a destructive habit. Moisture in the eye of the needle can cause it to deteriorate. Rust will cause the thread to snag and can cause damage to your project. If you have trouble threading a needle, use a needle threader.

The more you stitch, the more you'll find which kinds of floss appeal to you. Floss can be made from materials as diverse as rayon, wool, and silk. It can be metallic, glow-in-the-dark, or variegated in color. Flosses composed of different fibers will work differently on different types of fabric, so it is always helpful to test a few stitches on a scrap before beginning your project. Pairing similar fibers is often recommended as they are easier to stitch and to clean. For example, silk floss works well with silk fabric, and wool threads work well on heavy fabrics.

It is always helpful to test a few stitches on a scrap before beginning your project.

Commercial flosses are not your only option. Some artists, like Penny Nickels (see p. 386), create their own floss using a drop spindle or a spinning wheel. You can also dye floss using tea, Kool-Aid, food coloring, or natural dyes. Most hobby stores and textile shops will have information on how to dye fibers and the processes necessary to make your dyes colorfast.

Metal Head

Although they look pretty, metallic threads can be difficult to work with; many fray easily. If this happens to you, wrap a piece of cellophane tape around the tail ends of the thread. When cutting the thread, wrap tape around the area that you wish to cut through. Cut through the tape so that each end of the thread remains fixed together until you choose to unravel the tape and thread it though your needle.

About Bobbins

Embroidery bobbins are flat cards made for storing floss. While you can purchase readymade bobbins in plastic or cardboard, you can also make your own decorative bobbins by using cut-outs from re-purposed cardboard, such as a cereal box (trace Fig. 3.0 to use as a template on lightweight cardstock) or by re-purposing wine corks or film canisters to wrap thread around.

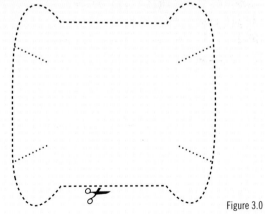

Figure 3.0

GODDESS EMBROIDERIES:
Sasha Webb

Sasha Webb lives in Vancouver, BC. Since finishing a multi-disciplinary degree in 2005, she has worked as a yoga teacher, waitress, cheesecake baker, federal tax employee, tree-planter, clothing designer, nanny, doula, and weaver. Inspired by an old costume book, the tiny works of Ray Materson, and Mary Lou Twinkwon's expansive samplers, Sasha Webb wanted to create works that could be hung in a series, and so she created Goddess Women. To make the pieces look timeless, she used natural dyes made from logwood shavings and simple embellished elements.

Find more of Sasha's textile work online at **imperialindigo .blogspot.com**

Sasha Webb, *Goddess Embroideries: Her Many Facets*, 2009, 7 ovals of hemp cotton, indigo, logwood, cotton thread, metallic thread, amber, pearls and glass beads, 7.5 × 5.5 in (19 × 14 cm). Photo: Sasha Webb

"I am enamored with the colors and elements of nature and focused on natural dyes in school. I thought it was crazy when I learned that some people dyed their own embroidery floss and was even more shocked when I started to do it myself! It seemed like too much work, but you simply cannot find thread that matches the luster and tones of natural dyes. I prefer to embroider on hemp cotton fabric using mercerized cotton thread."

Kat Siddle has designed a fun day-to-night project that uses both regular floss and glow-in-the-dark embroidery floss.

Not sure how to make those first embroidery stitches? See p. 114 for directions.

Rain and Snow Cowl

BY KAT SIDDLE

Named for a traditional folk song, the Rain and Snow Cowl offers a deceptively simple embroidery project. If you can sew a straight seam and embroider a backstitch, you can make this clever and fashionable accessory. The motif can also be transferred to a scarf or tote bag.

Tools and Materials:

EMBROIDERY FLOSS:

- 1 skein white DMC Glow-In-The-Dark Light Effects
- 2 skeins of DMC #3808 (Turquoise ULT VY-KD)

FABRIC:

- 23.5 × 9.5-in (59.69 cm × 24.13-cm) piece of medium to heavy fabric, such as a fine-wale corduroy (as in the example), a heavy woven cotton, felt, or canvas, in light blue. If using corduroy, ensure that the lines of cord run vertically across the cowl.

- 21.5 × 7.5-in (54.61 × 19.05-cm) piece light-weight white fleece fabric for the lining

- 3 in (8 cm) of turquoise ribbon, ⅛-in (3.5-mm) width

- 21.5 × 7.5-in (54.61 × 19.05-cm) piece of light weight muslin or waste fabric to test the size of the cowl (optional)

- 1 white button, 1 in (2.54 cm) diameter

- 4-in (10.16-cm) embroidery hoop

- embroidery needles, assorted sizes

- tracing paper: large sheet or sheets that can be taped together to measure at least 23.5 in (59.69 cm) long

- carbon or chalk transfer paper

- chalk dressmaker's pencil

- sewing thread

- sewing needle

- straight pins

- scissors

Stitches:

satin stitch   split stitch   straight stitch

Other skills:

sewing machine or hand sewing skills

KAT SIDDLE designs handknits, accessories, and the occasional embroidery template from her shabby-chic apartment in Vancouver, BC. Usually employed as a librarian, Kat also worked as the costume manager for the independent feature film *Outside Hope*. You can read about her thriftstore adventures, thoughts on fashion, and other crafty goings-on at **juniordeluxe.com**.

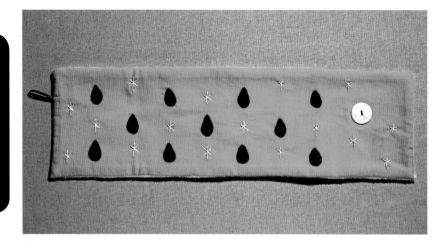

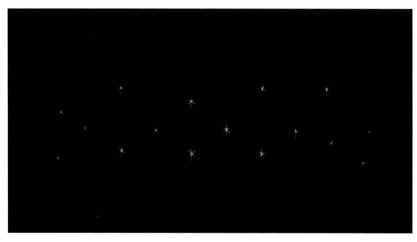

A NOTE ON SIZING: To ensure that your cowl will fit, cut out the lining on a scrap of test fabric before you cut out the good fabric. Pin back the seam allowance 0.5 in (1.27 cm) on each side, and test the size around your neck. This cowl was made to fit a 13-in (33.02-cm) neck. To make yours larger, measure your neck, then add 5–6 in (12.7–15.24 cm) for the overlap and seam allowances. This measurement becomes the length of the rectangle. Make sure you adjust the placement of the embroidered designs to match any of your alterations.

Preparation:

Cut a 23.5 by 9.5-in (54.61 × 19.05-cm) rectangle of the blue fabric. (Note: this piece will eventually be trimmed down to 21.5 × 7.5 in [54.61 × 19.05 cm]. Leaving a few extra inches of fabric to start will make it easier to stitch close to what will become the edge of the cowl.)

Trace the embroidery template (Fig. 3.1) onto tracing paper. Trim the tracing paper to a 21.5 × 7.5-in (54.61 × 19.05-cm) rectangle. Place the blue fabric right side up on a flat surface, place a sheet of carbon paper right side down on top of it, and then place the design template on top of the carbon. Make sure that the template is evenly centered in the middle of the fabric. You will have an excess border of fabric (approximately 1 in/2.54 cm) around the template. Using the carbon transfer method (p. 110), trace over the outlines of the raindrops and snowflakes with a blunt object. If the trace marks look faint on the fabric, retrace them with a chalk fabric pencil.

Secure the fabric in the embroidery hoop. Following the template (Fig. 3.1), embroider the raindrops using three strands of the DMC #3808. Fill each drop with a satin stitch (see p. 117) and outline the edges of each drop with a split stitch (p. 115), moving your hoop around the fabric as you need to. Work thread ends under after completing each element. If you want to make the raindrops pop more, use a padded satin stitch (see p. 117).

Embroider each snowflake using six strands of the Glow-In-The-Dark Light Effects floss (See Fig. 3.2 for the stitch pattern).

Once your embroidery is complete, wash and press your work (see p. 303–304). Then lay the tracing-paper template over the fabric again, matching the embroidery with the traced designs. Mark the boundaries of the 21.5 × 7.5-in (54.61 × 19.05-cm) rectangle. Pin the tracing paper to the fabric and use the paper as a guide for cutting away the excess fabric (approximately 1 in/2.54 cm around).

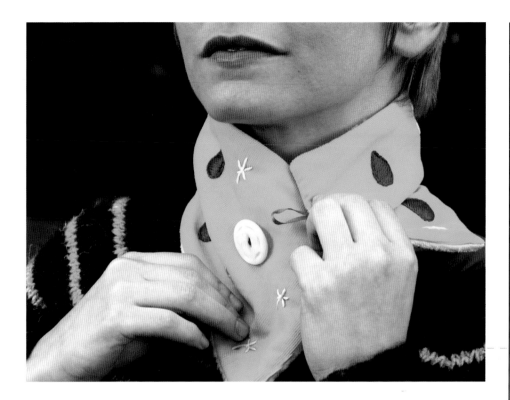

Place the exterior embroidery and the lining together, right sides facing each other. Pin a short loop (2 in/5.08 cm or less, depending on the size of your button) of the ribbon that will form your closure along the right edge. Sandwich the loop in place between the two layers of fabric and baste the loop in place.

Sew along the sides, 0.5 in (1.27 cm) from the edge. Leave a 2-in (5.08-cm) gap in the seam so that you can turn your work. Trim excess fabric from the corners by clipping the selvage edges diagonally. Turn the cowl right side out. Iron your seams to achieve a crisp edge. Press your work and then hand sew the open gap together.

Sew the button in place. Try on the cowl to make sure it fits comfortably. You are now prepared for rain or snow, day or night!

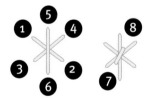

Figure 3.2: Snowflake stitches

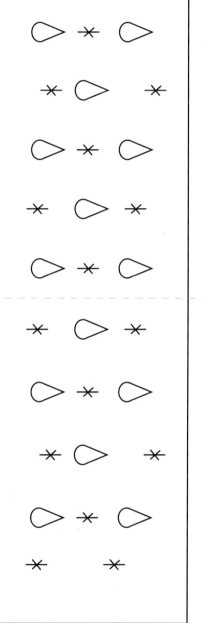

Figure 3.1: Rain and Snow Cowl Template. Copy and increase this template by 350 percent. In order for this to work on a standard photocopier, make separate copies of each half of the template (as noted by the dashed line), and enlarge each side, taping them together before copying the design onto tracing paper (p 109)

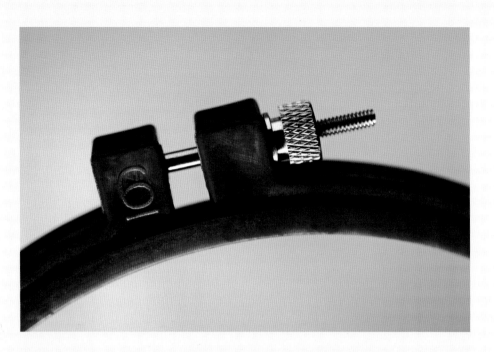

Hoop Dreams

Embroidery hoops come in all sizes but many beginners prefer a medium-sized 5 to 7-in (12.7 to 17.78-cm) hoop. Hoops can be made out of wood, metal, or plastic—every embroiderer seems to have an individual preference. Just look for something that is comfortable to hold and that tightly secures your fabric. If you are using a smaller hoop, don't worry if the entire design will not fit within the frame; you can always loosen your hoop and move it around to different areas of your fabric as you need to.

With traditional hoops, the upper piece of the hoop is the part that has the adjustable screw. This ring always goes on top of the fabric. The inner ring fits underneath the fabric. It's easiest to place the inner ring on a flat, clean surface. Lay the fabric over this hoop, smoothing out any gathers in the fabric, then place the upper ring on top. Gently tug any excess fabric from the hoop. Tighten the top ring with the screw at the top of the hoop, smoothing out any last wrinkles. When you begin to

embroider, the fabric in the hoop should be smooth and taut like the top of a drum, but it should not be stretched.

When taking a break from working on your project, release the fabric from the hoop until you return to stitching; this will prevent the hoop from creating a permanent ring-mark in the fabric.

Not all hoops are round. A new type of hoop is the Q-Snap. This clever apparatus, originally designed for quilters, is made out of PVC tubing, which won't crimp your fabric as traditional hoops can do. Square in shape, Q-Snaps can be found in embroidery-friendly sizes such as 6 × 6 in (15.24 × 15.24 cm), 11 × 11 in (27.94 × 27.94 cm), and 11 × 17 in (27.94 × 43.18 cm).

Some embroiderers forgo hoops entirely, preferring to use floor or tabletop standing frames. The advantage of these frames is that they keep the entire fabric taut, not just the part of the embroidery that is being worked. While frames are not overly mobile, and they take some work to set up, they are worth considering when planning a large-scale project.

Cut to the Chase

While you can use almost any type of scissors to trim your embroidery work, it can help to have a sharp, tiny pair dedicated to the task. Many embroiderers are drawn to the classic golden stork scissors, but any pair will do as long as you can cut easily with them. Use these scissors only for trimming thread or fabric; cutting paper or other materials will dull the blades and make them useless for embroidery work.

Choosing Your Fabric

While beginners are advised to start with a medium-weight cotton or linen, there are, of course, many kinds of fabric that can be embroidered. As you become more experienced, try to experiment with different fabrics in order to get a feel for how they work. Craft felt, denim, tweed, and even light upholstery can be fun to play with. Try stitching not only on colored fabric, but also on textiles with prints and texture. While stretch fabrics such as nylons, rayons, and knit cottons can be difficult to work with, sometimes the end result is worth the challenge.

If you're buying new fabric, the merchant should be able to tell you about the fiber contents of the cloth. Information is often printed on a sticker attached to the bolt of fabric. These labels will tell you how the fabric should be washed and dried, which will help you determine what type of floss will work best with it. If you happen to end up with material from "unknown fibers," be cautious—it may be made of flammable materials, which is potentially hazardous, especially if you are planning to use your finished work in a kitchen or on clothing. Try to use natural fibers whenever possible, whether they are purchased new or are recycled materials.

For counted needlepoint or cross-stitch, you will want to use Aida fabric—otherwise known as open-weave or even-weave cloth. Aida cloth can be purchased by the yard or meter from a fabric store or in small squares and rolls from most craft stores. Aida has different gauges or sizes, so purchase the gauge that is specified in your pattern.

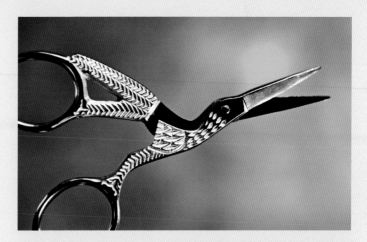

Embroidery on the Run

I saw a young girl in pigtails embroidering while waiting to board a plane. She gave me hope that the embroidery hoop continues to roll along creating future generations.
—SARAH HAXBY

Embroidery is a portable hobby. Here are some tips for taking your work with you:

1. Store your needles in those small medicine bottles and you won't stick yourself while rummaging through your bag.

2. Keep your stitching in a jumbo freezer bag. It will fold down nicely in your carry-on, is see-through for security, and will repel any crumbs that may be in your bag.

3. Transparent film canisters are great storage devices for extra floss. Your colors can be seen through the lids and your floss won't get tangled in transport.

4. Flying—and not allowed scissors? Dental floss containers have a blade that you can use to clip your thread.

For example, an 11-count Aida cloth has eleven holes per linear inch (2.54 cm). The open weave pattern will aid your stitching as you pass your needle through the holes in the fabric, not through the fibers themselves. Due to the thick weave, most Aida cloth is so stiff that you may choose not to use an embroidery hoop when stitching it.

Important note: While it is always advisable to wash cloth before beginning a sewing project, Aida cloth is the one exception. Do not wash it before you begin stitching! The fabric has a natural tendency to shrink and soften, which affects the even-weave characteristics that you will need to guide your stitching.

REUSE, REDUCE, AND UP-CYCLE

I try to use recycled materials such as bits of old clothes. I have friends who are weavers, quilters, and knitters, and they give me their scraps, which are the perfect size for me to use. —KIRSTEN CHURSINOFF

Embroidery enabled some of the earliest recycling of materials. Stitching has been used as a way to disguise recycled scraps of cloth, so that household linens could be sewn into articles of clothing and embroidered. When these garments were worn out, they would then be cut into dishrags and embellished with stitches.

Recycling cloth can eliminate unnecessary waste, and old fabric offers a wonderful worn texture that can add a soft look to your project. It feels good to know that you are taking something unwanted and making it useful again.

When up-cycling cloth, make sure that you read the washing instructions tag if you can, or try to find someone who can help you identify the fabric. If you are going to use a garment, wash and press the piece to remove any oils or dirt before you cut it apart. See "Home Invasion" on p. 254 as an example of how to bring new life to old linens.

Stabilizers

While stretch fabrics may cause some embroiderers nightmares, it can be fun to stitch on them if you have the help of a stabilizer or interface. Stabilizers create a strong foundation for your fabric; they keep the weave in place and create a thicker surface to stitch upon.

Stabilizers can come in many forms—iron adhesives, non-adhesives, stickers, tear-away stabilizers, and even a liquid paint. The trick is to choose a stabilizer that is suitable to your fabric and the cleaning methods you plan to employ. When purchasing new fabric, ask the sales person to recommend a stabilizer that will work well with that fiber. If you are working from thrifted fabric and are not sure what it's made of, begin with a tear-away stabilizer, which can be ironed into place on the wrong side of your fabric, and then be torn away or dissolved in water when you are finished.

The Humble Thimble

I don't like using thimbles, and I do like using thicker fabrics, which means I often prick my fingers, but those things don't deter me; my desire to make embroidery still wins. —TAKASHI IWASAKI

While not all embroiderers like using thimbles, they can help protect your fingers from sharp needles. Thimbles can be particularly helpful when stitching on heavy fabrics such as suiting or denim. Some people prefer to wear a thimble on their index finger to pull the floss. Others wear it on the finger that pushes the needle through the fabric. There is no right or wrong way to wear a thimble.

Thimbles come in small, medium, and large. Pick the size that corresponds to your glove size. Don't bother with the ceramic or glass thimbles that you come across in thrift stores; all the rage with tourists, these are mostly decorative, and because they can shatter are more trouble than they are worth.

How to Transfer Your Designs

Whether you like to use one of the patterns in this book as a starting point for your own pattern or create your own original work, you will first need to copy the image using a scanner or a photocopier. Use a hard copy of the image to trace the design onto fabric with a transfer pen, pencil, or paper.

Some of the designs in this book will need to be enlarged or reduced, so before you copy a design, read the Transfer Notes at the bottom of each diagram. A pdf of all patterns will be available for download at www.arsenalpulp.com/extras/Hooplapatterns.pdf.

SUPPLIES:
- a transfer medium: This can be a transfer pencil, a transfer pen, or carbon paper. (Note: carbon paper comes in colors that are suitable for transfer onto either dark or light fabrics; choose carbon color to contrast with your fabric; e.g., white carbon for dark fabric, black carbon for light-colored fabric.)
- a blunt object for tracing (such as a wooden or metal stylus, or dried up ball point pen)
- a photocopy of your design, increased to the desired size
- scissors for cutting paper
- a sheet of plain white paper (regular light-weight bond office paper or vellum will work well) (for pen and pencil transfers)
- a light source (for pen and pencil transfers)
- cellophane tape

NOTE: Before transferring an image, always pre-wash your fabric.

In Reverse

If you are creating your own design, remember that the image that you transfer using a carbon pen or pencil will be reversed from the design on paper. Therefore, any text in your design will need to be reversed on the hard copy before you trace it onto your fabric. Either flip the design on your computer before tracing it with the transfer medium or, if drawing freehand, trace the design from the reverse (wrong) side of the paper (where it should appear backwards) before tracing it with the transfer medium to achieve the same readability as the original drawing.

Unsure if you flipped your text correctly? Hold the design up to a mirror to proofread it.

Carbon Paper Tips

Carbon transfer paper comes in both wax and chalk finishes. Try out both kinds to see which you like best. Chalk transfer paper tends to work better on textured fabrics such as suiting material and corduroy, but it can be messier than wax finished carbon paper. Remember that carbon particles can rub off the sheets, so be careful not to place the sheets face down outside their packaging or to lay anything heavy on top of a package. Store any scraps from carbon sheets in the original packaging for future projects. And, after touching carbon paper, always remember to wash your hands!

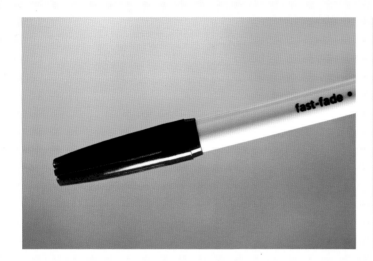

Pens vs. Pencils

Transfer pens tend to make a thicker, darker line on your fabric. While pens draw smoothly and can be easy to use, transfer pencils often come in many colors, which can be helpful if you choose to embroider on dark-colored fabric.

If you are working freehand and don't want the fuss of making a transfer, consider using a disappearing ink pen. It will allow you to draw your design but will fade away within a few days or several weeks. If you don't plan to stitch quickly, trace your design lightly in pencil.

THE CARBON TRANSFER PAPER METHOD

Cut out the pattern from the hard copy, taking care to trim it so that there is just a small margin (0.25 in/6.35 mm) of excess paper surrounding the image (this will give you an edge to hold onto when tracing without touching the design). Cut a piece of carbon paper to the same size as the pattern.

Lay your fabric down on a flat, clean surface. Then place the carbon piece face down onto your fabric, followed by your paper design on top, which should be face up. Secure both the pattern and the carbon paper to your fabric with tape so that they will not wiggle as you trace the image. Any movement may result in a line being repeated more than once, a mistake often referred to as "ghosting." Strive to make your transfer as crisp as you can.

Using a blunt object, trace your design with a firm hand. Press down hard along the artwork with enough pressure to transfer the image, but not so much that the pattern will tear. Work methodically from one corner to the other, until you have traced all parts of the pattern. When you are finished tracing, remove tape from the paper and carbon, and lift them away from the fabric—voilà! You now have a design to stitch!

THE TRANSFER PEN OR PENCIL METHOD

Transfer pens or pencils can be purchased at most fabric and craft supply stores. A pencil simply needs to be sharpened before use, whereas transfer pens need to be used a bit before their ink flows freely. Warm your pen up by testing it on a scrap of fabric.

To trace your image, find a light source with a flat surface to illuminate your design—a sunny window will do if you don't own a light box. Tape your image, right side up, to the light source with a piece of paper on top of it. Trace the image onto the tracing paper, or freehand your own design using the transfer pen or transfer pencil.

Once you've completed your tracing, treat the tracing paper with the image just as you would any other ready-made iron-on. Cut out the pattern and pre-heat the fabric so that it is warm. Lay your transfer tracing side down onto the pressed fabric, and iron it on the wrong side for ten to fifteen seconds, without wiggling the fabric against the cloth. Peel off your homemade transfer, and reveal your new stitching project!

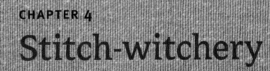

CHAPTER 4

Stitch-witchery

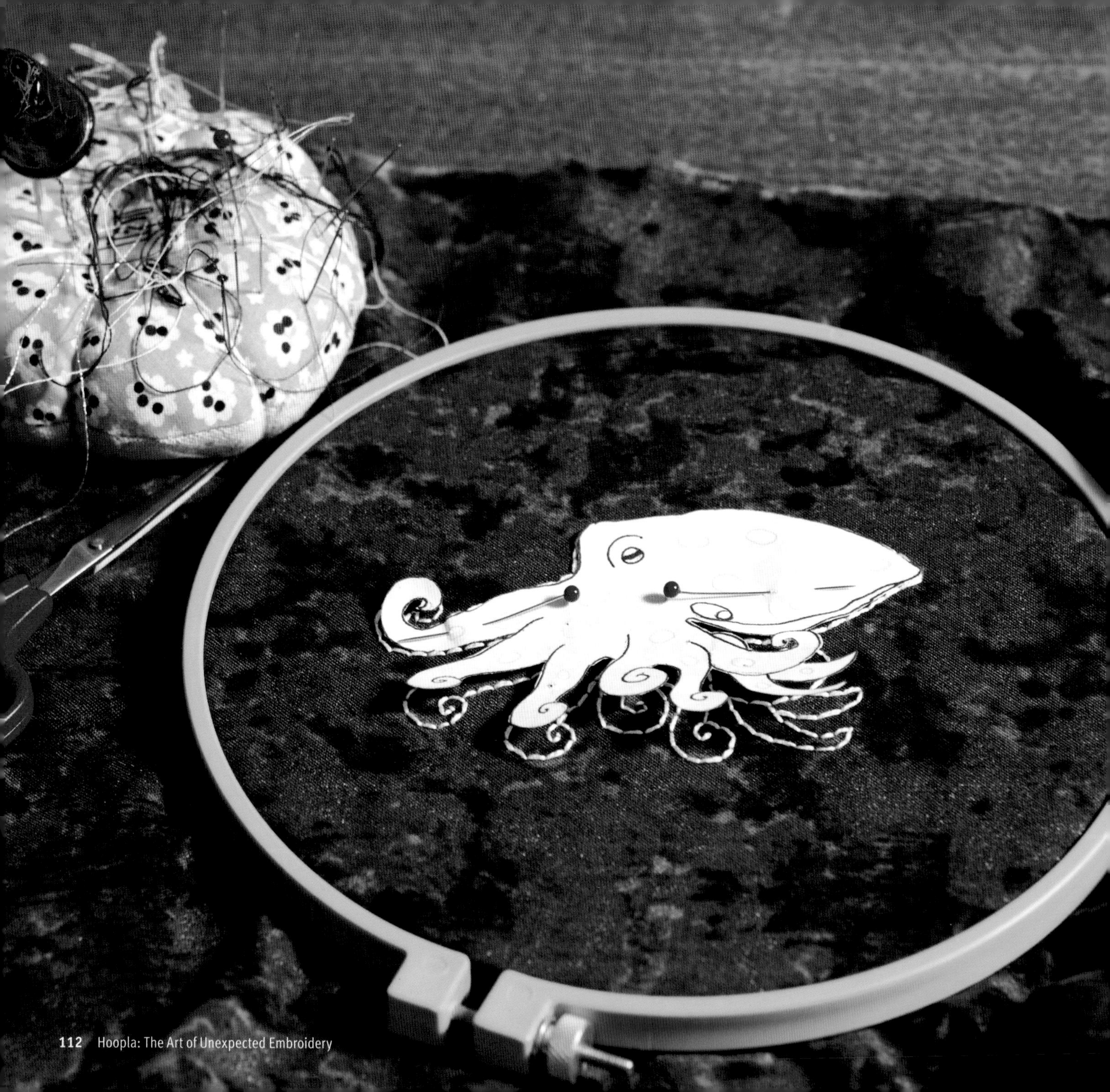

Once you have collected the basic tools, it's time to put your needle and thread to fabric. This chapter covers the simple stitches that you will need to complete the projects in this book. Remember that these stitches are merely an introduction to the world of embroidery, cross-stitch, and counted needlepoint. There are hundreds of stitch techniques that you can learn when you are ready to seek out new challenges.

Before you thread that needle, make sure that you do two critical things: 1) pre-wash and press your foundation fabric (see p. 303 for more details), and 2) wash your hands before you pick up your hoop! Any dirt or oil on your hands may stain your work.

Even those who know only one stitch can create an embroidered masterpiece—many of the artists profiled in this book use just a few types of stitches to create their work.

One-Stitch Wonders

I don't use many types of stitches—mostly running stitch and satin stitch. I kind of just draw with the thread. I just picked up a needle and thread one day and tied on a knot and started stitching. A lot of people say they only use a few stitches. —AUBREY LONGLEY-COOK

Even those who know only one stitch can create an embroidered masterpiece—many of the artists profiled in this book use just a few types of stitches to create their work. It is often not the stitch that matters, but the way that you choose to use it.

As you learn more stitching techniques, you may find that an embroidery stitch you know by one name has been given different names, or a stitch of the same name is worked differently than you

(FACING PAGE) Kirsten Chursinoff's *Octopus* in progress. Photograph by Kirsten Chursinoff.

were taught how to do it. Historically, embroidery was taught orally, so names of stitches were recalled from memory. The stitches in these chapters have been called by their most common names, and well-known pseudonyms have been provided. However, feel free to name your stitches in a way that will aid your memory.

I only know one stitch; the running stitch, so that's all I ever do, and I like to consider it, "the walking stitch." I'm embroidering these streets very slowly. My project is inspired by the Situationists, who encouraged people to get to know their city by walking. —LIZ KUENEKE

Basic Embroidery Stitches

Thread, needles, and fingers exist in the three-dimensional world, which can make written instructions for embroidery stitches somewhat confusing. If these directions make your head spin, find a friend who can teach you in person, or find some online videos that demonstrate stitches in real time. Remember that learning to embroider should be fun—choose the method that works for you!

Tips for Easy Stitching:

- Stitch with a length of floss as long as the space between your thumb and elbow.
- Floss should be smooth before you begin; make it so by separating the strands and smoothing them back together again. A floss conditioner may help.
- Always begin by pushing the needle through the fabric from the wrong side (the back) of the work. Leave a tail of floss at the back of your work at least 5–7 in (12.7–17.78 cm) long, and stick your needle through at the point where you want the stitches to begin.
- Use the correct size of needle for your floss (see p .95 for tips).

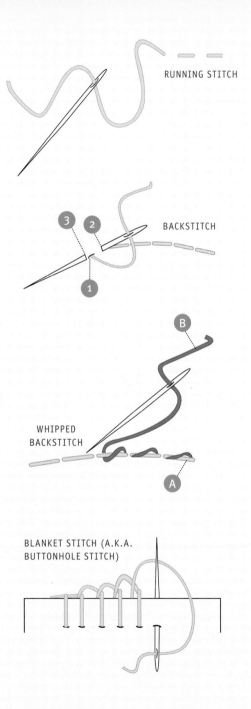

RUNNING STITCH

BACKSTITCH

3   2

1

B

WHIPPED
BACKSTITCH

A

BLANKET STITCH (A.K.A.
BUTTONHOLE STITCH)

RUNNING STITCH (A.K.A. THE HIDDEN STITCH): You may have encountered this stitch in early elementary-school craft projects. It creates a broken line that can be used for outlining a shape. To make a running stitch, move your needle in and out of the fabric at even intervals to create regularly spaced stitches of an even length.

BACKSTITCH: Learning the backstitch feels awkward at first, but eventually you will get used to it. **1** When you make your first stab at the fabric from the underside, anticipate where your stitch will end by pulling your needle through the fabric to the front. **2** Once the needle has been pulled through the right side of the fabric, stitch "backwards" by pushing the needle through the fabric one stitch-length behind the first entry point. **3** From the underside, draw the needle back up to the right side, one stitch-length away from where your last stitch ended. Repeat these three steps to create a continuous line of stitches. The backstitch can be worked in straight or curved lines.

> *Backstitch is my favorite stitch. It's very simple, and it gets the job done.* —ROSA MARTYN

WHIPPED BACKSTITCH: This is a more decorative version of the basic backstitch. Create a foundation row of large backstitches and leave a tail of thread (thread A) at the front of your fabric, close to where you began stitching. Secure the beginning and end tails of this thread to your work with several stitches, hiding the tails on the wrong side the fabric. Choose a new piece of floss as the whipping thread (thread B). Using your needle, wrap or "whip" thread B over and under thread A (the backstitches) without piercing the fabric. This should result in a neat, raised line. Whipping can also be applied to other stitches, including the running stitch, the stem stitch, the chain stitch, and satin stitch.

BLANKET STITCH (A.K.A. THE BUTTONHOLE STITCH): A looped stitch that can be worked in straight or curved lines, it can be used for surface embroidery or as a decorative finish for a hem. To create the blanket stitch, imagine that there is an invisible line running underneath the edge of your fabric. Working from left to right, bring the needle up on the invisible line and then down at right, over your fabric's edge. Moving one stitch length to the right, bring the needle up at the line, passing over the thread so that it becomes looped by your needle. Repeat these stitches to the right, ensuring they are evenly spaced and sized as you work along the edge of your fabric to create a continuous line of stitching. This stitch effect can also be achieved away from the fabric's edge if you can imagine a second invisible line instead of the fabric edge.

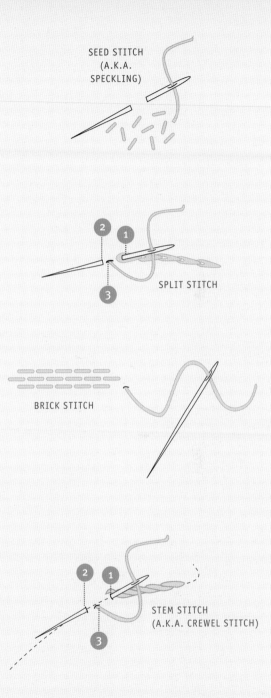

SEED STITCH (A.K.A. SPECKLING)

SPLIT STITCH

BRICK STITCH

STEM STITCH (A.K.A. CREWEL STITCH)

SEED STITCH (A.K.A. SPECKLING): This fun, erratic stitch is made by making a bunch of little backstitches (see p. 114) placed in random order.

SPLIT STITCH: ❶ Working with floss that has an even number of strands, create a single straight stitch, then bring the needle up through to the right side of the fabric in the middle of the straight stitch to split it, passing the needle through the thread itself. ❷ Push the needle through the fabric one stitch-length away from the end of the first stitch, and ❸ pass the needle up through to the front of the work in the middle of the area, thereby splitting the next stitch. The split stitch is great for outlines or can be used in rows for filling large areas of space.

The split stitch is the first one I learned. It is the easiest to do, and has the greatest effect. —JENNY HART

BRICK STITCH: This is a type of stitch that can be used to fill an area. It is created by making vertical or horizontal straight stitches of an even length in rows. The stitches fit together in a brickwork pattern of staggered stitches. The brick stitch is worked from left to right in a series of back stitches, and then back again from right to left.

STEM STITCH (A.K.A. CREWEL STITCH): The stem stitch can be used to create straight or curved lines and outlines. Each stitch should be approximately the same length and begin halfway along the previous

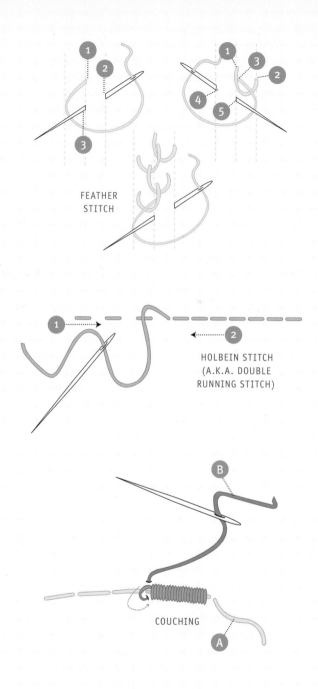

FEATHER
STITCH

HOLBEIN STITCH
(A.K.A. DOUBLE
RUNNING STITCH)

COUCHING

stitch. Working from left to right, create one straight stitch, then push the needle up into the right side of the fabric, close to your previous stitch. Finish this stitch just past the first stitch that you made. Repeat.

FEATHER STITCH (A.K.A. FEATHER CHAIN): This stitch is worked vertically. **1** Start by bringing the thread through the front of the work; **2** push the needle through to the back in along a parallel line, a stitch-width down from where you started. Do not pull the thread all the way through to the back, but **3** poke the needle back through the fabric halfway between where you began and ended your first stitch. Catch the thread under the needle to tack the stitch in place. **4** To create a second stitch, move one stitch length to the left. **5** Repeat the stitch, working from left to right and right to left.

HOLBEIN STITCH (A.K.A. DOUBLE RUNNING STITCH): Similar to the backstitch, the Holbein stitch is worked in a fine line and is often used in blackwork patterns (see p. 232). Usually created on even-weave fabric, this stitch is worked in two steps. **1** A running stitch is created, working left to right, along the line to be covered. **2** A second running stitch, which fills the spaces between the first set of stitches, is worked from right to left on the same line.

COUCHING: A decorative thread is laid onto the fabric (thread A), which is then embellished and held in place by a second thread (thread B). The decorative thread is often referred to as the "laid" thread, and stitchers have used string, cords, metallic threads, and some unusual materials for this. The second or "couching" thread should be made of smooth and shiny fibers. Two to three strands of embroidery floss are recommended for the couching thread.

Begin to make the stitch by securing the couching thread to the fabric with a few backstitches. Place the laid thread onto the fabric, leaving an extra 1.5 in (4 cm) of space around your backstitches. Use the couching thread to make evenly spaced vertical stitches over and around the laid thread. Place the couched stitches close together or far apart to achieve the desired effect.

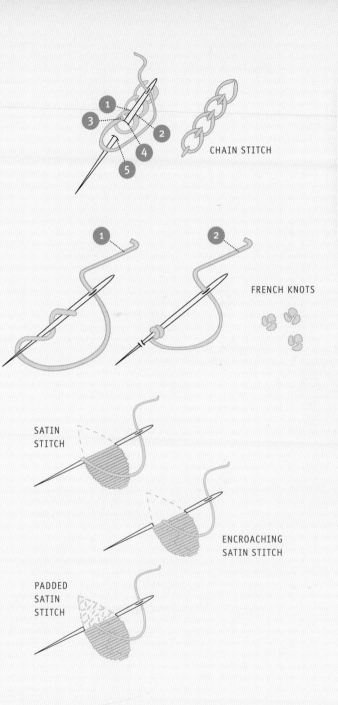

CHAIN STITCH: The basic chain stitch resembles links in a chain: it is slightly raised and can be used to create straight or curved lines. **1** Begin by bringing the needle through to the front of your work, then **2** bring the thread back through at the top of the stitch to create a loose loop. **3** Before you pull the thread taut, hold the loop down with your thumb, and reinsert your needle into the back of the work where you placed the first stitch. **4** While still holding down the loop, bring the needle out to the front, one stitch width away from the original starting point. **5** With the loop of thread underneath your needle, pull the thread taut in order to create the first chain link. Repeat as necessary to create the rest of the chain.

CHAIN STITCH

FRENCH KNOTS: These dramatic stitches, once mastered, are fun to make. **1** Bring your thread to the front of the work. Holding it taut with a finger, wrap the thread around the needle twice. **2** Insert the needle into the fabric close to the point where the thread emerged from the back of the work. Pull the needle and thread to the back, leaving the perky-looking knot at the front of your work.

FRENCH KNOTS

> *There is nothing so satisfying as a carpet of delicate French knots. Each one adds just the right amount of surface texture.*
> —IVIVA OLENIK

SATIN STITCH: This stitch is used to fill in, or shade, areas with color. A basic satin stitch is a series of straight stitches that are worked close together. To make satin stitching look shiny and silky, ensure that the stitches measure no longer than 0.25 in (6.35 mm).

SATIN STITCH

If a piece requires filling in a large area, use an ENCROACHING SATIN STITCH by working in rows that are staggered enough to disguise an obvious join-line.

ENCROACHING SATIN STITCH

You can also create depth and shadow in your work by creating a PADDED SATIN STITCH, made by working a foundation of stitches (such as a running stitch or chain stitch) underneath a satin stitch. The foundation stitches give the satin stitch a raised or padded appearance.

PADDED SATIN STITCH

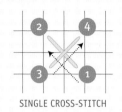

SINGLE CROSS-STITCH

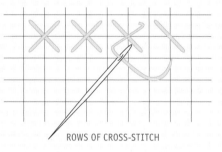

ROWS OF CROSS-STITCH

COUNTED CROSS-STITCH

The patterns in this book that have charts (such as the "Modern Cuckoo Clock," "Bite the Hand That Feeds You," and "Along for the Ride") are created using a simple cross-stitch. Cross-stitch is almost always stitched on Aida fabric (see p. 107) where the spaces between the vertical and horizontal threads are the same. Cross-stitch work that uses a chart or graph, where the pattern for the design is followed precisely, is known as counted cross-stitch.

The SINGLE CROSS-STITCH is created by a single cross in an invisible square. You can eyeball the square by looking at four spaces clustered together on a piece of Aida fabric. Bring the needle through to the right side of the fabric, moving diagonally from the bottom right-hand corner to the top left-hand corner of the square. From the underside of the work, move the needle diagonally down through the bottom left-hand corner of the square to the upper right corner, and you have a finished x!

Try cross-stitching your favorite number. Once you've tried it in a relaxed environment, you'll realize the pleasure that stitching brings. From there, all you need is imagination, and you're away. —JAMIE CHALMERS, MR X STITCH

ROWS OF CROSS-STITCH can be efficiently created by stitching half of the xs in one direction and completing the cross-stitches in the opposite direction. Working right from left, move your needle from each bottom right corner to upper left corner. Repeat until you reach the end of the row. Then return back along the row, working left to right, completing each x with a bottom left to top right motion.

Once you've mastered the simple cross-stitch, you'll find many new stitches that you can add to your repertoire...such as the half cross-stitch, the three-quarter cross-stitch, the quarter cross-stitch, and the double cross-stitch.

TIP: In cross-stitch, counted needlepoint, and satin stitch, keep the direction of your stitches consistent to achieve an even sheen.

To Knot or Not

Traditionally, knots were thought to make a finished work look lumpy so it was thought better to leave a tail of thread behind the work instead of a knot. Embroidery has usually been worked through the fabric well enough that it will not unravel. However, if you are embellishing a piece that will be well-handled, such as a piece of clothing, you may want to use a knot. Begin your piece with knotted thread and end your stitches with a small backstitch on the underside.

COUNTED NEEDLEPOINT

Needlepoint is stitched on an even-weave canvas that follows a chart or a screen-printed image. To create the final image, the stitches are counted so that the picture is precise. Needlepoint designs can be worked in a variety of stitch patterns, but tent stitch or half cross-stitch are the most popular. As with an Aida cloth, the open, even weave will determine where the threads should be placed. Counted needlepoint projects in this book include "Ode to the Ones and Twos" and "Bosom Buddies."

TENT STITCH (A.K.A. PETIT POINT OR CONTINENTAL TENT STITCH): Working diagonally through the weave of the canvas openings, this stitch produces a diagonal effect on both sides of the canvas. Start new stitches in the hole next to where the previous stitch began. Take care not to distort your canvas by pulling your stitches too hard; this diagonal stitch has a tendency to pull and make the canvas appear to "lean." Tent stitch can be worked from right to left and vice versa, as your pattern requires.

HALF CROSS-STITCH: This resembles the tent stitch, but the back side is created as a straight bar, rather than a diagonal stitch.

TENT STITCH (A.K.A. PETIT POINT OR CONTINENTAL TENT STITCH

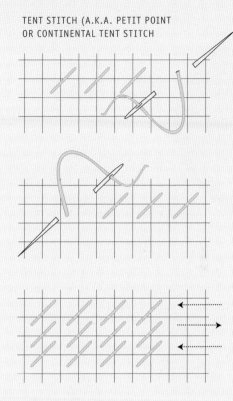

Wolftastic Scarf

LAURA MCMILLAN

Making a few simple stitches on a line drawing can result in a compelling embroidery project. Laura McMillan has developed two basic wearable projects for you to try. Follow the stitches she suggests, or try your own variations using the stitches described in this chapter.

This project was inspired by an experience Laura had during a summer of tree planting. One day while she was working, she felt someone watching her from the trees. Returning to camp, she found wolf prints on the muddy road. That night she dreamt that she was running through the forest with a wolf guiding her way.

Tools and materials

FLOSS:

■ 1 skein of DMC #310 (Black)

■ 1 skein of DMC #645 (Beaver Gray VY - DK)

FABRIC:

8 × 8-in (20.32 × 20.32-cm) square of white cotton-linen blend

1 yd (0.91 m) of black linen (to make the scarf)

light interfacing

fusible interfacing (to aid in attachment to scarf)

embroidery needle, size 1–3

6–8-in (15.24–20.32-cm) embroidery hoop

carbon transfer paper

pen or pencil

sewing machine thread

sewing machine (optional)

scissors

Stitches:

backstitch   running stitch

Other Skills:

basic sewing machine operation

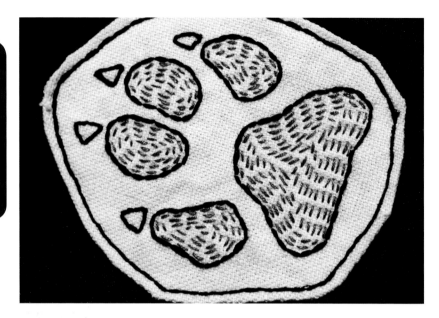

Make Your Wolf Tracks

Transfer paw designs (Fig.4.1) onto the white fabric using the carbon paper method described on p. 109. Place light interfacing underneath fabric, and place hoop over both interfacing and fabric.

Using DMC #310, outline the design using a backstitch. Next, follow the contour of the outline with a running stitch in DMC #645, gradually working around to the center. The circles will become smaller as they fill in the inside of the paw print.

Once finished, remove the fabric from the hoop, and trim the light interfacing close to the embroidery. Set aside while you are making your scarf.

To Make the Scarf

Cut along the length of the black fabric to make a 15-in (38.1-cm) wide strip. Fold the fabric in half lengthwise with right sides together and iron. Sew one short end and the long edge together to create a tube. Iron open the seams of your sewn edges. Turn the tube right side out. Turn under the open end of the tube 0.5 in (1.27 cm) and iron the seam into place. With your fingers, roll each sewn edge so that the seam edge looks crisp and flat. Press the scarf. Close the open end with hand stitching.

Attach the Embroidered Design

Cut the fusible interfacing in the size of the paw print appliqué shapes. Remove one side of the interfacing, arrange on back of embroidery and iron, fusing the interfacing to the back.

Cut excess fabric from around the stitched design, leaving 0.25–.5 in (6.35 mm–1.27 cm) around the edge of the fused interfacing shape. Clip the seam allowance with small cuts to make it easier to turn the seam.

Peel off the second side of the fusible interfacing. Arrange the paw prints, right side up, on the scarf in desired location. With a needle or pin, slowly turn the

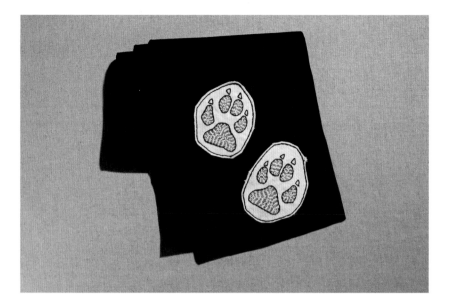

small, snipped edge flaps under along the edges. When a clean edge has been achieved, take the top point of a warm iron and press this part of the design.

Once the entire edge has been turned under, press the iron onto the design several times to fuse the patch to the garment.

Finishing the Scarf

Use three strands of black embroidery thread to backstitch around the edge of the appliqué to secure the edges of the patches. Don your finished scarf, go outside, and howl at the moon!

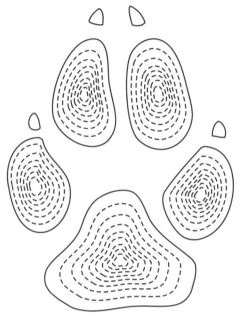

Figure 4.1. Copy at 100 percent

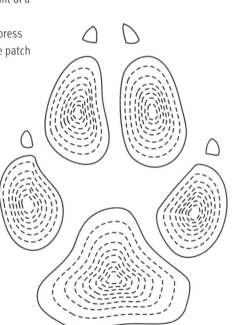

Eye to the Sky Pocket Protector

LAURA MCMILLAN

Laura says, "This project was inspired by the eye troubles of a relative. I started taking a keen interest in the anatomy of the eye and discovered just how intricate and beautiful it is. The anatomical drawings I found seemed so drab, so I decided to add rainbows to my design to up the fun and magical qualities!"

Tools and materials

FLOSS:

■ 1 skein of DMC #310 (Black)

■ 1 skein of DMC #645 (Beaver Gray VY - DK)

(Colors of your choice can be substituted for colors in the example project:)

■ 1 skein of DMC #817 (Coral Red VY - DK)

■ 1 skein of DMC #740 (Tangerine)

■ 1 skein of DMC #972 (Canary - Deep)

■ 1 skein of DMC #905 (Parrot Green - DK)

■ 1 skein of DMC #824 (Blue VY - DK)

FABRIC:

8 × 8 in (20.32 × 20.32 cm) of white cotton-linen blend

a pair of jeans or another garment (optional: you can stitch this project on any piece of fabric)

Embroidery needle, size 1–3

6–8-in (15.24–20.32-cm) embroidery hoop

light interfacing

fusible interfacing

carbon transfer paper

pen or pencil

scissors

Stitches:

backstitch   covered backstitch

seed stitch   blanket stitch

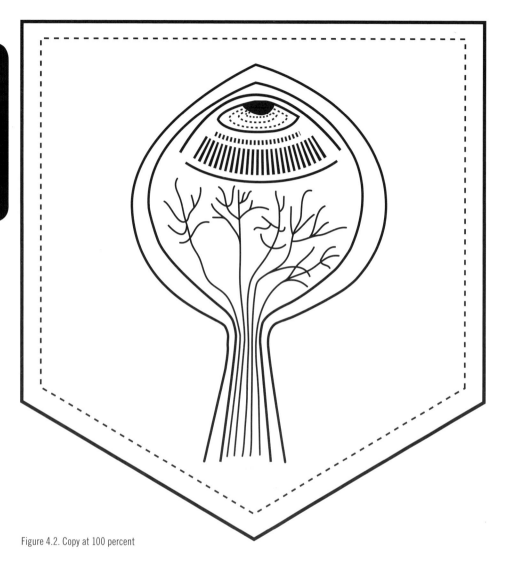

Figure 4.2. Copy at 100 percent

Keep Your Eye on the Prize

Transfer the design (Fig. 4.2) onto the fabric using the carbon paper transfer method (p. 109).

Note: If applying the pocket to a garment, as in the example project, you may need to enlarge or reduce the size of the design before transferring it so that it will fit onto your pocket. Measure twice, trace once!

Place the interfacing under the fabric and center the design in the hoop. Stitch the pattern in a variety of colors and stitch patterns as shown. The example project uses a rainbow of colors and backstitch, satin stitch, and running stitch. Begin with DMC #310 to outline the eyeball, and follow this by stitching in the veins with colors of your choice. When the stitching is complete, trim the interfacing around the edge of the embroidery to reduce the size of the patch.

Cut a portion of fusible interfacing in the exact size and shape of the pocket to which you wish to attach the patch.

Peel away one side of the interfacing and fuse it to the back of the embroidered design.

Draw a generous (up to 1 in/2.5 cm) hem allowance around the fusible interfacing shape on the underside of the embroidery. Make small snips at the corners to allow for folding and hemming.

Fold the hem allowance under, and iron only the edge of the patch where the two layers of fabric meet. These two layers will now be fused.

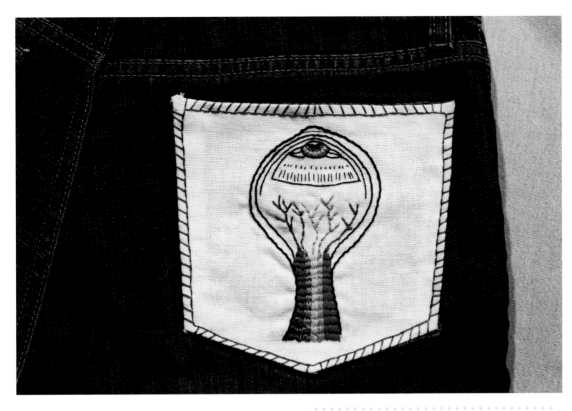

Preheat garment with an iron. Place the patch on the garment and use the iron to fuse the embroidery to the fabric. Add a decorative stitch around the edge to attach the patch more securely. If you require a guide for stitching, use a pencil to draw a straight line around the edge of the pocket.

Use the edge of the pocket to create a slanted blanket stitch around the edge of the patch, always working back to your drawn line. Make a backstitch around the line you drew in pencil, covering all marks. A thimble may help you push your the needle through all the layers of fabric.

Put on your new gussied-up garment and feel like you have a third eye!

LAURA MCMILLAN is a textile and mixed-media artist living in British Columbia. Her creativity is fueled by her experiences in nature. She began stitching on a regular basis a few years ago while attending the textile arts program at Capilano University in North Vancouver, BC. She realized that everything looks better when stitched and became hooked! Laura's other work can be found on her blog dropspindletimes.blogspot.com, Etsy shop **www.dropspindletimes.etsy.com**, and portfolio **laura-mcmillan.com**.

PAINTING WITH THREAD:
Kirsten Chursinoff

Beaded octopi, translucent jellyfish, shimmering starfish—the detailed work of Vancouver artist Kirsten Chursinoff is a pleasure to behold. By creating her own techniques that combine hand stitching, raw-edge appliqué, and free-motion machine embroidery, Kirsten's layered nature studies are detailed and charming. Seen from across the room, they can convince a viewer that they are paintings rather than fiber.

Q: **How long have you been interested in embroidery?**

A: My grandmother taught me when I was quite small. I used to do those iron-on transfers of butterflies and flowers. My mother did a lot of needlepoint while she was pregnant with me, and I feel like I assimilated it by osmosis.

I didn't call myself an artist, because I couldn't draw very well. My sister was the artist in the family, as she could always draw and paint, but I discovered myself through stitching.

The first time I went to college, I took environmental studies, but I found that I was up late at night knitting or crocheting instead of cramming for exams. Luckily, when I returned to college the second time, I found the textile program at Capilano College.

Octopus and Anemones, 2010, floss, yarn, thread, beads, fabric, 5 × 6.5 in (12.7 × 16.51 cm). Photo: Ernst Schneider

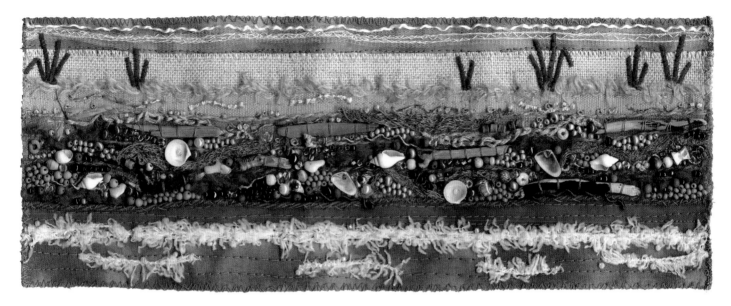

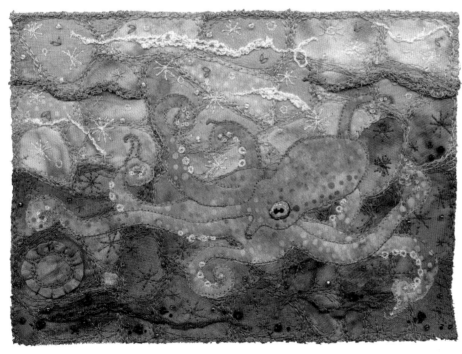

(TOP) Kirsten Chursinoff, *Seaweed Cove*, 2009, floss, thread, yarn, beads, shells, fabric, 10.5 × 4 in (26.67 × 10.16 cm). Photo: Ernst Schneider

(BOTTOM) Kirsten Chursinoff, *Octopus's Garden*, 2009, floss, yarn, thread, fabric, 7.5 × 5.25 in (19.05 × 13.34 cm). Photo: Ernst Schneider

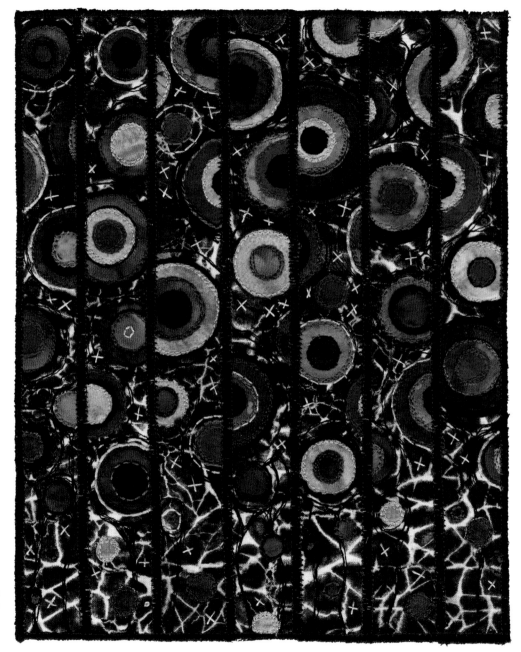

Kirsten Chursinoff,
Momentum, 2008, floss,
thread, beads, thread fabric,
8 × 10 in (20.32 × 25.4 cm).
Photo: Ernst Schneider

Kirsten Chursinoff, *Moonlight Umbels*, 2010, floss, thread, beads, thread fabric, 5 × 6.5 in (12.7 × 16.51 cm). Photo: Ernst Schneider

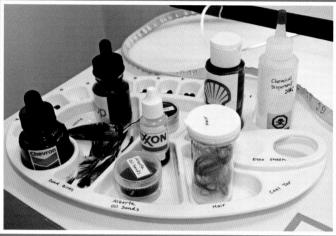

PHOTO BY ANGELA READY

I n 2008, when I applied for an art show called Low Tide, I knew that I wanted to work on a piece about the west coast of British Columbia and explore the seashore. But in the last few months, as I was working on the pieces, all I could hear on the news was that this oil spill in the Gulf [of Mexico] kept growing larger. I knew that I had to do something [about it] with my show. In my art, I try to find beauty in unusual things such as spiders, octopi, or even tubeworms. This oil spill was something that I couldn't find beauty in.

I came up with the idea of staging an oil spill that would happen on one of my pieces of art. I decided to destroy an embroidered landscape that contained a sea-shore with flotsam and jetsam—driftwood and seashells made of glass and wooden beads. I added yarn to represent seaweed and embroidered trees to represent the west coast.

I immersed that piece in a tray of water. To the side of that, I had an art palette of materials. I filled these jars with black inks and paints and some shimmery materials. I covered the labels with the logos of all the corporate oil companies—Exxon, Shell, BP.

The piece of work that I decided to destroy was an embroidered and beaded landscape. It looked like a seashore with flotsam and jetsam. I have never ruined a piece of art before—I was quite nervous. I submerged the piece in this thick, black oil slick and doused the seashore with the "chemicals" of the oil companies, changing the landscape.

Kirsten Chursinoff re-enacts the 2010 oil spill off the Gulf Coast of Mexico on one of her textile pieces at The Opening of Low Tide, her art show at Crafthouse Gallery in Vancouver, 2010. Photo: Angela Ready

Q: **Your education explains the environmental interest in your work.**

A: Yes, I've been able to bring the two elements together with textile design and with the oil spill that I recently created at a gallery.

Q: **What techniques do you use?**

A: I used to do primarily hand-embroidery with French knots. I loved the denseness that they gave to the cloth—it transformed a flimsy piece of cloth into this heavy, rich textural surface.

To avoid repetitive stress injury, I started to use my sewing machine as an embroidery tool. I disable the feed dogs (the mechanism that pulls the fabric forward) so that I can move my fabric in any direction underneath the needle and do free-motion embroidery using zigzag and straight stitching. Sometime I use a hoop, but often I work on an artist canvas. I don't use a lot of stitches. I use basic stitches but combine them in different ways with techniques that make them unusual.

Q: **What's the biggest challenge with the sort of work that you do?**

A: One of the challenges is to figure out how representational I want to be with the image or how illustrative or how abstract, and where it will lie across that spectrum. Some of the pieces become more like botanical or scientific illustrations, but then I'll do something different, make one element—like the eye on an octopus—bigger, so that it shows up in the composition.

I take photos, and do a little bit of sketching, but a lot of it happens like collage. I cut a fabric piece, stitch it into place, and just play with the elements. I like to try to find a way to

Kirsten Chursinoff, *Red Anemones*, 2010, floss, yarn, thread, beads, fabric, 2.5 × 2.5 in (6.35 × 6.35 cm). Photo: Ernst Schneider

capture change and motion with a material that is meticulous and time-consuming.

I like to look for beauty in unusual places and sometimes get a bit quirky with unusual subject materials. The message might be, look at things more closely. Art can be made using many materials; it doesn't have to be just drawing and painting. You can create your imagination out of other materials.

(FACING PAGE) Kirsten Chursinoff, *Jellyfish*, 2010, floss, thread, beads, thread fabric, 4 × 4 in (10.16 × 10.16 cm). Photo: Ernst Schneider

(THIS PAGE) Kirsten Chursinoff's octopus in progress; Kirsten Chursinoff at work in her studio.

See more of Kirsten's work at **chursinoff.com/kirsten**.

Like Kirsten's undersea creatures? She has designed a
pattern so that you can make one of your own.

A Creature of Curiosity

BY KIRSTEN CHURSINOFF

*Marine life—specifically, the octopus—fascinates Kirsten Chursinoff. The eight
twisting arms, lined with suckers, presented an interesting embroidery challenge.*

Tools and materials

FLOSS:

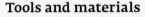 1 skein of DMC #3021 (Brown Gray VY - DK)

FABRIC:

14 × 14-in (35.56 × 35.56-cm) or larger piece of medium-
weight cotton in off-white, cream, or subtle prints. Try
using vintage fabric from clothing, pillowcases, or napkins.
NOTE: The size of fabric determines the size of the pattern.

embroidery needle size 1–3

7-in (17.78-cm) embroidery hoop (or different size of hoop,
if the image is enlarged or reduced)

picture frame without glass (vintage or second-hand).

TIP: Find the frame first and scale the pattern proportionally
within the space of the frame.

hardware to hang the frame

2 pieces of acid-free mat board, cut to the size of the
opening of the picture frame

1 spool of sewing thread in a color that matches your fabric

scissors

Stitches

backstitch   French knots

Preparation

Before you begin, wash and iron the fabric.

Measure the frame opening and scale the pattern
(Fig. 4.3) to fit, allowing some space on all sides of
the image when centered within the frame.

Determine the size of your other materials based
on the frame size. For example, if the pattern needs
to be sized up by ten percent, then other measure-
ments should increase by ten percent.

Transfer the image to the center of the fabric
using the carbon paper transfer method (p. 110).

Capture Your Creature

Mount the fabric in the embroidery hoop. Separate
the floss into one or two strands to create a thin
line. Use three strands if you prefer a thicker
embroidery line or if you've chosen a larger frame.

TIP: When embroidering with dark floss on a
light fabric, avoid carrying the thread across the
back of the work, as it may show through the fabric.

Using a backstitch, outline the octopus. Use
French knots for the suckers on the octopus. Remove
finished embroidery from the hoop and press the
finished project.

To Frame Your Octopus

Lay the fabric on top of the mat board, embroidery side up. Center the pattern/image on the mat board. Temporarily tuck the excess fabric around the back of the board to see if the embroidery fits in the frame. If the fabric is too bulky, you may need to trim the mat board so that it fits within the frame with the excess fabric stretched behind it.

Once you know that they will fit, gently remove fabric and mat board from the frame. Placing your embroidery face down with the mat board on top of it, fold the right and the left sides of excess fabric toward each other. Using the sewing thread, stitch these sides up around the mat board in a large zigzag stitch. Repeat this step by sewing together the excess fabric from the top and the bottom of the piece. The sewing will stretch the fabric taut and ensure that it is held in place without glue.

Insert mounted embroidery in the frame. Secure any hardware that you wish to use, and hang your piece. Step back and admire your new undersea friend!

Figure 4.3. Enlarge or reduce to fit your picture frame before transferring this design to fabric.

CHAPTER 5

Freeform Work

S ome artists prefer not to work with patterns, even those of their own making. They design as they stitch, guiding their needle and thread in whatever direction feels right. Freeform embroidery is an intuitive act in which the results are often joyful and mysterious.

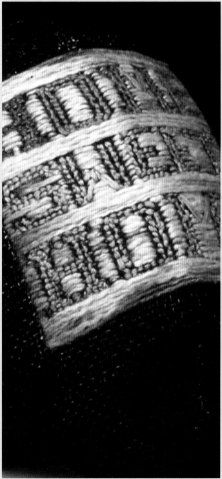

(LEFT TO RIGHT) Sarah Haxby, *Peargirl* (*Yellow*), 2008, embroidery thread on found linen, 8.5 × 8.5 in (21.59 × 21.59 cm).

Jacque Lynn Davis, *Silly Little Dolls*, 2009, dolls made from upholstery fabric samples and other notions from the St. Louis Teacher's Recycle Center, filled with recycled bags, each approx. 12 in (30.48 cm) tall. Photo: Jacque Lynn Davis

Andrew J. Phares, *Home Sweet Home*, 1999, fencing mask, embroidery floss, 10 × 7 × 9 in (25.4 × 17.78 × 22.86 cm). Photo: Andy Krause

Rebekah Nathan, *untitled*.

COLORFUL ABSTRACTIONS:
An Interview with Jacque Lynn Davis

The work of Jacque Lynn Davis invariably makes people smile. Jacque Lynn works as a blood-bank specialist in St. Louis, Missouri, but also finds the time to create her playful embroideries. Her art has embellished abstract canvases, decorated dolls, and has even been used for guerrilla-style adbusting. Throughout the online embroidery community, her abstract works are well-known for combining vivid color, embroidered texture, and humor.

Q: **What makes your stitchwork unusual?**

A: I like to make my abstract embroidery unplanned, so I often stitch without drawing a pattern. Since I don't have a pattern to transfer, I can easily work on black fabric. I start by stitching a large element or group of geometric shapes and then add more and more to play off each other.

My supplies also influence my embroidery. I live near the St. Louis Teachers' Recycle Center, where I have gotten pieces of fabric from upholstery sample books. The pieces are small and great for embroidery art. I have selections of 100-percent silk, nubby wools, and wonderful linens that I bought for one dollar a pound. I also play with embroidery on items from the ninety-nine cent store, stitching on stuffed toys, small bags, and coin purses.

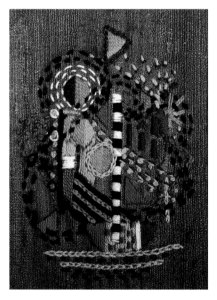

Jacque Lynn Davis, *Signal Flags*, 2010, freeform embroidery, recycled silk, 5 × 7 in (12.7 × 17.78 cm). Photo: Jacque Lynn Davis

(FACING PAGE) Jacque Lynn Davis, *Untitled*. 2009, freeform embroidery on recycled silk/ wool fabric, approx. 13 × 13 in (33.02 × 33.02 cm). Photo: Jacque Lynn Davis

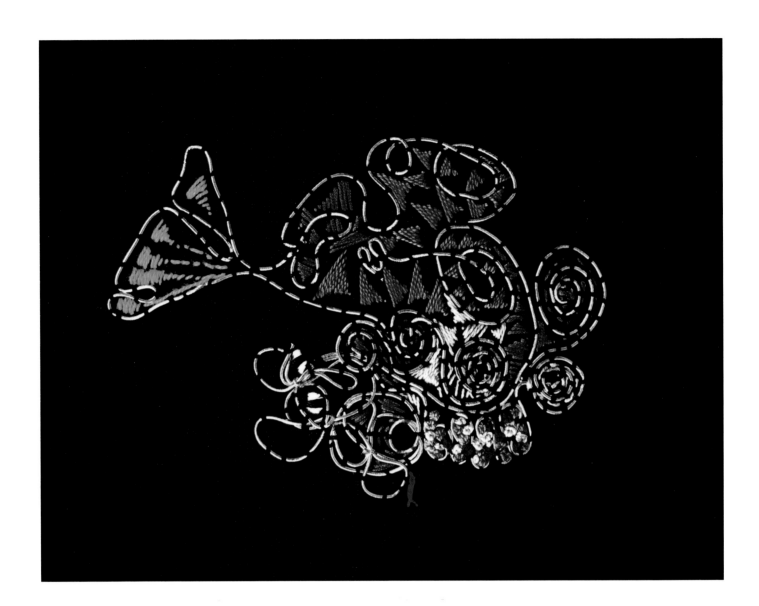

Jacque Lynn Davis, *Untitled*, 2010, freeform embroidery
with gold elastic, 5 × 7 in (12.7 × 17.78 cm). Photo: Jacque
Lynn Davis

Jacque Lynn Davis, *Chain Stitch on Red*, 2010, freeform
embroidery stitched on recycled upholstery example fabric,
8 × 9 in (20.32 × 22.86 cm). Photo: Jacque Lynn Davis

(ABOVE) Jacque Lynn Davis, *Alien Doll*, 2010, stuffed toy and china doll from a dollar store, approx 9 in (22.86 cm) tall. Jacque says, "To make this weird alien doll, I combined two dollar store finds, a stuffed toy and a china doll, then I hand-embroidered the whole thing, 'cause sometimes, you know, you just gotta do weird." Photo: Jacque Lynn Davis

Jacque Lynn Davis, *Why Not?* Mixed Media for Transit Art, 2010, freeform hand embroidery on fabric, matte paper printed with digital art, 70.75 × 45 in (180 × 114 cm). Produced for V-TARP: The Vancouver Transit Ad Re-Appropriation Project curated by Jerm IX and Vegas in Vancouver. A team of participants covertly installed artwork in the Vancouver, BC, transit system to reclaim adspace that corporations use to communicate with the public. Photo: Jacque Lynn Davis

Jacque Lynn Davis, *Conversation on Green*, 2010, doodled embroidery on recycled green upholstery fabric, 5 × 7 in (12.7 × 17.78 cm). Photo: Jacque Lynn Davis

Q: **What is your favorite embroidery stitch?**

A: I usually do lots of chain stitch circles and triangles, then add satin stitch rectangles, lots of French knots, and bullion-stitch dots. If I'm wondering what to sew next, I'll think about a different stitch to use and let it guide the shape and look of the element.

When I embroider, I use six strands of floss—it's sort of the equivalent of drawing with fat markers—it's big and bold and fast. My stitching is far from neat, but I really do have fun.

Q: **What do you like about embroidery?**

A: When I do freeform embroidery, it is like doodling very slowly. As I work on one element, I can start to think about what I want to add next. The textures of the thread, fabric, and embroidery knots seem to give the doodle an importance that it wouldn't have on paper.

Q: **Where do you get your inspiration for your embroidery work?**

A: I'm fascinated about what causes a drawing to seem humorous. What is it about the style of drawing that has that cartoon appeal? I like to use talk-balloons, pie eyes, Ben-Day dots, dotted lines, and black-and-white checks. I think those elements, in bold bright colors, convey a lot of happy, silly energy!

Find more of Jacque Lynn's work online at **flickr.com/photos/ jacquedavis**.

Wide-Ruled Scrawl

AMY ADOYZIE

When Amy Adoyzie was inspired to recreate a piece of loose-leaf paper using her sewing machine, she knew that she had to return to her doodling roots to embellish the project. She says, "This is an attempt to celebrate the little creative things that we may feel are insignificant—to painstakingly stitch the seemingly frivolous scrawls of my younger teenage self, who helped to mold and shape who I am today." Stitch Amy's design, or unearth some old doodles of your own to commemorate in thread.

Tools and materials

FLOSS:

(colors are optional, but this is what was used in the example project)

- 1 skein of DMC #797 (Royal Blue)
- 1 skein of DMC #535 (Ash Gray VY - LT)
- 1 skein of DMC #310 (Black)
- 1 skein of DMC #3837 (Lavender - ULT DK)
- 1 skein of DMC #307 (Lemon)
- 1 skein of DMC #3807 (Cornflower Blue)
- 1 skein of DMC #321 (Red)

FABRIC:

10.5 × 13-in (26.67 × 33.02-cm) white, bottom-weight, plain-weave (60 percent cotton, 40 percent polyester)

embroidery needle, size of your choosing

9 × 18-in (22.86 × 45.72-cm) embroidery frame or 8-in (20.32-cm) embroidery hoop

sewing machine thread in red and blue to create the loose-leaf paper. (The example project uses Gutermann No. 227 100m and Gutermann No. 323 100m)

disappearing fabric pen

rotary cutter

cutting mat

quilter's ruler

8.5 × 11-in (22 × 28-cm) sheet of loose-leaf paper

sewing machine

zipper foot attachment for sewing machine

scissors

Stitches:

split stitch   straight   satin stitch

Skills required:

basic sewing machine operation

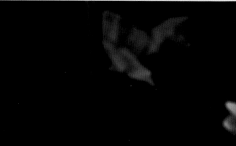

Make the Loose-leaf

Using an erasable fabric pen, mark a square measuring 8.5 × 11 in (21.59 × 27.94 cm) on the fabric. Your finished project will be trimmed to this size, so you will want to use these marks as guidelines for stitching.

Use the fabric pen and a ruler to draw a vertical line 1.5 in (3.81 cm) from the left 11-in (21.59- cm) edge. This line will guide where to sew two lines to denote the red margin of the lined paper. Draw a horizontal line 2 in (5.08 cm) below the top of the page to mark where you should sew the first blue line. Using your sewing machine, stitch both the red and the blue lines following the guides that you have created. To maintain clean rule lines, do not use backstitch.

After you have sewn the initial blue line at the top, use the zipper foot as a guide to sew evenly spaced blue lines all the way down the page. Leave a 0.5-in (1.27-cm) margin at the bottom of the page.

Stitch Your Doodles

When brainstorming about what to place on your "notebook paper," remember that old journals and notebooks can be inspiring!

Doodle with the disappearing ink pen, then embroider over it, using floss in single strands. The thread colors in the example project are indicative of classic doodling tools: pencil markings, ballpoint pens of various colors, and yellow highlighter.

TIP: To achieve the appearance of the transparency of a highlighter, stitch with a very loose and open satin stitch. You can also re-stitch the page rules on top of the yellow thread.

Finishing

When you've completed the stitching, press the fabric and lay it on a cutting surface. Use a quilter's ruler and rotary cutter to trim the fabric into the finished

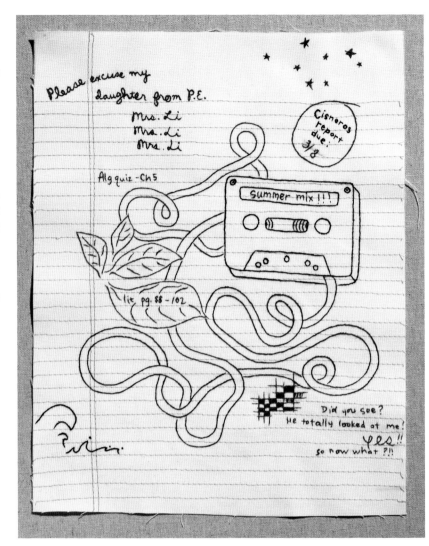

8.5 by 11-in (21.59 × 27.94-cm) size, lining up the cuts parallel with the stitched lines.

Now that you are finished, hang your page, displaying it old-school classroom-style on binder clips or pushpins.

Figure 5.1. While this project encourages you to create original drawings, you can also use Amy Adoyzie's doodles by copying this diagram and increasing it 120 percent to fit your looseleaf page.

Did you see? He totally looked at me! yes!! so now what?!!

AMY ADOYZIE calls Portland, Oregon, home. She is a recovering ex-pat who spent several years abroad volunteering in Bangladesh and China. Amy has been doing free-hand embroidery since 2005 and just recently discovered the magic of erasable fabric pens. She is self-taught, and her free-hand style exemplifies her non-traditional designs. She enjoys writing, designing, and embroidering. Find Amy online at **amyadoyzie.com** and on Etsy at **amyadoyzie.etsy.com**.

Cisneros report due; 3/8

Summer mix !!!

ELEVATING ORDINARY OBJECTS:
An Interview with Andrew J. Phares

A mixed-media artist who works with found objects, Andrew J. Phares lives on Alameda, an island in the Bay Area of California. Andrew holds both a BFA and MFA in jewelry and metalworking from the California College of Arts & Crafts. His stitchwork projects have included clothing vintage nudie cards and embroidering weapons onto military drop cloths. His gender-bending work is surprising yet maintains a sense of humor.

Andrew J. Phares, *Home Sweet Home*, 1999, fencing mask, embroidery floss, 10 × 7 × 9 in (25.4 × 17.78 × 22.86 cm). Photo: Andy Krause

Q: How did you get into needlework?

A: When I have an idea for a work of art, I don't let the media restrict me. Whatever that piece needs to be, I figure out how to realize it. I went to my local library and checked out a couple stitching-for-beginners books to create my first embroidery piece, *At Needle Point*.

Q: What sort of subject matter do you focus on?

A: I enjoy playing with the concept of opposites such as good and evil, male and female, wholesome and unwholesome, etc. Humor is always a part of my work. I'm also interested in gender roles, specifically the eroding of masculinity in popular culture. This is what drew me to embroidery.

In the past, a man was what he wore, what he did for a living, and what he did with his leisure time. That's not true today. As part of my investigation of what it means to be a heterosexual male in today's society, I enjoy taking art and craft media that are normally associated with women's work, such as embroidery or imagery, and reinterpreting them through a male lens. A couple of non-embroidery artworks of mine that illustrate this are a pair of

bulletproof oven mitts and a tin dollhouse deconstructed and rebuilt in the form of a large revolver.

Q: **Do you do other types of stitch-work?**

A: Once I cross-stitched the traditional sampler motto "Home Sweet Home" onto the face of a fencing mask.

Q: **What is your creative process like?**

A: I like to incorporate found objects into all of my artwork, and the embroidery pieces are no different. The objects I start off with and finish with are important to me, regardless of whatever conceptual angle there might be. I really covet "things," so a large part of my creative process is to just stare at whatever object I'm about to alter and to think about it.

Q: **What sort of feedback have you had on your work?**

A: I have had positive responses to my art, and I believe that's mostly due to

Andrew J. Phares, *Cover Your Shame*, 2008, vintage pin-up playing cards, embroidery floss 2.5 × 3.5 in (63 × 88 mm). "I have taken a complete of deck of 1954 vintage pin-up girl/naked-lady playing cards, and I have embroidered a different outfit on each card." Photo: Andrew J. Phares

Andrew J. Phares, detail of *Cover Your Shame*. Photo: Andrew J. Phares

Andrew J. Phares, detail of *Cover Your Shame*. Photo: Andrew J. Phares

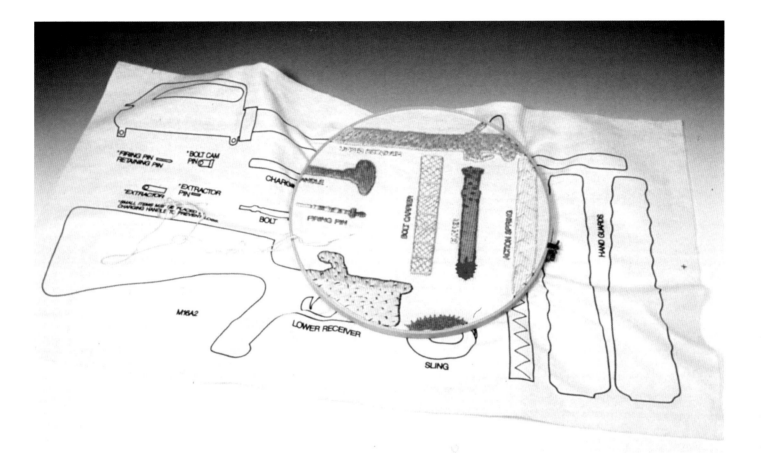

Andrew J. Phares, *At Needle Point*, 2000, military drop cloth, embroidery floss, 20 × 32 in (50.8 × 81.28 cm). According to Andrew, "It's a US Army-issue drop cloth used by soldiers to keep track of all the parts of their M16 assault rifles when they are disassembled for cleaning. I was given this drop cloth by someone who was retired from the military. When I first saw the cloth, I thought it looked so much like a store-bought pre-printed embroidery pattern that I just put a hoop on it and stitched everything within the hoop in a fleshy color to complement the phallic shapes of the gun parts. I left it in the hoop with a threaded needle stuck through it as if Grandmother had just set down her work for a moment." Photo: Andrew J. Phares

my use of humor and the best possible workmanship that I can come up with. If you use those things, you can talk about almost any subject and make it palatable. I don't mean for any one specific message to be carried by my art, but I would like it to act as a tool to provoke a dialog. I don't care what that dialog entails, but the sharing of stories is an important part of the human experience.

Find Andrew's work online at: **flickr.com/photos/22171451@ N08/3857736852**

Photo Feelism

SIOBHAN LONG

Inspired by Andrew Phares' playing cards? Why not experiment with stitching on photographs?

Introduce a tactile element by embellishing your photos with a little embroidery; you can stitch what may not have been captured by the camera. Add a rainbow to an idyllic landscape, place hearts around the one you love, or put a mustache on a serious-looking baby.

Tools and Materials

embroidery thread, selection of your choice

embroidery needle, size of your choice

photographs, printed on heavy card or photographic paper

a pen or pencil

a strong light source

scissors

Stitches:

double running stitch
satin stitch

any other stitches that you like!

Get Ready for Your Close-Up

Begin by assessing your photo collection. Some photos are great, but they might be lacking that special something. What's missing? Does your friend's arm need a tattoo? Does that cloud need more raindrops? Does that lake need a sea monster? Chances are, the answer is yes!

Here are some ideas for stitched motifs:

- rain clouds
- rainbows
- lasers
- glasses
- hats
- flags
- fish

This is not a pattern as much as it is an example that can kick-start your work. What you create will rely on the particular subject matter of the photo that you have and what you want to make of it.

Let's use the rainbow photo (facing page) to demonstrate the process:

Using a pen or pencil, draw the rough outline of your stitch pattern on the back of the photo. Press lightly, but still hard enough that your drawing

makes an imprint on the photo. As you embroider, remember to periodically hold the photo up to a light source; your sketch marks will indicate where to stitch.

To embroider a rainbow, begin by tracing the outer arc of the rainbow on the back of the photo. Thread your needle with three strands of red floss and pierce the paper from the back, where the rainbow begins. Tie a knot in the floss on the back of the photo. Use a double running stitch to trace along the arc, holding the photo up to the light see your sketch marks.

When you get to the end of the rainbow, your embroidery should look like a dashed line, so stitch back in the other direction to fill in the gaps. Once you've retraced the line, tie a knot in the thread.

Repeat with the remaining colors—orange, yellow, green, blue, indigo, violet—following the contour of the previous color. Be sure to stagger the points where your needle enters the photo; if the holes are too close together, the paper may tear.

You can use this technique to create any scene you like. For elements that you want to fill with a solid block of color, such as a mustache, a satin stitch is more suitable. Experiment with what works best for you.

Finishing

Display your photo with pride or glue it on to the front of a greeting card for a friend. Whatever you choose to do, remember that a picture is worth a thousand stitches!

SIOBHAN LONG is an all-round crafty girl based in Vancouver, BC. She's always up for learning a new craft, and usually does so by picking up some supplies and muddling her way through, using a mix of experimentation and imagination. Siobhan spends a great deal of time dreaming about color and is a sucker for the notions section of the fabric store. Follow Siobhan's blog on crafting and living a creative life at **magpieandcake.com**.

CLEVER CANADIANA:
An Interview with Sarah Haxby

Hailing from Bowen Island, a small community off the west coast of Canada, Sarah Haxby balances working at a school with her many pursuits as a fine artist. During a residency in Wales to complete an MFA, she began to experiment with embroideries in order to exhibit gallery work. Her unique approach to tackling Canadiana through stitching is defiant proof that she did not need to heed the advice she heard at art school that belittled her handicrafts.

Q: **How did you learn to do embroidery?**

A: After a terrible accident with a sewing machine, my mother was afraid to sew. At our house, the dangerous sewing machine sat in the corner, untouched. I was afraid of that machine and never used it, but I did learn to sew from an elderly lady [who lived] in the woods. She taught me how to hand-sew, hand-quilt, and do some basic embroidery techniques. When I was twelve years old, I purchased an electric sewing machine with my paper-route money. I used that sewing machine to sew a hundred dolls with hand-embroidered faces. Since that time, I have embroidered regularly.

While earning a BA in Fine Arts, I was advised to not show anyone my "little embroideries" and to focus on "real" art forms. I took all the put-downs as a challenge, which inspired me to have my first solo textile-art exhibit in 2007. The show almost sold out.

In 2008, while working on a Masters' degree in Wales, I found there was a different attitude; there is an established respect for historic and contemporary textile art in Europe that is underdeveloped in Canada. In Wales, however, my embroidery work was often referred to as "twee." I was again challenged to metamorphose the hobby-ishness into gallery-ishness.

The work got bigger, more focused, and I explored new territory. I wanted the thread to speak with the language of drawing and painting as well as stitching. I began to take raw painter's canvas and stretch it around canvas stretchers and old furniture—chair backs, table tops, and table legs—so that the hoops became part of the work.

Q: **What sort of work do you do?**

A: I've never been particularly brilliant at following patterns...Mostly, I would buy old embroidery books and then try out different stitches on my own drawings, as in my Canadian identity series, or I come up with my own design and then replicate it many times. I bounce around with my techniques; I like to learn lots of different types of stitches, from Renaissance Italian blackwork to those in a 1970s Holly Hobby embroidery kit. If I'm not amused or intrigued by the work, the piece is less likely to be completed.

My favorite embroidery stitches were created using some vintage Welsh embroidery thread that had belonged to an elderly lady. She kept her mother's sewing supplies for over half a century before she gave them to me. I estimated that some of the materials, including the bone buttons and wool embroidery floss, might have been a century old. It was one of the greatest gifts ever.

Q: **Do you believe that your gender or social class has any bearing on your attraction to and involvement with needlework?**

A: I feel grateful for all the textile artists who made political statements about equality in the 1960s and 1970s. I feel I'm embroidering in a pretty egalitarian time, and that I can embroider what I

(THIS PAGE) Sarah Haxby, *Canadian Modesty, 2010*, embroidery thread and vintage wool on canvas, 22 × 22 in (55.88 × 55.88 cm).

(FACING PAGE) Sarah Haxby, *Canadian Economy, 2009*, embroidery thread and vintage wool and metallic thread on canvas, 19 × 19 in (48.26 × 48.26 cm).

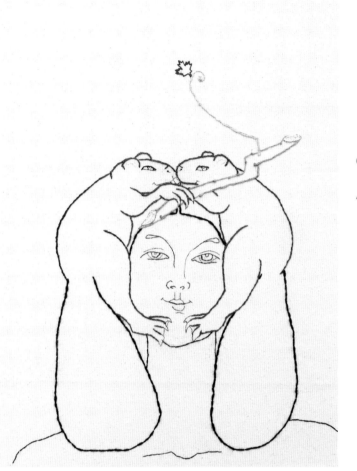

want to without reflecting on my gender or class, unless I want to. I know as many male embroiderers as female and find that the prejudices toward embroidery are based less on gender or class these days and more on the classifications of high- and low-brow, the hobby versus the "real artwork."

Q: **Where do you get your inspiration for your embroidery work?**

A: This latest series began when I was in Wales researching historic textile icons, specifically the Welsh hat. Canadian beaver pelts were imported to the UK to create the hats, and Welsh wool was exported to Canada to create the iconic Canadian hat, the toque. I became giddy when I learned about the connections between iconic headware and my own ancestral roots! I began drawing people wearing beavers and sheep on their heads and then embroidering these images using wool and traditional threads. My return to Canada has expanded into exploring other symbolic animal-based imagery tied to my national identity.

Q: **If you were trying to convince someone else to take up embroidery, what would you say to convince them?**

A: Think about the passion, not the perfection! Try a small project first, and have fun with your mistakes. Don't worry about how the back looks.

(THIS PAGE) Sarah Haxby, *Beaver Snood (A Softwood Agreement)*, 2010, embroidery thread and vintage wool on canvas, 22 × 22 in (55.88 × 55.88 cm).

(FACING PAGE) Sarah Haxby, *Canuck (Canadian Greenman)*, 2010, embroidery thread and vintage wool on canvas, 22 × 22 in (55.88 × 55.88 cm).

Sometimes, I actually end up liking the random mess on the back of the piece as much as the front! There are no shoulds and should-nots in embroidery anymore.

Find out more about Sarah Haxby online: **peargirl.weebly.com**.

(FACING PAGE) Sarah Haxby, detail of *Monogamy Rocks! (A Canadian Relationship)*, 2009, Embroidery thread and vintage wool on canvas, 17 × 17 in (43.18 × 43.18 cm).

(LEFT) Sarah Haxby, *Free Trade Agreement, 2009*, embroidery thread and vintage wool on canvas, 17 × 17 in (43.18 × 43.18 cm).

(ABOVE) Sarah Haxby on Bowen Island.

BLISS IN A TEACUP:
An Interview with Rebekah Nathan

Originally from New Zealand, Rebekah Nathan lives with her Canadian husband Richard in Vancouver, BC. Together they run an Etsy business called Bliss in a Teacup. Their product line includes handcrafted items that are often embroidery-themed, including chalkboards and clocks inset into embroidery hoops. Despite not having much success at cross-stitch as a young girl, Rebekah fell in love with embroidery when stitching an empowering bell hooks quote.

Q: How did you come to embroidery?

A: It was always something that I was interested in but never thought I could do until I tried it a few years ago after I found, on the blog Meet Me at Mikes, a tutorial for embroidering patterns on Christmas stockings.

I enjoyed the stitching, rather than following a pattern. Around the same time, I participated in a feminist craft swap. One of the pieces that I traded included a portion of a bell hooks quote, "I will not have my life narrowed down," about how she would not put herself in a box and would stand up to people. There was something really meditative about stitching for me, and especially with this quote to think about.

I always enjoyed art, but I never felt like I was good at it. When I started to enjoy doing free-hand embroidery, I came to the realization that it was art. Anything can be art.

My husband and I started making things to sell. I started to create a free-hand woodgrain pattern and stitch it onto clock faces. It was cool to sell our work rather than having it pile up around the house.

Q: What techniques do you use in your stitch-work? I notice that you use a lot of recycled fabrics.

A: I mostly use a backstitch of sorts. I approach stitching as if I were drawing. I begin by stitching the shapes that I see in my mind's eye, and if it doesn't work, I unpick it.

We thrift a lot because there is so much out there that can be reused. We look for wool suiting or upholstery fabrics, as I like to use a thicker needle in my work.

Rebekah Nathan at work in her home studio, 2010.

Q: How would you describe your work?

A: Because we have the shop, I think that I should be doing something that has a purpose and is decorative. I would like to branch out into more artistic things that don't have a purpose besides being beautiful or expressing an idea.

Q: If you were trying to convince someone else to take up embroidery, what would you say to convince them?

A: That it can be whatever you want it to be. Embroidery is mark-making. If you are interested in creating, embroidery is another skill to add to your repertoire. There is nothing to be afraid of!

Find Rebekah online at **blissinateacup.blogspot.com** and on her Etsy site **blissinateacup.etsy.com**.

Against the Grain

REBEKAH NATHAN

Rebekah Nathan has created a variation of her embroidered clocks to share with you. Try your hand at freeform embroidery with these woodgrain wall hangings. This pattern will make a set of three hoops which can be hung together on a wall, or you can choose to make just one to adorn a special indoor space that needs a touch of needle-made nature.

Rebeka says, "My husband and I work a lot with wood, and I find myself often mesmerized by its intricate, movement-filled patterns. I must admit, my embroidery style is more about making it up as it goes than following a pattern, so one day, using thrifted brown wool suiting and thread, I started stitching knots and wood grain. Leaving them in their embroidery hoops for frames is like having little slices of wood adorning your walls."

Tools and Materials

FLOSS:

8 skeins of DMC White or another white cream-colored embroidery floss

FABRIC:

1 yd (0.91 m) of medium- to heavy-weight fabric (twill or suiting) in brown

1 of each: 5, 6, 7-in (12.7, 15.24, 17.78-cm) wooden embroidery hoops

embroidery needle, size 1–3

fabric glue

heavy stock cardboard

scissors

utility knife

pencil (optional)

invisible pen (optional)

Skills required:

backstitch

Prep Your Woolen Woodcuts

Prepare the cardboard for backing the project(s). Take the inside hoop of each embroidery hoop and use a pencil to trace the inside ring onto heavy stock cardboard. Cut out the piece(s) of cardboard to save until you are ready to finish your piece.

Gently stretch the fabric into the embroidery hoop(s) and use scissors to trim the fabric edge until you have approximately 1–1.5 in (2.54–3.81 cm) of overhanging fabric.

For reference, you may want to first sketch out the woodgrain pattern on paper or trace it onto the fabric with an invisible marker. However, because this type of pattern varies so greatly, if you want to forgo a formal pattern, try to stitch freeform! Just remember that the final work is going to be framed in an embroidery hoop, so, with this in mind, decide where you'd like to begin the wood knot, either in the center of the hoop or set asymmetrically.

To Stitch Each Hoop

Using all six strands of floss, thread your needle and make a double-knot at the tail of the floss. Create a circular or oval woodgrain "knot" using a backstitch stitching circular shapes around this initial shape, varying the width between circles and also the shape. It's okay if your stitches vary a little, but try to keep their length between 0.5 in (1.27 cm) and 2 in (5.08 cm) to create the desired woodgrain effect.

Begin to create the long grain lines to curve around the knot. These can run horizontally or vertically; variation makes this project interesting.

From the wrong side of your work, insert your needle into the fabric at an angle as close to the edge of the work as possible, so that if you were to stitch a straight line it would slightly overlap with the knot. Begin stitching a line to follow around the curve of the knot that finishes in a straight line close to the edge of the work.

Insert the needle close to where you finished the first wood grain line, and stitch the next line by mimicking the shape and curve of the first one. Continue this pattern, moving up and down the work. When stitching the knot, vary the width between grain lines, and begin to straighten out the grain line as you go. Remember that an actual woodgrain pattern isn't perfectly straight, so there is no need for this to be! Complete one side before moving on to the other side.

Once you're happy with your completed pattern, loop your thread through a stitch on the wrong side of your fabric to secure the thread.

To Frame

Place a small amount of fabric glue around the inside edge of your hoop(s). Carefully fold over the fabric overhang, pressing it down into the glue to hold it in place. Continue until all the excess fabric has been folded inside. Now press the cardboard circle that you made earlier into the back of the hoop to hold the excess fabric in place. You may need to trim the circle slightly to fit, but it should be pretty snug. If need be, secure it with something heavy while the glue dries.

Use a hook to hang up your hoop of woodsy goodness!

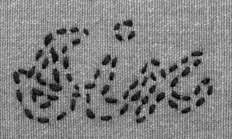

CHAPTER 6

Graphically Inclined

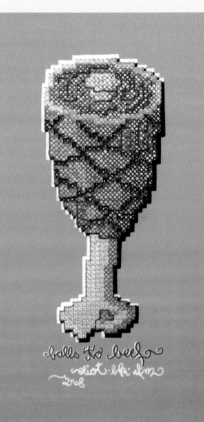

The artists profiled in this chapter are influenced by the disciplines of graphic design, media, and commercial illustration. Their muses may be comic artists, horror movies, animations, or their own drawings. Whether they are revolutionizing traditional illustration, animating their stitching, or creating their own stitched characters, each has a unique perspective on how embroidery and modern imagery can converge.

(FACING PAGE) Takashi Iwasaki, *Negadegrow*, 2010, embroidery floss and fabric, 10 × 10 in (25.4 × 25.4 cm). Photo: Takashi Wasaki

(FROM TOP LEFT) Esther Oh, *Jimmy and Timmy*, 2009, embroidery on fabric, 11 × 14 in (27.94 × 35.56 cm). Photo: Esther Oh

Eliot M. Henning, *Balls to Beef* from *Opus 1* series, 2008, cross-stitch work on canvas, 24 × 24 in (60.96 × 60.96 cm). Photo: Eliot M. Henning

Aubrey Longley-Cook, *Midas*, 2009, embroidery floss, fabric, 6 in (15.24 cm) in diameter. Photo: Aubrey Longley-Cook

Cate Anevski, *Green Face*, 2010, re-purposed fabric, embroidery floss, wooden embroidery hoop, hot glue, 6 in (15.24 cm) in diameter. Photo: Cate Anevski

Brette Gabel, *Omen 2*, 2009, freeform machine embroidery on paper, 12 × 12 in (30.48 × 30.48 cm). Photo: Jason Cawood

ANIMATED EMBROIDERY:
An Interview with Aubrey Longley-Cook

"Give us this day our daily thread, and lead us knot into temptation" is the tagline
of *Spool Spectrum, Aubrey Longley-Cook's* blog, which chronicles his ever-growing body of work
and collection of thrifted needlework. Based in Atlanta, Georgia, Aubrey began embroidering
while studying animation at the Rhode Island School of Design and wishing to produce personal work,
free from classroom critique. He has applied his stitch-witchery to studying the skeletal structure of
animals and the iconography of mortality, and he has even created an embroidered animation.

Q: **I came across your work online through *Runaway*, a haunting animated .gif of an embroidered golden lab who is endlessly running.**

A: Gus is my roommate's dog. Before I moved in, he found Gus running in the street. He's a super sweet dog. We've had him for two years. He's calmed down now, but for a while you'd take him outside, and he'd just bolt as fast as he could. It was interesting that there was this call-of-the-wild that we could not train out of him. At heart, he is a runaway.

I knew that I wanted to combine embroidery with animation technique. A run or walk cycle is a really simple animation test. You study how gravity and weight work together. If you take an animation 101 class, chances are it will be your first assignment. I thought that a run cycle of an animal would be a perfect project.

Q: **It is a complex animation that could have been shown in an art gallery, but it seems like it was made for the Internet.**

A: That piece was inspired by Internet animated .gif culture. It was produced for the Internet as a gallery space. The Internet makes it is so easy to get your work out to so many people.

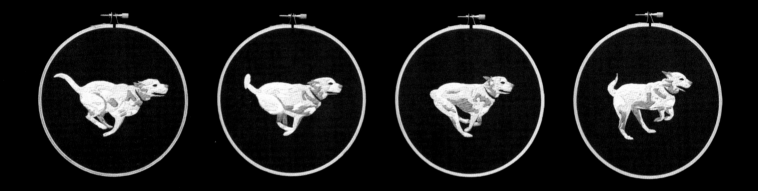

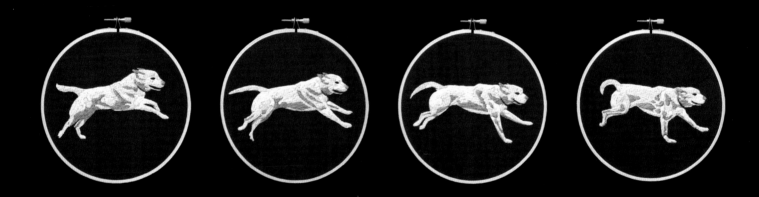

Aubrey Longley-Cook, *Runaway*, 2010, thread on cotton; each embroidery is 6 in (15.24 cm) in diameter. An animated .gif of 14 frames of motion. Photo: Aubrey Longley-Cook

another day
shot
to hell!

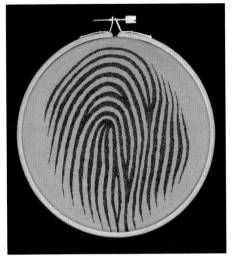

Q: **How many embroidery works did you have to make in total to create the animation?**

A: Fifteen 6-in (15-cm) works, which all took about a week each to make. I ended up not even using one of them. That's what happens when you animate—sometimes a frame isn't necessary.

Q: **You've also animated the "wrong" side of the embroidery. Watching the animation of Gus's body render itself in a mess of threads is really interesting to see.**

A: If you turn it around, the animation still works. You get all the crazy texture and the knotting and the connections. The motion is more telling on that side. It is not a realistic or literal portrait of Gus, but there is something really emotional about all of the knotting which hints at the chaos in Gus's head, [as he is] trying to make connections, but it's impossible; it's like trying to do undo a knot.

Q: **It's stunning. How did you learn to do embroidery?**

A: I'm pretty much self-taught. My mother did embroidery when I was young, but she passed away when I was fifteen, so I was too young to learn from her. When I started to get interested, I definitely needed to find a way to connect with my mother. I was past grieving, but I was leaving home and school. I think that embroidery was a way of finding personal support and a connection with my mother. There was something comforting that reminded me of her.

Q: **I've noticed that you seem to be an avid collector of second-hand embroidery and that your tastes are broad, from very formal-looking needlepoint with kittens to 1980s Garfield images. Why do you collect these works?**

A: There's something wonderful about that kitsch. There was so much work that was made in the 1970s that is still sitting around in people's attics, basements, and thrift stores. It's not archived or documented in the same way that artwork is. All of these [pieces are made by] unknown artists who didn't sign their work—housewives, grandmas, and people working on these pieces for their families. I see these pieces at thrift stores and want to buy every single one. I preserve them by displaying them with my work on my blog. It puts my work in context, but also it puts these pieces in a new context as well. I think these pieces should be re-examined and appreciated as works of art and not just "a craft project."

Q: You've incorporated a lot of stitched patterns into the backgrounds of your work.

A: I like to use geometry, pattern, and gradients to create space. In classical two-dimensional animation, pattern has traditionally been used to create space and depth. If you look at the backgrounds of old Warner Brother cartoons, for example, you can see examples of this. I like the connection between being an animator and an embroiderer.

Q: Tell me about some of your other series.

A: I stitched a series of my own fingerprints to evoke how important the notion of touch is to embroidery. The work is hand-done, and when I stitch a piece, my fingers touch every single bit of the fabric. Every single stitch was done with my fingers, and the stitch-work could not look the same if done by someone else.

Soon after finishing the fingerprints, I began to explore the concept of death, creating the Midas piece and the black rose piece, which is a symbol of imminent death. Following this, I wanted to explore the idea of spirit

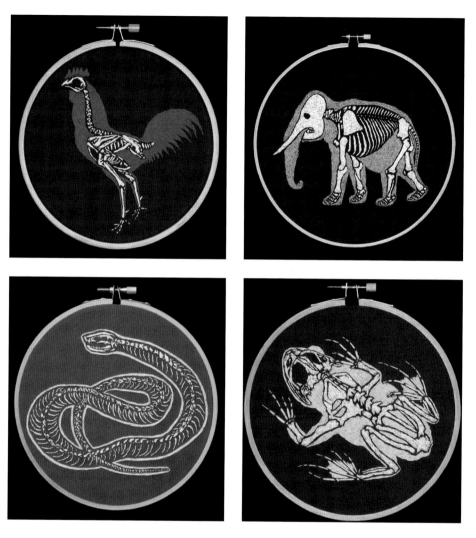

(CLOCKWISE FROM TOP LEFT) Aubrey Longley-Cook, *Coop Spook*, from the series *Zombie Zoology*, 2009, thread on cotton, 5 in (12.7 cm) in diameter. Photo: Aubrey Longley-Cook

Aubrey Longley-Cook, *Elephantom* from the series *Zombie Zoology*, 2009, thread on cotton, 8 in (20.32 cm) in diameter. Photo: Aubrey Longley-Cook

Aubrey Longley-Cook, *Croaker*, from the series *Zombie Zoology*, 2009, thread on cotton, 5 in (12.7 cm) in diameter. Photo: Aubrey Longley-Cook

Aubrey Longley-Cook, *Shedding* from the series *Zombie Zoology*, 2010, thread on cotton, 8 in (20.32 cm) in diameter. Photo: Aubrey Longley-Cook

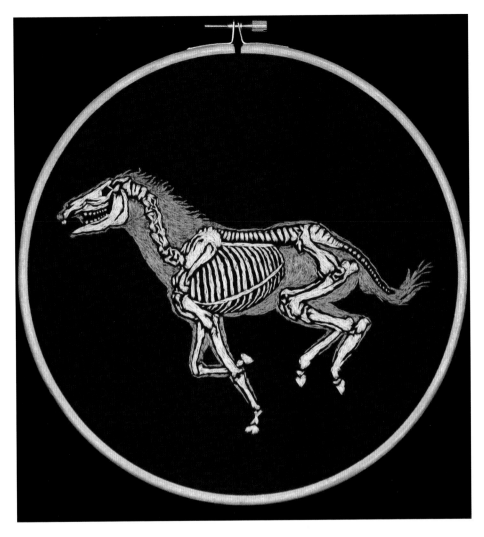

Aubrey Longley-Cook, *Undead Thoroughbred* from the series *Zombie Zoology*, 2009, thread on cotton, 8 in (20.32 cm) in diameter. Photo: Aubrey Longley-Cook

animals and animal bone structures using bright colors. Having the profiles of these animals combined with their skeletons is playful but haunting. These profiles are ingrained into us, but their interiors are very bizarre. I remember researching all of these skeletons and looking at the elephant and thinking, this is the creepiest thing ever. This is really terrifying. It needed the blue skin to balance it, to make the idea of living death work—an oxymoron that is important to the piece.

Q: **Do you have any fantasy projects that you would like to tackle?**

A: Making an animated short film is something that I've wanted to do for a while in order to combine my two loves. It's definitely a little daunting. It took five months to make Runaway, which was a five-second film. I'd also like to continue on the path that I'm on and see where it takes me. There's something incredibly calming and meditative about embroidery. The speed of it is completely the correct pace for me. The animator in me loves letting the world slow down. Frame by frame, stitch by stitch.

See more of Aubrey's original works and collected pieces online at **spoolspectrum. blogspot.com.**

CROSS-STITCHING PIXELS:
An Interview with Eliot M. Henning

A beatboxer, graffiti artist, painter, cartoonist, and production manager from Berlin, Eliot M. Henning was first drawn to experiment with cross-stitch when a brightly colored display of thread caught his eye. The intense colors of embroidery floss and the metallic yarns reminded him of the aerosol cans that he used for spraying graffiti. Having learned to cross-stitch as a child, he began using it to create art, comparing the pixel-like look to digital graphics.

Q: **Tell me about your first stitched work.**

A: I want to combine spray paint, markers, and other tools from my graffiti work with floss. My first cross-stitch piece was a robot, and I learned that "easy looking doesn't mean easy doing." My stitching was all over the place, but the result was still fascinating.

I quietly worked for almost two years on ten 24 × 24-in (60.96 × 60.96-cm) canvases displaying the tools of graffiti: a spray can, a marker, a pencil, a cutter, and a roller, as well as icons such as ice, beer, beef, a microphone, and a dildo. I first showed all the pieces as a series with the other famous street artists of Berlin.

Q: **Why embroidery?**

A: The colors—this is why I love graffiti and its pixel-like look, as I grew up with Pac Man—and the durability. Graffiti usually disappears pretty fast, so I like the idea of the floss being there for the next 1,000 years or so.

Q: **Do you believe that your gender has any bearing on your attraction to and involvement with needlework?**

A: I was surprised that so many people were surprised that I am a man doing needlework. I knew it was rather new territory to mix a traditional art like embroidery with the urban attitude, but I didn't expect that embroidery was such a gender- and age-dependent activity. I am happy to reach so many different people through this art. I love seeing happy and surprised faces enjoying the pieces.

Eliot M. Henning, *Opus 1* series, 2007–08, cross-stitch work on canvas, 10 works measuring 24 × 24 in (60.96 × 60.96 cm). Photo: Eliot M. Henning

(FACING PAGE) Eliot M. Henning, *Embroidoid 2*, 2010, yarn on canvas with spraypaint and marker, 19.5 × 16 in (49.53 × 40.64 cm). Photo: Eliot M. Henning

(THIS PAGE) Eliot M. Henning, *Embroidoid 1*, 2010, yarn on canvas with spraypaint and marker, 19.5 × 16 in (49.53 × 40.64 cm). Photo: Eliot M. Henning

Eliot M. Henning, *Loader*, 2009, markers, cross-stitch
on canvas, 31 × 39 in (78.74 × 99.06 cm). Photo:
Eliot M. Henning

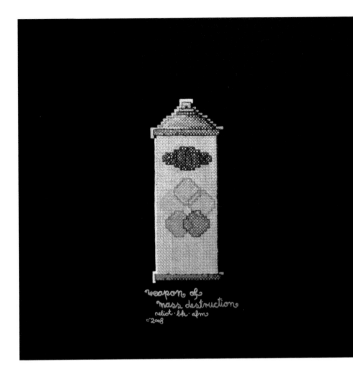

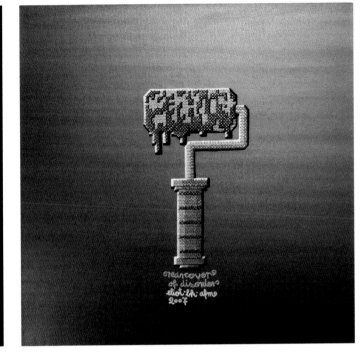

Q: How do you develop ideas for your pieces?

A: I like to have a theme. Then I think about the size, basic colors, and the background elements. In a series of different characters, like the robots, I may have an idea on the fifth piece to give it some pimples, and if I like it, I sometimes go back to already-sketched pieces and add pimples on those as well. If I feel that something is missing, I have to search for the idea of the "missing link." In general, it's a lot of decision-making. Most important is the discipline; ideas come easy, but you are stuck with the work of creating it.

See more of Elliot's work at **flickr.com/eliotbk** or **myspace.com/ beatboxeliot**.

(LEFT) Eliot M. Henning, *Weapon of Mass Destruction* from *Opus 1* series, 2008, cross-stitch work on canvas, 24 × 24 in (60.96 × 60.96 cm). Photo: Eliot M. Henning

(RIGHT) Eliot M. Henning, *Rediscover of Disorder* from *Opus 1* series, 2007, cross-stitch work on canvas 24 × 24 in (60.96 × 60.96 cm). Photo: Eliot M. Henning

Eliot M. Henning at work on *Robot*. Photo: Eliot M. Henning

Along for the Ride

ERIN STANTON

Whether you're an experienced New Yorker or someone who's only visited once, this counted cross-stitch NYC MetroCard Pouch is for you! It's the perfect compromise between carrying your everything-in-it wallet or making do with bulging pockets. This pouch is sized to hold your cash, a few cards, a pen, and a lip balm or two. With that bright MetroCard design on the front, it's easy to keep track of when you're out on the town.

Tools and Materials

FLOSS:

- 1 skein of DMC #310 (Black)
- 1 skein of DMC #741 (Tangerine - MD)
- 1 skein of DMC #742, (Tangerine - LT)
- 2 skeins of DMC #746 (Topaz - LT)
- 1 skein of DMC #798 (Delft Blue - DK)
- 1 skein of DMC #3776 (Mahogany - LT)

FABRIC:

8 × 5-in (20.32 × 12.7-cm) piece of white 18-count Aida cloth

Fabric for the pouch:

5 × 6.5-in (12.7 × 16.51-cm) piece of medium-weight cotton, linen, or muslin in a natural color

2 5 × 6.5-in (12.7 × 16.5-cm) pieces of cotton (patterned cotton is recommended) for lining

tapestry needle, size 22

6-in (15.24-cm) zipper

scissors

white thread for sewing machine

sewing machine (optional)

zipper foot for sewing machine (optional)

Skills required:

basic counted cross-stitch

basic machine sewing skills
(to construct the pouch)

You can now create a row of half stitches. Following the pattern, note that the bottom of the "r" in the middle of "MetroCard" requires three full stitches. Stitch three half stitches from left to right, then complete these stitches by stitching three half stitches from right to left.

From here, all you have to do is count your stitches and match them to the pattern. Remember, you will need to thread a new piece of floss several times throughout the pattern. Once you get to the end of the current piece of floss, leave the leftover thread as a tail at the back of the fabric. Seal your completed stitches by overlapping them with stitches from your new thread.

To Construct the Pouch

To make a zippered pouch, begin with four pieces of fabric: your stitched piece, a piece of solid-colored cotton for the back of the pouch, and two pieces of cotton for the lining.

To add the zipper, place one piece of the lining fabric right-side up, match the zipper edge to it, and place the outer fabric wrong-side up so that it faces the zipper. Match up all three raw edges, and baste the pieces together with a straight stitch running along the zipper edge.

Using a zipper foot on your sewing machine, top stitch along the edge of the fabric, catching both layers, which are sandwiched around the zipper teeth. Repeat these steps on the other side of the zipper. Remove basting stitches with the use of a seam-ripper.

Once the zipper is in place, pin together the right sides of the lining to one side of the zipper and the right sides of the outer fabric to the other side. Baste around both the lining and the outside of the pouch. Unzip the zipper at least halfway (you will need this space to be able to turn your pouch right-side out).

Sew all the way around both the lining and outer fabrics, staying as close to the edge as you can. Leave a 2-in (5-cm) opening on the bottom of the lining side. Clip

On the Move

Begin by folding the Aida cloth in half vertically, then fold it again horizontally to find the center of your fabric. Mark the center with string or a pin. Once you've found the center, put the fabric in a hoop and pull it taut.

Stitching

Begin stitching the center of the pattern (marked with a red dot in Fig. 6.1). Separate the lengths of floss into six individual strands. Thread the needle with two strands of DMC #798. Push the needle from the underside to the front of the Aida cloth and leave a 5–7-in (12.7–17.78-cm) tail of floss behind. Cross over to the upper right-hand hole, making the first half of a crossed stitch. On the back of the fabric, pass your needle through the loop created by the first stitch; this will seal the ends of your stitching.

Complete your first cross-stitch by crossing the initial stitch. Keep the direction of the stitches consistent (the initial stitch should always be in the same direction) so as not to affect final sheen of the piece.

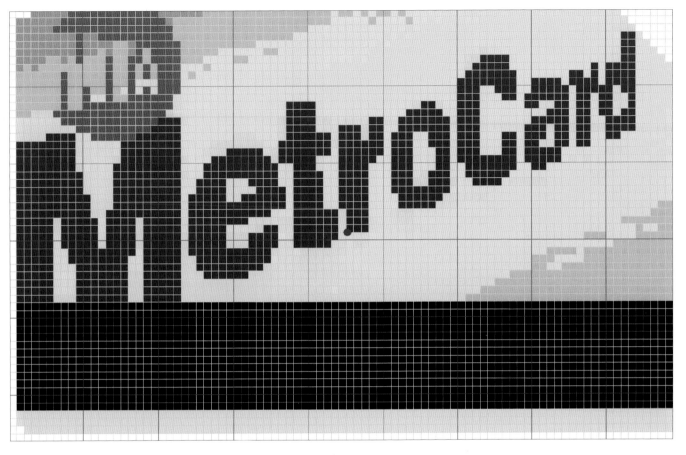

Figure 6.1

the corners diagonally to achieve sharp-edged corners when you flip the pouch inside out. Iron all seams and turn the pouch right-side out. Close the opening in the lining by hand, using a straight stitch.

Push the lining inside, and it's done! Throw in your stuff and you're ready to go!

For Erin Stanton's biography, see p. 196.

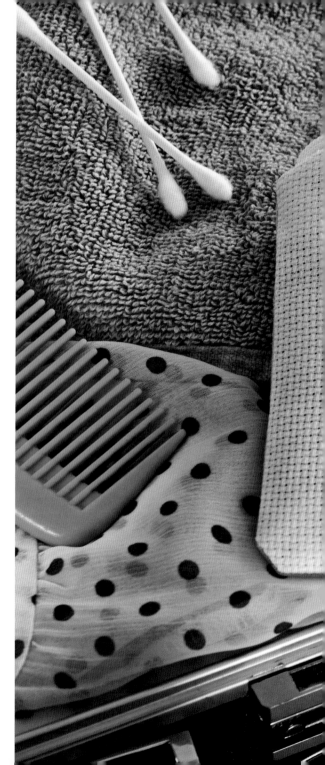

The "Always Prepared" Pouch

ERIN STANTON

When choosing fashion over function, stylish shoes can leave you with blisters on your heels. This little pouch is the perfect first-aid kit! It's just the right size to hold some Band-Aids, a small bottle of painkillers, land other essential items. You're prepared for whatever the night might bring with this kit tucked in your bag.

Tools and Materials:

FLOSS:

■ 1 skein of DMC #3779 (TerraCotta - ULT VRY)

FABRIC:

8 × 5-in (20.32 × 12.7-cm) piece of white 14-count Aida cloth

Fabric for the pouch:

5 × 6.5-in (12.7 × 16.51-cm) piece of medium-weight cotton, linen, or muslin in a natural color

two 5 × 6.5-in (12.7 × 16.51-cm) pieces of cotton for lining

tapestry needle, size 22

6-in (15.24-cm) zipper (optional for pouch)

scissors

white thread for sewing machine

sewing machine (optional)

zipper foot for sewing machine (optional)

Stitches:

basic counted cross-stitch   French knot

Other skills:

basic operation of a sewing machine

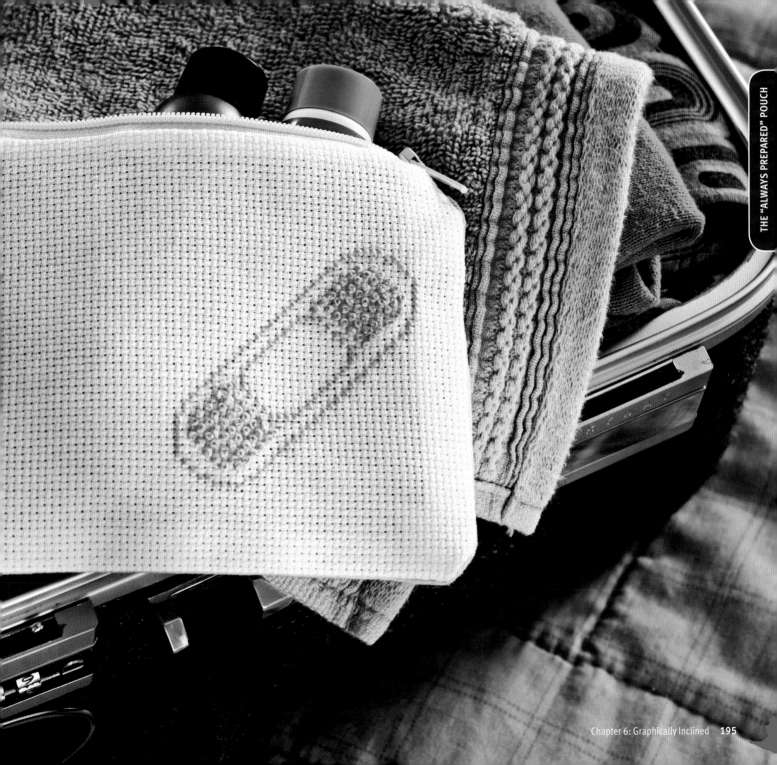

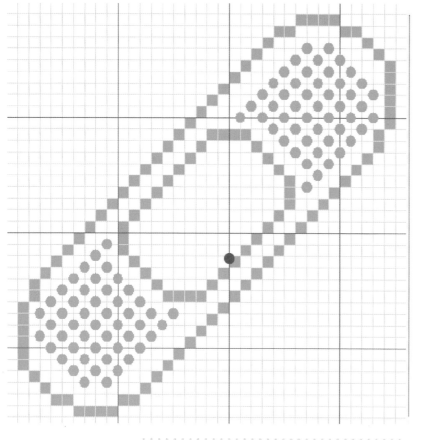

Figure 6.2

A Stitch a Day Keeps the Doctor Away

Begin by folding the Aida cloth in half vertically, then fold it again horizontally to find the center of your fabric. Mark the center with a string or a pin. Once you've found the center, put the fabric in a hoop and pull it taut.

Separate your length of floss into six individual strands. Thread the needle with two strands of DMC #3779. Begin stitching at the center of the pattern (marked with a red dot in Fig. 6.2).

Push the needle from the underside to the front of the Aida cloth, leaving a tail of floss 5–7 in (12.7–17.78 cm) in length. Cross over to the upper right-hand hole, making the first half of a crossed stitch. On the back of the fabric, pass your needle through the loop created by the first stitch; this will seal the ends of your stitching.

You can now create a row of half stitches.

Each circle in the Band-Aid pattern indicates the location of a French knot (see p. 117). French knots start the same way as the cross-stitch, with two strands of DMC floss.

This pattern can be made simply by counting your stitches and matching them to the pattern. You will need to thread a new piece of floss several times throughout the pattern. Once you get to the end of the current piece of thread, leave the leftover on the back of the fabric. Seal your completed stitches by overlapping them with stitches from your new thread.

Pouch Construction

To make the pouch, follow the sewing directions on p. 192.

You are now your very own Florence Nightingale!

ERIN STANTON enjoys rethinking classic needlework techniques and using them to create fun, modern patterns. She learned to cross-stitch as a child, and returned to it as an adult as a creative outlet and stress-buster. She designs and sells her patterns on Etsy: **etsy.com/shop/slipcoveryourlife**. Erin tries not to take herself too seriously, and her patterns express that!

INTENTIONAL ABSTRACTS:
An Interview with Takashi Iwasaki

In 2002, Takashi Iwasaki moved from Japan to Winnipeg, Manitoba, Canada.
He began to embroider when an art school assignment required that a creation be made of
"decorative art." Using satin stitch, Takashi creates whimsical embroideries in striking
color palettes. His embroidered work is modern, arresting, and unconventional.

Q: Your work is very colorful and graphic. What influences your stitch work?

A: My basic philosophy is, "Life is too short to take gravely all the time. I want to delight in what I can, when I can." Colors have a psychological influence on people, and I always try to make people, and myself, feel uplifted and cheerful when looking at my work.

The "graphic" quality of my work is the result of creating symbolic shapes and forms in my own way. Some may think that the forms that they see in my work could be purely abstract and design-oriented, but most of them have origins and meanings that I recognize. I transform the shapes of things in a way that I still recognize them, but it may be hard for others to recognize what they are, so that there's some room for them to imagine and expand their own ideas.

Takashi Wasaki, *Chochinger*, 2010, embroidery floss, fabric, 10 × 10 in (25.4 × 25.4 cm). Photo: Takashi Wasaki

Q: **What do you like about embroidery?**

A: I generally like artwork that shows evidence of labor intensiveness, the patience of the creator, and the time spent in creating it. Embroidery is definitely one of those [art forms]. Why do I spend so much time and effort on this one thing? I think making an embroidery piece could seem to be a very trivial thing, but for me it's part of my life, and I'd like to continue doing this for as long as I am able. I like to imagine how I will think about it by the time I'm eighty years old!

Q: **Your work has been exhibited as art and also used as illustration. Do you think there is a difference in the way you create work for art galleries verses work that is used for illustrative purposes?**

A: When I create work for a gallery setting, I can basically create anything that I like. I have more freedom in my creation, because my work is the main focus in this setting. But when it's for illustrative purposes, I have to communicate with the client and meet their needs, such as following their storyline or capturing a required "feel," because the illustration is a supportive element.

(THIS PAGE) Takashi Wasaki, *Gokakupristabletoble*, 2010, embroidery thread, fabric, 12 × 12 in (30.48 × 30.48 cm). Photo: Takashi Wasaki

(FACING PAGE) Takashi Wasaki, *Chiroruhouten*, 2010, embroidery floss, fabric, 14 × 14 in (35.56 × 35.56 cm). Photo: Takashi Wasaki

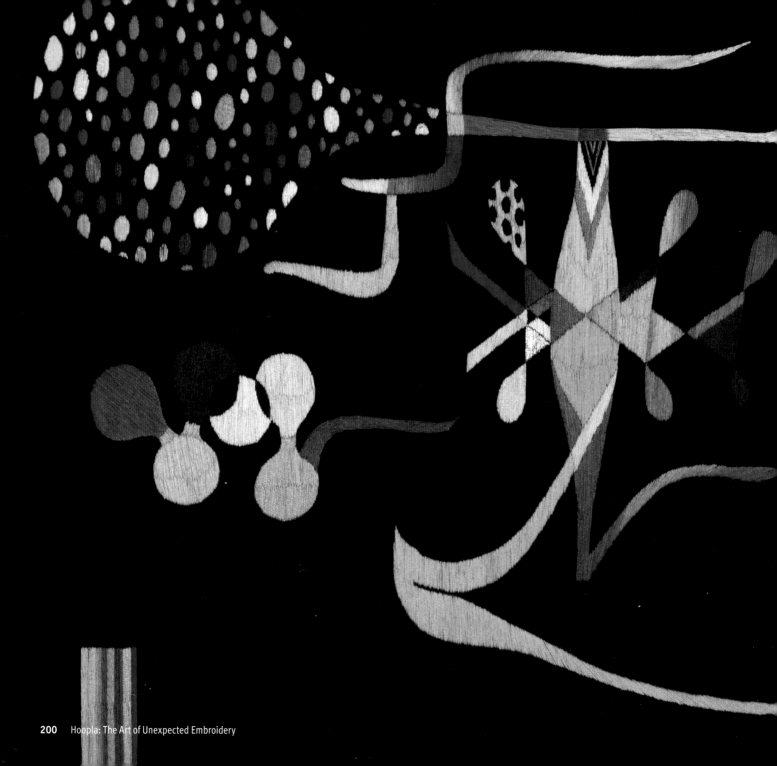

(FACING PAGE) Takashi Wasaki, *Nijiawapaip*, 2008, embroidery floss, fabric, 16 × 16 in (40.64 × 40.64 cm). Photo: Takashi Wasaki

(THS PAGE) Takashi Wasaki, *Minotogetenti*, 2009, embroidery thread, fabric, 14 × 14 in (35.56 × 35.56 cm). Photo: Takashi Wasaki

Q: **Do you believe that your gender or social class has any bearing on your attraction to and involvement with needlework?**

A: I believe that there are some people who think I'm uncommon or strange. Men don't embroider very much in Western society. I'm not aware of any evidence that they do in Japan, either, where I'm originally from.

In this fast-paced world, people tend to think that the faster, the better. I'm sort of going against the grain by refusing to use a machine for embroidery, only my hands and needles.

> In this fast-paced world, people tend to think that the faster, the better. I'm sort of going against the grain by refusing to use a machine for embroidery, only my hands and needles.

Q: **Which embroidery artists do you find inspiring?**

A: To be honest, I'm more inspired by non-embroidery artists like Rex Ray, Aaron Horkey, James Roper, and unknown East Indian artisans and Tibetan Buddhist monk painters. It's not only the medium that I'm inspired by, but the artists' work ethics and practices—whatever I feel resonates with mine.

Find more about Takashi online at: **takashiiwasaki.info.**

UNNERVING NEEDLEWORK:
An Interview with Brette Gabel

Brette Gabel was taught the chain stitch by a friend so that they could make T-shirts for an imaginary rock band named Seam-Ripper. Drawn to macabre subject matter like taxidermy, horror movies, and accidents, Brette's hand- and machine-stitched work is a world apart from conventional embroidered motifs.

Q: What sort of work do you do?

A: I usually work on fabric, sewing by hand. Once a piece is finished, I stretch it onto a frame, as if it were a painting. Recently, I started using a sewing machine on paper to make images. I use a straight stitch and color in my image by sewing back and forth on the paper. I have started using this technique to embroider my favorite scenes from horror movies.

(FACING PAGE) Brette Gabel, *It's a Feeling I Get* from the *One a Day* series, 2010, embroidery floss, cloth, 12 in (30.48 cm) in diameter. Photo: Brette Gabel

Brette Gabel, *You Feel So Alone*, from the *One a Day* series, 2010, embroidery floss, cloth, 12 in (30.48 cm) in diameter. Photo: Brette Gabel

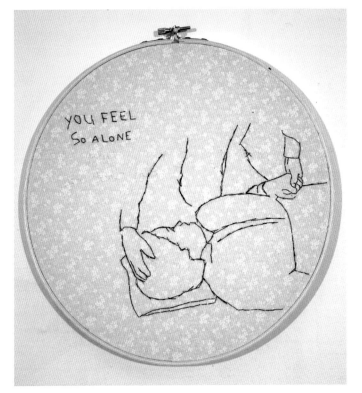

Q: **Do you have a signature embroidery style?**

A: I really like simple line drawings using a single strand of embroidery floss for a line. I feel like my work is meticulously sloppy but also changing and developing all the time. I use embroidery in video work, in my quilts, and I like to think that my embroidery is similarly a medium for getting my ideas across.

I always tell myself that I can complete a piece way faster than I actually can. It's beautiful because it's slow, but it's frustrating too. I want results!

Q: **Do you have a favorite piece among your work?**

A: I'm the most proud of The Omen pieces. I really enjoy using a sewing machine to embroider, and I love the effect of the loose threads. I love the scenes in horror movies that, for better or worse, have such an effect that their audiences can't forget them. I rarely take a shower in a hotel room without thinking about poor Janet Leigh [in Alfred Hitchcock's *Psycho*].

I also made a piece for a project I did with Rachel Ellison called One a Day. I embroidered something every day for a week, and she did a project called We Paint every day for the same week. In that week, I made one piece of a sinking ship with the caption "It's just a feeling I get." I think it really expressed how I was feeling.

Q: **If you were trying to convince someone else to take up embroidery, what would you say to convince them?**

A: Not only will you be able to make beautiful art objects, but you will increase your hand/eye coordination and you will ultimately be better at hand-sewing all things. Think about what a great skill it will be to have during post-apocalyptic times. Take up the needle arts for survivalist reasons alone!

Find more about Brette online at **brettegabel.blogspot.com**

(ABOVE) Brette Gabel, *Omen 1*, 2009, freeform machine embroidery on paper, 12 × 12 in (30.48 × 30.48 cm). Photo: Jason Cawood

Brette Gabel at work. Photo: Jason Cawood

(FACING PAGE) Brette Gabel, *Omen 2*, 2009, freeform machine embroidery on paper, 12 × 12 in (30.48 × 30.48 cm). Photo: Jason Cawood

ODDNESS AND ILLUSTRATION:
An Interview with Esther Oh

Esther Oh is a freelance illustrator who began embroidering in college during an experimental illustration class that she took from the accomplished illustrator Daniel Lim. Her subject matter echoes her illustration style—she says that, for her, embroidery is like drawing with a pencil, except with string. A self-described "little Korean lady living in Koreatown, Los Angeles," Esther likes to eat, draw, sing karaoke, and embroider.

Q: **What sort of embroidery work do you do?**

A: I like to incorporate linoleum-block printing, watercolor, or fabric. I mostly stitch on canvas or muslin. I like to add humor whenever possible. Also Bill Murray. The primary function of my work is to make people laugh or think in a different way or just tilt their head and ask, WTF?

I embroider this one character named Jimmy who has a large benign tumor growing out of his head that has grown eyes and arms. The tumor's name is Timmy, and Jimmy doesn't like him much because he is quite a bother.

Q: **What do you like about embroidery?**

A: I like embroidery because it's a medium that not a lot of people use for illustration purposes. My mom learned how to embroider in middle school back in Korea. I guess it was more useful back then, but I think it's important to keep old skills alive. With the

rise of DIY and craft culture, the old-world medium has fused with modern ideas and images, which makes for very fun and interesting artwork.

Q: **What is the biggest challenge with the sort of embroidery work that you do?**

A: Getting my fabric to not wrinkle! I often don't use any stabilizer, so everything comes out wrinkly. But the more imperfections, the more special it is.

Q: **Do you believe that your gender or social class has any bearing on your attraction to and involvement with needlework?**

A: As a girl, it's almost a given that I know how to do this kind of handicraft. I guess I was attracted to this medium because it is historically feminine, though I don't think it should be left for only women to do. I've read of men in prisons doing needlepoint work. I think that's super cool. But embroidery should not only be an activity for the freedom-challenged—it should be enjoyed by everyone.

Q: **What is your creative process like?**

(FACING PAGE) Esther Oh, *Jimmy and Timmy*, 2009, embroidery on fabric, 11 × 14 in (27.94 × 35.56 cm). Photo: Esther Oh

(THIS PAGE) Esther Oh, *Dance (Napoleon Dynamite)*, 2009, embroidery on fabric, 5 × 7 in (12.75 × 17.75 cm). Photo: Esther Oh

I like to add humor whenever possible. Also Bill Murray. The primary function of my work is to make people laugh or think in a different way or just tilt their head and ask, WTF?

A: First I draw a sketch. Then I get stumped and start Googling. Then I draw some more. Then I listen to some music or watch a movie. Then I go buy materials. Then, at the last moment, I start and finish the project as quickly as I can. Preparation time usually takes longer than execution time.

Q: **Where do you get inspiration for your embroidery work?**

A: I get inspired by people. All people are different, and it's those differences that make people so cool. Extremely different people, like those in the Mütter Museum's exhibit of odd human specimens in Pennsylvania, are the coolest.

Find more of Esther's work online at **estheroh.com**.

(FACING PAGE) Esther Oh, *That Silver Haired Daddy of Mine*, 2010, linoleum print and embroidery on paper, 9 × 12 in (22.86 × 30.48 cm). Photo: Esther Oh

(THIS PAGE) Esther Oh, *Ben with Dog*, 2010, embroidery, fabric, thread, fiberfill, 5 ft (1.52 m) tall, width variable dimensions. Photo: Esther Oh

Paulo and Stella

ESTHER OH

Esther Oh has created a unique and odd illustration for you to stitch. Paulo and Stella are conjoined twins who are fighting over what they should eat for dinner: international pancakes or Chinese takeout. As an only child, Esther always wondered what it would be like to have a sibling. She noticed that brothers or sisters bicker a lot, which really didn't make her want any siblings. Arguing would be difficult to avoid since the siblings would often be together and bonded by blood. In this case, Paulo and Stella are bound to each other by their heads.

Tools and Materials

FLOSS:

- 1 skein of DMC #964 (Seagreen - LT)
- 1 skein of DMC #962 (Dusty Rose - MED)
- 1 skein of DMC #956 (Geranium)
- 1 skein of DMC #951 (Tawny - LT)
- 1 skein of DMC #312 (Baby Blue VY - DK)
- 1 skein of DMC #310 (Black)

FABRIC:

- 15 × 16 in (38.1 × 40.64 cm) piece of medium-weight blue cotton fabric

transfer paper and pencil

embroidery needle—size of your choosing

10-in (25.4-cm) embroidery hoop

scissors

FOR THE TOTE BAG:

- a second piece of 15 × 16 in (38.1 × 40.64 cm) medium-weight blue cotton
- 2 pieces of 15 × 16 in (38.1 × 40.64 cm) medium-weight cotton in a contrasting color or print (to be used for the bag lining)
- 2 long rectangles 3 × 9 in (7.62 × 22.86 cm) of medium weight blue cotton for the bag handles

blue sewing-machine thread to match the blue cotton fabric

straight pins

measuring tape

iron and ironing board

sewing machine

Other skills:

basic sewing machine operation (to create the totebag)

Stitches:

running stitch   back stitch
split stitch   satin stitch

Figure 6.3. Enlarge Paulo and
Stella 120 percent to fit tote bag.

Double Trouble

Transfer Fig. 6.3 using the transfer pen or pencil method (see p. 110). Stretch the fabric taut into your embroidery hoop.

Bringing the Twins to Life

Start with DMC #951. Divide floss into a three-strand thread. Using satin stitch, block in the color of the two faces, arms, and the girl's legs.

TIP: For the faces, keep the stitches short (half the height of the face) so that the stitch doesn't get too loose. To achieve a smooth surface, vary the lengths of every other stitch to make the next row of stitches interlock.

Stitch the eyes separately. Make horizontal satin stitches for the eyelids, leaving a space between upper and lower lids for the pupil. The alternating direction of satin stitches in the head will give a different sheen to the eyes and face.

Satin stitch the arms and legs width-wise, producing short stitches.

Split a skein of DMC #964 into two three-strand strings and satin stitch the boy's shirt.

Using three strands of DMC #962, satin stitch the top half of the girl's dress in two vertical rows. Stitch the bottom of the dress with two rows of interlacing satin stitches.

With six strands of DMC #956, satin stitch two stitches at the ends of each sleeve on the dress. Add two satin stitches to make the belt accent at the waist.

Use a variation of the running stitch to add little dashes to the skirt of the dress. Start at one side of the skirt and continue to make short sparse stitches around the edge. Use a backstitch to add the collar outline onto the dress.

With six strands of DMC #310, split stitch the outline of the characters. For little curved areas like the ears and facial features, use the backstitch for your outline. The mouth and pupil should be filled in with a satin stitch.

The whites of the eyes can be left unstitched so the blue fabric shows through, but this area could also be covered with white floss.

Use a satin stitch in DMC #310 to fill in the shoes.

The extra arms in the background should be back-stitched with three strands of DMC #310.

Stitch the lines of the hair and background with DMC #312.

Use a combination of backstitch and running stitch to achieve the desired pattern for the strands of hair.

Use running stitch to fill in the ground. The rocks are sewn with a running stitch in a circular design. The embroidery should now be finished. Take the fabric off of the hoop and say hello to the twins!

To Sew the Totebag

Press and trim the piece of fabric that has the embroidery on it so that it measures 15 in wide (above and below the embroidery) by 16 in tall (38.1 × 40.64 cm). Ensure that the embroidery is centered squarely before trimming the fabric down to size. Pin this panel to the other piece of light blue fabric with right sides together. Using a straight stitch, machine stitch around the perimeter of three sides of the bag, leaving a 0.25-in (6.35-mm) seam allowance. Do not stitch the top of the bag (the 15-in/38.1-cm side of the square). Iron and press the seams.

Repeat this step with the lining. With right sides together, stitch around the three sides of the lining. When stitching the bottom of the lining, leave a 3-in (7.62-cm) gap to turn the bag inside out. Iron the seams.

To make the handles, fold each rectangle width-wise, so that you have two straps that measure 1.5 × 9 in (3.81 × 22.86 cm). Stitch down the length of each of these pieces. Press seams, and turn straps inside out. Stay-stitch the seams of each handle by running a straight stitch ⅛ in (3 mm) from the edge down the length of the handle.

Place handles on the upper portion of the tote so that the right sides of the handles meet the right side of bag exterior. Baste straps into place.

Place lining on the inside-out bag, sandwiching the handles (tucked in so that the upper loops face down into the center of the bag and the raw edges of the handle ends poke outward), in between the two pieces of fabric. Pin or baste together all three layers of fabric. Stitch around the perimeter of the bag, leaving a 0.25-in (6.35-mm) seam allowance. Trim any excess fabric close to the stitching. Press seams and remove the basting.

Turn the entire bag inside-out through the gap at the bottom of the lining. Press and hand-stitch closed the hole in the lining. The tote bag is now complete, so you can take Paolo and Stella out for a jaunt on the town!

DOUBLE-TAKE:
An interview with Cate Anevski

Cate Anevski is an artist, illustrator, and maker interested in every form of art that she can get her hands on. She enjoys blending traditional crafts with digital media in fun and unexpected ways to express her personal vision and to keep her hands busy. She has exhibited her work internationally.

Q: **Your embroidery work appears to be based on illustration techniques. Is this true?**

A: In embroidery, my focus is the image more than the technique. I use simple stitches, usually just stem stitch, running stitch, French knots, and satin stitch. I like to explore paradox and juxtaposition. My favorite response to my work is the double-take, which I tend to get a lot. At first glance, it seems cute and innocent, but there is always a slightly creepy edge.

Q: **Why embroidery?**

A: I am particularly drawn to embroidery because it forces me to slow down. There is no immediate gratification with needlework, but that makes the end result all the sweeter.

Q: **What is the biggest challenge with the sort of embroidery work that you do?**

A: The hardest part is altering my illustrations so that they will work well with thread. When I first started doing illustration, I worked exclusively in digital media and ink. Some things that work well with those media simply don't translate well to embroidery, but I always enjoy the challenge.

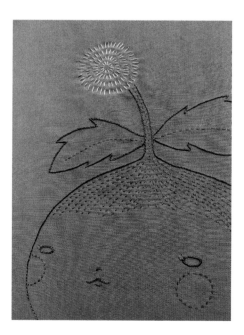

My favorite response to my work is the double-take, which I tend to get a lot. At first glance, it seems cute and innocent, but there is always a slightly creepy edge.

(FACING PAGE) Cate Anevski, *Dandelion Sprite*, 2010, fabric, embroidery floss; 6 × 8 in (15.24 × 20.32 cm). Photo: Cate Anevski

(THIS PAGE, LEFT TO RIGHT) Cate Anevski, *Green Face*, 2010, re-purposed fabric, embroidery floss, wooden embroidery hoop, hot glue, 6 in (15.24 cm) in diameter. Photo: Cate Anevski

Cate Anevski, *Blue Face*, 2010, fabric, embroidery floss, wooden embroidery hoop, hot glue; 4 in (10.16 cm) in diameter. Photo: Cate Anevski

Cate Anevski, *Big Red*, 2009, fabric, embroidery floss, wooden embroidery hoop, hot glue; 7 in (17.78 cm) in diameter. Photo: Cate Anevski "I enjoyed playing with textures on a mainly monochromatic piece. Also the teeth were tons of fun to stitch," says Cate.

Q: **Where do you find inspiration for your embroidery work?**

A: I am inspired by virtually everything I see. I watch a lot of movies and read constantly. I also spend a great deal of time in nature. I find that I am most inspired when I keep my mind open. Some of my best ideas have come from splotches on the floor or the blurry shapes I see when I don't wear my glasses.

Any time an idea strikes, I grab a sketchbook and write it down immediately. Whenever I'm in a creative mood (usually late at night), I flip through my sketchbook and refine these ideas. Once it seems ready, I choose a medium and begin. Generally, I have the idea completely hammered out by the time I begin working on the finished product, but it seldom resembles the original sketch.

Q: **What would you say is the primary function of your work?**

A: I use my work as a means of communication. I have been working on bringing in more functional elements, particularly with embroidered clothing, because I enjoy art in all the parts of my life. I believe that form and function can live in perfect harmony if each challenge is met with creativity and careful thought.

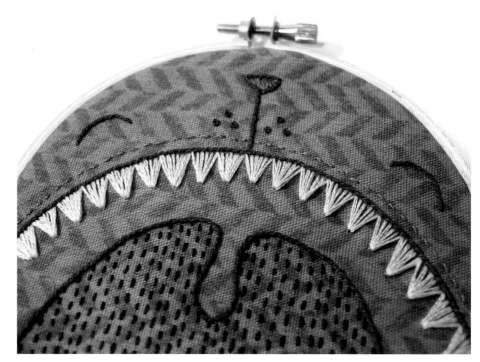

Cate Anevski, detail of *Blue Face*, 2010, fabric, embroidery floss, wooden embroidery hoop, hot glue; 4 in (10.16 cm) in diameter. Photo: Cate Anevski

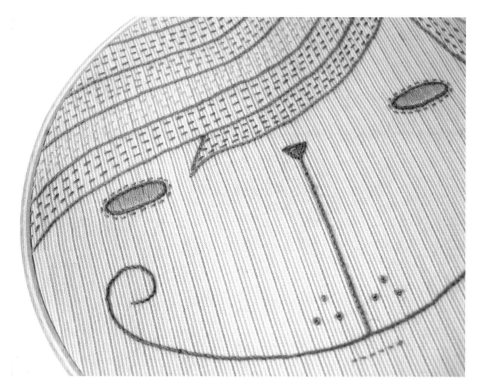

Cate Anevski, detail of *Green Face*, 2010, re-purposed fabric, embroidery floss, wooden embroidery hoop, hot glue, 6 in (15.24 cm) in diameter. Photo: Cate Anevski

Q: **Do you believe that your gender or social class has any bearing on your attraction to and involvement with needlework?**

A: I consider myself a die-hard feminist, and one of the most important elements of this, to me, is to learn the things that my foremothers knew. I spend a lot of my spare time doing traditional women's work, particularly housekeeping and cooking, and being able to use embroidery in my art as an extension of this part of myself has been a wonderful revelation.

Q: **Do you have any fantasy projects that you would like to tackle?**

A: I want to start embroidering elaborate superhero capes for myself. I'll begin once I figure out just what kind of superhero (or super-villain) I am.

See Cate's online portfolio at **cateanevski. com.**

One Mutant to Another

CATE ANEVSKI

Cate Anevski thinks that every mutant should be as fortunate as the four-leafed variety. She created this simple and beautiful illustration for a watercolor painting and adapted it to embroidery so that you can stitch your very own lucky mutant!

Tools and Materials

FLOSS:

- hair: 1 skein of DMC #435 (Brown VY - LT)
- skin: 1 skein of DMC #758 (Terra Cotta VY - LT)
- dress: 1 skein of DMC #3810 (Turquoise - DK)
- spots: 1 skein of DMC #223 (Shell Pink - LT)
- eyes and clover: 1 skein of DMC #581 (Moss Green)

FABRIC:

- 15 × 18 in (38.1 × 45.72 cm) piece of natural-colored linen
- 15 × 18 in (38.1 × 45.72 cm) piece of low-loft/thin quilt batting
- 15 × 18 in (38.1 × 45.72 cm) piece of white fabric
- 2 canvas stretcher bars 9 in (22.86 cm) long
- 2 canvas stretcher bars 12 in (30.48 cm) long
- staple gun and staples
- sawtooth hanger
- scissors

Stitches:

running stitch   stem stitch

Preparation

Center the design (Fig. 6.4, p. 222) on the fabric. Transfer design to fabric using the transfer pen or pencil method (p. 110).

Make Your Mutant

Embroider the design in the specified floss colors or a palette of your choice. All the dashed lines were created in running stitch, and all solid lines were created using stem stitch. The stitches in the example project are very small. To make small stitches, insert your needle ¹⁄₁₆ in (1.5 mm) or less away from the end of the last stitch.

Finishing

If applicable, remove the design transfer by spraying with water until the marks come out entirely.

Assemble the stretcher bars. Center the frame over the quilt batting. Cut away excess batting to eliminate bulky corners when stretching the embroidery. Sandwich the quilt batting between the embroidered fabric and the white fabric. The embroidery should face out. Place the "sandwich" on your working surface with the embroidery facing the table and the white fabric facing upward.

Center the stretcher bar frame over the fabric. Staple the center of each edge of the fabric to the

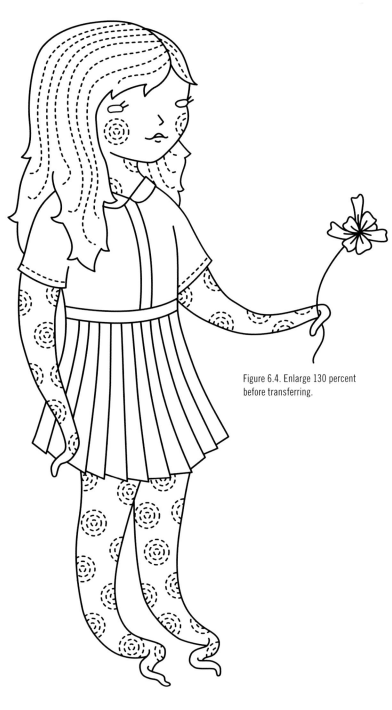

Figure 6.4. Enlarge 130 percent before transferring.

stretcher bars, moving from left and right, and continuing from top to bottom.

Fold the point of each corner diagonally over the stretcher bars and staple it in place. Then fold the edges over the stretcher bars and staple those in place. The goal is to have tidy corners, so check how each looks from the front before you staple. Repeat this step for each corner.

Attach the sawtooth hanger to the top of the stretcher bar frame, nailing through the layers of fabric and quilt batting. You now have a framed mutant that you can hang on the wall for all to see!

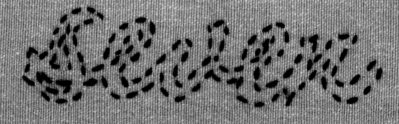

CHAPTER 7

Unexpected Stitching

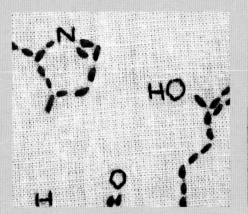

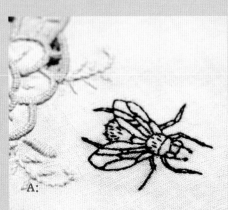

W hile many of the artists profiled in this book stress the importance of not following patterns, sometimes a template can serve as a valid creative kick-start. The designers featured in this chapter possess diverse aesthetics and artistic backgrounds. Each has conceptualized an original stitch project for you to enjoy. Personal choices in stitch patterns, materials, and color can make your handiwork unique! Choose to follow these projects step-by-step using your own creative sensibilities or adjust the ideas to suit your own imaginative whims.

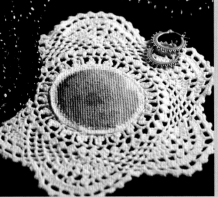

All Good in the 'Hood

SARA HERNANDEZ

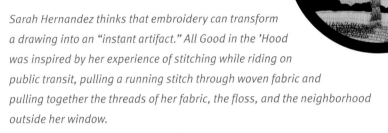

Sarah Hernandez thinks that embroidery can transform a drawing into an "instant artifact." All Good in the 'Hood was inspired by her experience of stitching while riding on public transit, pulling a running stitch through woven fabric and pulling together the threads of her fabric, the floss, and the neighborhood outside her window.

The embroidery design pictured here is a composite of photos from Chicago neighborhoods where Sarah has lived. Find images of your own neighborhood to use in a project that is unique to you. You can use this idea to create an entire blanket, or to stitch a single dwelling on a small object like a pillow or a potholder.

Tools and Materials

FOR THE EMBROIDERED PANEL:

Floss in an assortment of colors

FABRIC:

54 × 36 in (137.16 × 91.44 cm) piece of light blue broadcloth

fabric scraps in contrasting colors to use as appliquéd buildings

10-in (25.4-cm) or larger embroidery hoop

embroidery needle—size of your choice

sewing needle

disappearing ink pen

double-sided fusible interfacing

dressmaker's pencil

scissors or rotary cutter

measuring tape

Fray Check, Craftguard, or fabric glue (optional)

pinking shears (optional)

iron (optional)

To make the blanket:

FABRIC:

exterior side of blanket:

beige cotton: 70 × 76 in (177.8 × 193.04 cm)

blue cotton: 36 × 22 (91.44 × 142.24)

blanket lining:

cotton or light flannel: 105 × 76 in (266.7 × 193.04 cm)

9 yd (8.23 m) of 1-in (2.54-cm) double-fold bias tape

sewing machine

straight pins

polyester or cotton thread in a color that matches the blanket fabric

Stitches:

backstitch	blanket stitch
couching	feather stitch
running stitch	satin stitch

Other skills:

basic sewing machine operation

Preparation

Wash all fabric and trim in order to release extra dye and pre-shrink the cotton.

Collect printed images of your neighborhood online or from your own collection of photos. Arrange pictures on broadcloth panel. If you would like to have all of the buildings a uniform size, enlarge or reduce the images on a photocopier to achieve the desired effect. You may wish to include other design elements such as trees, fences, animals, and cars.

The design can be drawn freehand, or the printed pictures can be used as a stencil. If you prefer to use the images as a stencil, cut out each paper building and trace its outline onto the broadcloth using a dressmaker's pencil. If you wish to make the embroidered panel into a blanket, remember to leave a 2-in (5.08-cm) border around the broadcloth piece so you can stitch the seams of the blanket.

Choose building elements—such as windows or doors—that should be appliquéd onto the broadcloth. Trace these onto the fabric scraps using the dressmaker's pencil. To prevent the appliquéd pieces from fraying, apply fabric glue or an anti-fray product to the edges of each cut-out piece, or trim with pinking shears.

Build Your Appliqué

Lay the appliqués onto the broadcloth right-side up. Tack the pieces to the blanket with straight pins to keep them from shifting. Once these are in place, sew (either by hand or sewing machine) the appliqué into place using a running stitch, starting with the larger foundation pieces, such as building outlines, and then applying smaller pieces, such as doors and windows.

TIP: When applying small bits of appliqué, it can help to use a fusible interfacing to hold them in place. Cut the interfacing a slightly smaller size than the fabric and place it between the two pieces of fabric. Fuse the materials together with a hot iron. You can then sew the small appliqué into place without straight pins.

Techniques Used in the Sample Project
(Fig. 7.1)

OFFICE BUILDINGS: The grid pattern on the office buildings was backstitched. To make a perfect grid, draw it using a ruler and disappearing ink pen before you stitch. Using a large hoop when stitching will keep your work taut without having to adjust the hoop.

CLOUDS: The silhouette of each cloud was drawn behind the buildings, and a split stitch was used to articulate the outline. The outlines were filled with concentric circles. Different shades of white and blue floss were used to suggest depth.

TREES: The trees were approached like a paint-by-number painting. Each of the leaves was divided into shapes according to shade, and satin stitch was used to fill each shape. Varying the direction of the stitch gives the texture of the leaves variety. The tree trunks were created with half a skein of gray floss couched in a switch-back pattern.

PARK: A rectangle was drawn to represent a lawn, and the grass was filled in using blanket stitch. It is recommended that two to three different shades of green floss are used to represent light and shade. The park's border was created using satin stitch.

FARAWAY BUILDINGS: Split, running, and back-stitches were used together to make the buildings in the background. Once these were in place, the tree line was drawn and filled with satin stitch.

FOREGROUND BUILDINGS: The buildings on the left side of the piece were made with blanket stitches of varying sizes to represent differently sized bricks. To create the perspective of buildings in the foreground, lay a ruler along the bottom of the tree line and trace a line through the foreground buildings. This creates the horizon

line, and all lines above it should gradually angle up to the left until they reach the roof. All lines below the horizon line should gradually angle down until they meet the ground. The bricks are drawn bigger on the left and smaller on the right to achieve the notion of perspective.

STREET: Fve different colors of floss were used in a running stitch.

FINISHING TOUCHES: Climbing vines were added onto the yellow appliquéd building using a feather stitch, finished with a split stitch. Strands of silver bugle beads were added to one of the office buildings to give a sense of sunlight reflecting from a wet surface. The blanket stitch rainbow was added last.

Once you get started, you'll probably feel that you could work on this blanket forever—appliquéing on things like cars and dogs and people playing Frisbee!

To Make the Blanket

Pre-wash all fabrics and press all pieces, including your newly finished embroidery piece.

To create the center panel of the blanket, cut the blue cotton piece in half so that you have two pieces of fabric measuring 36 × 11 in (91.44 × 27.94 cm). Align and then pin together the right sides of the two 36-in (91.44 cm) lengths of blue cotton to the 36-in (91.44-cm) right sides of the embroidered work, so that the embroidery work is

Figure 7.1
LEGEND:

Back Stitch

Blanket Stitch

Feather Stitch

Running Stitch

Satin Stitch

Split Stitch

Couching

now flanked on each side with blue fabric. Leaving a 0.25-in (6.35-mm) seam allowance, use your sewing machine to straight stitch the two seams. Trim extra thread and press all seams. The center panel of the quilt is now complete.

Cut the beige fabric asymmetrically so that one piece measures 76 × 22 in (193.04 × 55.88 cm)—for the top blanket panel—and a second piece measures 76 × 48 in (193.04 × 122.92 cm) for the bottom panel. Attach the top panel by matching the raw edges of the right sides to the center panel (which measures 76 in/193.04 cm across) to the 76-in (193.04 cm) side of the top beige panel. Leaving a 0.25-in (6.35-mm) seam allowance, stitch together. Attach the bottom panel by matching the right sides of the center panel with the beige bottom panel along the 76-in (193.04-cm) side, and stitch together. Trim all threads and iron all seams.

Lay the blanket and the lining fabric out on a flat surface, matching the raw edges of the wrong sides together. Baste around the perimeter of the blanket to stitch the two pieces together. Finish the blanket by stitching bias tape around the raw edges of all four sides of the blanket.

Enjoy sleeping in your cozy 'hood!

SARAH HERNANDEZ finds inspiration in woodblock prints like those by Ando Hiroshige and Tugboat Printshop, illustrations by Jill Bliss, Leonard Tsuguoharu Foujita, and Lart Cognac Berliner, wallpaper, and Scandinavian kitsch. In 2004, Sarah moved from Dallas to Chicago to paint at the School of the Art Institute of Chicago. She took an embroidery class, and immediately identified with the process. She likes the rhythm of it, and that she could choose simple or complex stitches to work with and be equally satisfied with both results. Sarah also makes felt animals and greeting cards for her Etsy shop, Paper Tiger Cards. Find Sarah's online shop at **etsy.com /shop/papertigercards.**

Eat the Kitch

HEATHER BAIN

Heather Bain's skull 'n' utensils apron was inspired by a late night in her kitchen:

"It was the summer of 2006, and [rock critic] Lester Bangs' specter was hangin' with me in my kitchen. He was spewing a litany of expletives over the newest cracker-jack band to come out of... and just couldn't believe how far down the sewer music had gone. You know, sure, he hated Lou, but at least he respected him and liked his music, but the... really? People actually... But I digress. So it's me and specter Bangs. Now, I'm no rock critic, but Lester and I shared one thing: a sense of boredom over the mass-produced dribble that was being spoon-fed to the youths of our generation. Lester thrived in the absurd, was depressed by mediocrity. I know, this is just a skull with a knife and fork below it; it's not like I brought back Johnny Thunders from the dead. But hey, isn't it better than another apron covered in flowers that has no skull with a knife and a fork below it?"

Tools and Materials

FLOSS:

■ 2 skeins of DMC #310 (Black)

FABRIC:

10 × 10-in (25.4 × 25.4-cm) square of 10-count tear-away waste canvas for needlepoint

10 × 10-in (25.4 × 25.4-cm) square of heavy weight white cotton

thrifted or handmade apron

6-in (15.24-cm) embroidery hoop

embroidery needle (size of your choice for three strands of floss)

upholstery-weight sewing needle

thread in a bright color

transfer pen or pencil

scissors

Stitches:

backstitch   basting/running stitch

Boning Up

Transfer Fig. 7.2 onto the cotton square by tracing the pattern directly onto the white cotton with a disappearing ink pen (see p. 110). Secure the fabric in the embroidery hoop.

Stitch the outline:

Separate the floss into three strands. Using a backstitch, stitch the outline of the skull and utensils. Be sure to delineate the lines where the utensils cross, the holes of the skull's eyes and nose, and the teeth.

Release the cotton from the hoop and iron the fabric. Center the stitched design onto a piece of waste canvas. Using the waste thread, stitch around the edges of the canvas to baste it to the material. Make an x-shaped pattern through the center of the canvas so that the two pieces of fabric don't slip against each other.

Transfer the stitch pattern onto to the waste canvas by laying the waste canvas on top of the material. Trace the border of the design using the disappearing ink pen.

The Blackwork Pattern

Stitch through both the fabric and the waste canvas to create a fill pattern using this simple blackwork technique:

A. Working from left to right, make a series of vertical straight stitches, using the waste canvas as a guideline. Leave one "square" of space between each stitch. Continue until you reach the outline.

Figure 7.2. Transfer
image at 100 percent.

Next, working right to left, move your needle one square down and repeat the same stitch, so that you have two lines of parallel stitches with one "square" between them. Continue until you reach the edge of the design outline.

B. Working left to right, join every two vertical stitches with a horizontal stitch at their tops and bottoms, so that the four stitches resemble a square.

C. Add a short vertical stitch in-between each box. Continue this pattern until you reach the left edge of the design. Working from left to right, make a horizontal stitch below the base of each box. Make the stitch the same width as the base of the box and one "square" below the stitched box.

D. Repeat steps A–C. Repeat the blackwork pattern through the skull and utensils, except for the tines of the fork.

Once you have completed the fill, remove stitching from the hoop, and discard the waste canvas following the manufacturer's directions (usually this means tearing the canvas off in loose threads). Press your work.

To turn your project into a patch for an apron, press each raw edge back 0.25 in (6.35 mm), fold, and press 0.25 in (6.35 mm) again. Sew the patch to an apron by using black embroidery thread and a running stitch ⅛ in (3 mm) from the patch's border. Trim any loose threads.

Wear your new rock 'n' roll apron with panache! Bone Appetite!

HEATHER BAIN is a self-taught crafter who often has bloody fingers and calloused hands. She learns primarily through exploring and manipulating techniques, while making numerous mistakes and accepting them as unique. Heather has experimented with many mediums, including textiles, knitting, woodworking, bookbinding, printing, and needlecraft. Mostly, she makes art for herself and uses her work as a way to better relate to her surroundings. She also uses it as a way to locate herself and other queers in a predominantly straight world. Heather has been on the fringe of the Toronto drag scene and performing arts community, including performing with KingSize Kings, whose work focuses on queering communities through gender, sexuality, and fat politics.

Evolution or Revolution

BARBARA RANDALL

We live in a world in which science is obsessed with proving everything. Instead of dog-faced boys and saints with miraculous visions, we have hereditary diseases and mental disorders. Science is the killjoy at the party, rolling its eyes at the sideshow oddities like the Fiji mermaid in the room. It is more fun to believe that jackalopes are hiding out in their jackalope huts or caves (or whatever they live in), and laughing at how easily they have tricked mankind into believing they aren't roaming than to listen to science explain their non-existence. This piece is for all the jackalopes out there, living their lives and, by doing so, proving everybody wrong.

Tools and Materials

FLOSS:

- 1 skein of DMC Ecru
- 1 skein of DMC #434 (Brown - LT)
- 1 skein of DMC #738 (Tan VY - LT)
- 1 skein of DMC #801 (Coffee Brown - DK)
- 1 skein of DMC #803 (Dark Navy Blue)
- 1 skein of DMC #3045 (Yellow-Beige - DK)
- 1 skein of DMC #3328 (Salmon - DK)

FABRIC:

18 × 24-in (45.71 × 60.96-cm) piece of cotton fabric. A subtle white-on-white or cream pattern is recommended.

18 × 24-in (45.72 × 60.96-cm) piece of plain medium-weight cotton in white

embroidery needle, size of your choice

10-in (25.4-cm) embroidery hoop

10–20 T-pins or straight pins (used for framing, so they should have metal pinheads, not decorative tops)

tracing paper

transfer pen or pencil

acid-free Elmer's 3/16-in (4.76-mm) foam core (available at most craft stores)

8 × 10-in (20.32 × 25.4-cm) picture frame

scissors

Stitches:

running stitch   satin stitch

EVOLUTION OR REVOLUTION

NOTE: The example project is stitched with two strands of floss separated from a six-strand skein.

Use a basic running stitch to trace the jackalope's body, antlers, and the banner. Use satin stitch to fill in the eye, nose, and text. Using DMC #801 in a running stitch, outline the body, ear, mouth, and eyebrow of the jackalope. Use a running stitch to outline the antlers in DMC #3045. Use a satin stitch on the jackalope's face to fill in his nose with DMC #3328 and his eye with DMC #803.

To finish the jackalope, highlight the tufts of fur in the ear with a line of DMC #434 stitched directly next to the previously stitched lines. Repeat this method on the legs, knee, and tail.

To outline the banner, use DMC #738 in a running stitch. As in the highlights of the jackalope's fur, use DMC Ecru to place a second line of stitches inside the banner. Stitch the text using DMC #803. Finally, combine the two colored stitches by using a running stitch on the thin lines and a satin stitch to fill in the thicker lines.

Preparation
Transfer the image (Fig. 7.3) onto the patterned fabric using the transfer pen or pencil method (p. 110).

The (R)evolutionary Process
If you chose a patterned fabric that is thin, ensure that the tail of the floss cannot be seen through the back. If the fabric is transparent, place a plain white piece of fabric behind the patterned piece. Then place both pieces into your hoop. As you sew, your embroidery work will stitch the two pieces together.

Finishing Your Jackalope
Press the embroidery work. Cut an 8 x10-in (20.32 × 25.4-cm) piece of acid-free foam core.

To frame, place the embroidery on top of the foam core, positioning the stitched image in the middle of the composition. Fold the excess fabric over the edge and press T-pins straight into the edge of the foam core. Work around all four edges, pulling the fabric tight; this tension will help to eliminate wrinkles. Once all four sides are pinned, use your embroidery needle and a length of the DMC Ecru to whipstitch the fabric to the board. Trim any excess fabric from the back and place the jackalope into a frame.

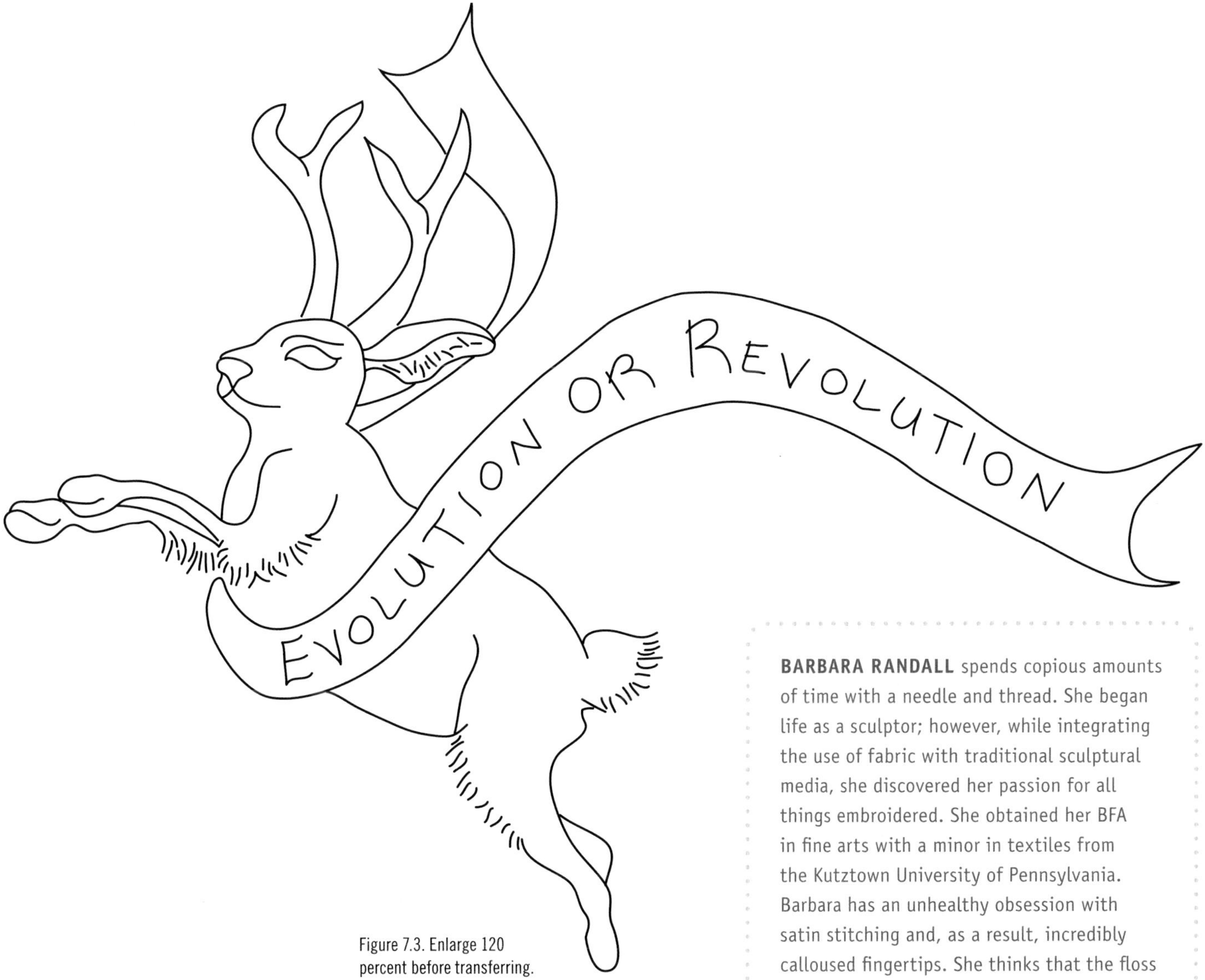

Figure 7.3. Enlarge 120 percent before transferring.

BARBARA RANDALL spends copious amounts of time with a needle and thread. She began life as a sculptor; however, while integrating the use of fabric with traditional sculptural media, she discovered her passion for all things embroidered. She obtained her BFA in fine arts with a minor in textiles from the Kutztown University of Pennsylvania. Barbara has an unhealthy obsession with satin stitching and, as a result, incredibly calloused fingertips. She thinks that the floss color #3847 is DMC's greatest accomplishment. Barbara sells some of her embroidered goodies at **stlucybelle.etsy.com**.

Knuckle Tattoo Church Gloves

LYNN KEARNS

Tattoo You

The beauty of these gloves is you can embroider all of the designs or pick just one element. The instructions for each image are therefore written separately.

TIP: Stitch the lettering ("love" and "hate") first, then stitch the cross and spider web around the words.

LOVE and HATE

Try on the gloves one at a time and make a fist. Using a pencil, mark the letters between the first and third knuckles of each finger for ease of embroidering.

Trace the letters onto transfer paper and roughly cut around each one. Position and transfer one letter at a time by tracing the letters with the carbon paper underneath. Remember to check that the letters face the right way up before embroidering!

Using two strands from the skein, outline the letters using a backstitch. Finish the letters by filling them in satin stitch. Stitch through only one layer of fabric so that you do not stitch the fingers of the gloves together!

The Spider Web

Try on the glove on which you will stitch the web; in the example project, the web radiates out from the bottom knuckle of the thumb.

Using a pencil or a disappearing-ink pen, draw radiating lines out from the knuckle to the thumb gusset. Draw slightly arced lines across them, spaced evenly apart until you achieve the effect of a spider web.

Lynn Kearn's love of tattoos and embroidery led her to create the Knuckle Tattoo Church Gloves. Whether they are done at home or in prison, hand tattoos still carry a social stigma and are often seen as defiant and rebellious. Not being sufficiently brave enough to carry off something as permanent as a tattoo, Lynn came up with the idea of substituting ink for thread and transferred the iconic tattoo images onto gloves. She enjoyed playing with the contrast between the prim and proper church gloves and the imagery of the tattoos, as well as comparing the stereotypical idea of a woman sitting at home alone stitching with the isolated person scratching words or pictures into his or her skin with ink.

Tools and Materials

FLOSS:

■ 1 skein of DMC #939 (Blue VY - DK)

FABRIC:

white gloves (found at thrift stores or on Ebay)

embroidery needle, size 5–10

carbon transfer paper

pencil or disappearing ink pen

tracing paper

scissors

Stitches

straight stitch   stem stitch

satin stitch   backstitch

To stitch the spider web, thread your needle with two strands of floss. Embroider the radial lines with stem stitch. Thread your needle with one strand of thread and use a back stitch to follow the web lines.

The Cross

Transfer the pattern (Fig. 7.4) using carbon transfer paper (see p. 110) between tracing paper and the glove.

Using two strands of floss, backstitch the outline. Then re-thread the needle with one strand of floss, and backstitch the inner outline.

Use one strand of floss to create shading. Cover the perimeter of the shaded areas with a straight stitch. Satin stitch in the shaded areas between the ribbon and cross.

Finishing

Hand wash the gloves carefully to remove any marks left from the transfer. Press your gloves gently with an iron, first laying a damp tea towel on the gloves so the iron doesn't come into direct contact with the embroidered surface.

Wear your stitched tattoos with pride!

LYNN KEARNS lives in Te Awamutu, New Zealand. She works part-time as an office administrator and makes artwork to counter the effects of a day job. As a child of the 1970s—the heyday of craft—she was always busy embroidering the obligatory tray cloths, creating macramé pot-plant holders, and picking up skills from family, friends, and books. Today, she focuses on repurposing thrift shop finds, embellishing and customizing garments and textile art with embroidery in order to transform them from mundane items to special one-off creations.

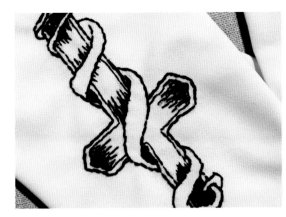

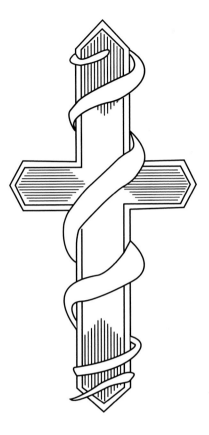

LOVE

HATE

Figure 7.4. Customize images to suit glove size.

Microbe Hankies

JO SAFFERTON

Once upon a time, before Jo picked up a needle and thread, she was a scientist who specialized in microbiology. Although that qualification isn't particularly useful in her day-to-day life now, she is still fascinated by the different shapes of microbes. It occurred to her that she should combine this love with her love of embroidery and that the most perfect place to stick an embroidered microbe would be, of course, where they reside anyway, the handkerchief!

There are four microbe designs with this project. They can be embroidered on separate handkerchiefs or all together on one.

Tools and Materials

FLOSS:

- **For the bacillus:**

  1 skein of DMC #550 (Violet VY - DK)

  1 skein of DMC #796 (Royal Blue - DK)

- **For the virus:**

  1 skein of DMC #740 (Tangerine)

- **For the E.coli:**

  1 skein of DMC #3760 (Wedgewood - MED)

  1 skein of DMC #937 (Avocado Green - MD)

  1 skein of DMC #550 (Violet VY - LT)

- **For the amoeba:**

  1 skein of DMC #444 (Lemon - DK)

FABRIC:

10 × 10-in (25.4 × 25.4-cm) square of white cotton-linen blend (choose a soft fabric) for each handkerchief.

8 × 8-in (20.32 × 20.32-cm) "retro pattern" cotton print for the back of each handkerchief.

embroidery needle, size of your choice

8-in (20.32-cm) embroidery hoop

white sewing-machine thread

sewing machine

blunt object such a crochet hook, chopstick, or pair of closed scissors, to turn out corners

iron

water-soluble pen

set square

straight pins

scissors

Stitches:

split stitch   satin stitch

Other skills:

basic sewing machine operation

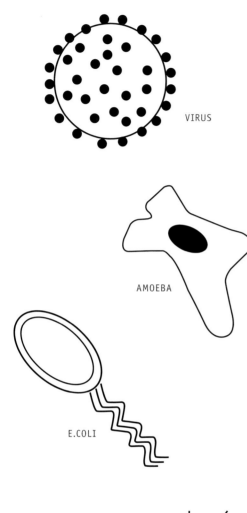

VIRUS

AMOEBA

E.COLI

Figures 7.5 a–d. Choose to trace one microbe or all four onto your handkerchief. Copy at 100 percent of size.

BACILLUS

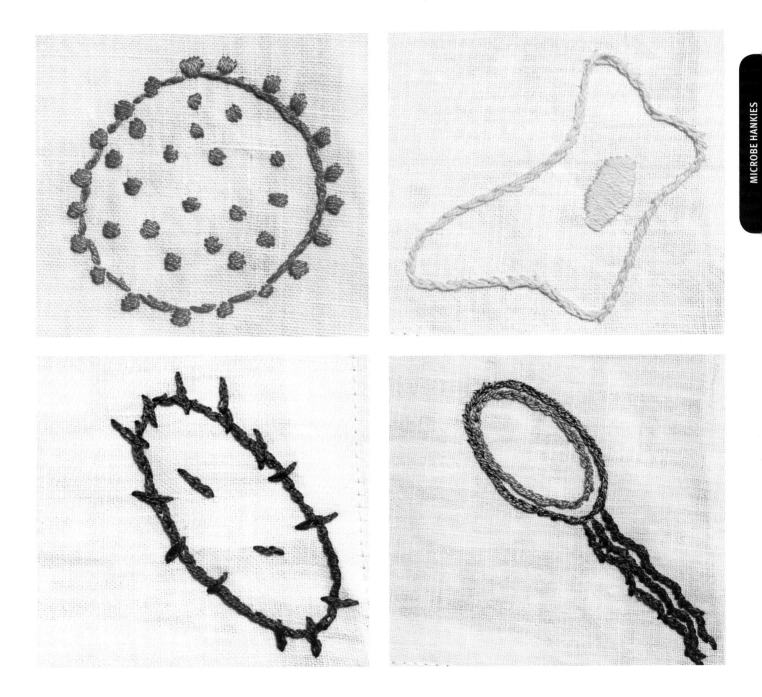

Go Viral

Before you begin, machine wash and dry the fabric at the same temperature that you will wash your handkerchief once you've used it.

When the fabric is dry, press it with an iron.

Using the edge of your cotton-linen square as a guide, draw an 8-in (20.32-cm) square on the top right-hand corner of the white fabric with the water-soluble pen, so that there is a border on the bottom and left-hand side of the fabric. This will show you where the lining will be placed, but the extra 2-in (5-cm) border also allows the fabric to fit comfortably in the hoop while you embroider the microbe.

Transfer the microbe design(s) (Fig 7.5) onto the fabric using chosen transfer method (see p. 110 for details) in the bottom left-hand corner, remembering to leave some space for the seam.

Make the Microbes

Using three strands of floss, stitch the outline of the microbes in split stitch. Use satin stitch to fill in the details of the amoeba and the virus.

Remove the finished embroidery from the hoop and cut the fabric along the lines that you marked, so that this piece of fabric is 8 × 8-in (20.32 × 20.32-cm) square. Wash the water-soluble pen off the cotton-linen fabric, let it dry, and then press gently to remove any creases.

Sew the Hankie

Pin the right sides (the side with the embroidery and the side with the retro pattern) of the two squares of fabric together.

Using a 3/8-in (0.95 cm) seam allowance, machine stitch around the perimeter of the handkerchief. Begin to stitch at the center point of one of the raw edges and pivot around each corner. Stop 2 in (5 cm) from your starting point to allow a gap big enough to turn handkerchief

JO STAFFERTON, otherwise known as Mrs Lacer or just plain Lacer, blogs at Lacer's Life (lacer.wordpress.com) about crafting, cooking, reading, writing, and raising two kids, who are her biggest and best clients. After a previous life as a scientist, Jo became interested in embroidery. She wanted to recapture the crafting that she did with her mum, school, and even her Brownie pack while her children were still small. Jo still can't "draw for toffee," but is pleasantly surprised that, with a bit of practice, she didn't turn out too bad with a needle! She has an online shop, Mrs Lacer's Attic (**etsy.com/shop/lacer**), and writes regularly for the popular embroidery blog Feeling Stitchy (**feelingstitchy.com**).

right-side out. To finish, remember to backstitch at the start and end.

Snip the corners of the handkerchief diagonally. Cut close to the seam, but be careful not to cut the sewn corners. Hand roll and then press all seams. Turn the handkerchief right-side out. Use a blunt object to gently push out the corners.

Gently press the handkerchief and then top stitch around the entire edge of the square by lining up the edge of the sewing machine foot against the edge of the handkerchief. This stitching will close the hole.

Pop your finished hankie in your pocket to be ready for a microbe moment!

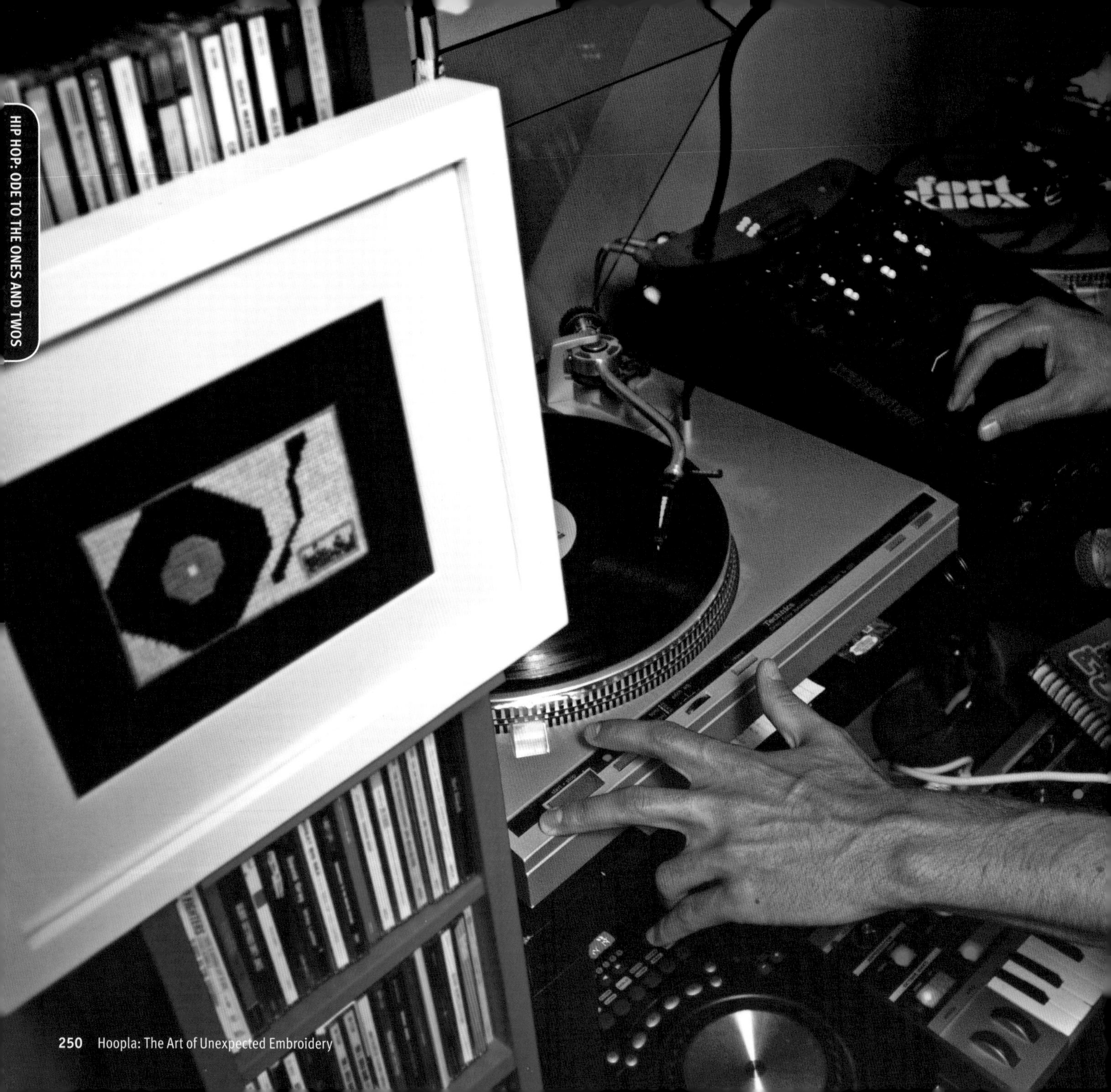

Hip Hop: Ode to the Ones and Twos

JENNIFER BAKER

Jennifer Baker was inspired to combine two things that she loves—old school hip hop and crafts. She thought it would be fun to take needlepoint, a traditional craft, and combine it with contemporary urban culture. By pushing the boundaries of traditional stitching, she hopes to introduce needlepoint to a younger audience and make art that is more relevant to their generation.

Tools and Materials

FLOSS:

- 2 skeins of DMC #E310 (Black Antique Effects)
- 1 skein of DMC #E130 (Mixed Jewel Effects)
- 2 skeins of DMC #E940 (White Glow in the Dark)
- 1 skein of DMC #310 (Black)
- 1 skein of DMC White
- 1 skein of DMC #700 (Green - Bright)
- 1 skein of DMC #414 (Steel Gray - DK)

FABRIC:

- 4 × 2.5-in (10.16 × 6.35-cm) piece of Aida 14-count cross-stitch fabric in black
- 6-in (15.24-cm) embroidery hoop
- tapestry needle (blunt ended), size 24
- waste sewing thread, for basting
- masking tape, min. 1-in (2.54-cm) width
- scissors

Stitches:

counted needlepoint

Turn up the Volume

Line the edges of your canvas with masking tape in order to keep them from fraying as you work with the waste thread. Mark the center of the canvas by stitching two intersecting lines across the length and width of your piece. Place fabric in the center of the hoop and pull taut.

Put the Needle on the Record

Start at the center point and follow the chart (Fig. 7.6). Work the stitches using the colors defined by the chart. Stitch the smallest areas of color first, and then work on the larger areas.

When all the stitches are complete, add a gray border around the piece, doubling a backstitch over the existing stitches.

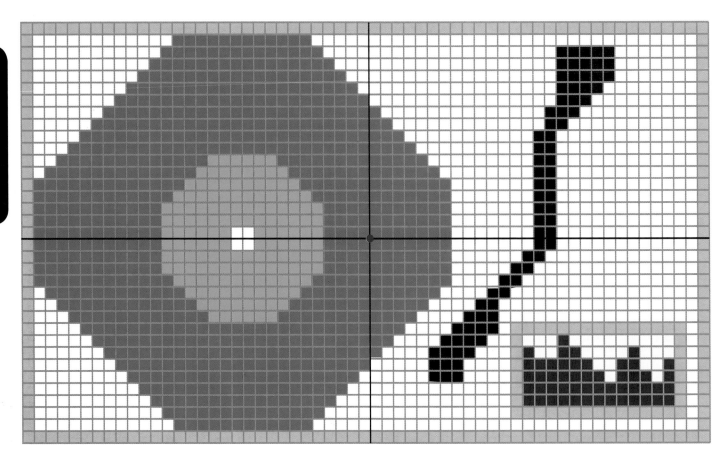

Figure 7.6.

LEGEND:

- DMC #E310 (Black Antique Effects)
- DMC #E130 (Mixed Jewel Effects)
- DMC #E940 (White Glow in the Dark)
- DMC #310 (Black)
- DMC White
- DMC #700 (Green - BRIGHT)
- DMC #414 (Steel Gray - DK)

JENNIFER BAKER is a New York-based multi-media artist. Raised in a small northern Minnesota mining community, she discovered her passion for art as a young child. Jennifer is pursuing her dream of making a living from art or, as she likes to say, "making art work." She uses her art as a form of self-expression and as a medium for social commentary. A self-proclaimed "hip hop head" with unquenchable wanderlust, Jennifer is humbled and inspired by her world travels. She hopes that her art will create a positive impact on the world and touch the lives of others. An Ode to the Ones and Twos is the first piece in *Hip Hop*, a needlepoint series homage to the four pillars of hip hop culture. Find Jennifer online at **minacraft.com**.

Home Invasion

SARAH TERRY

Shock and amaze your guests with this creepy-crawly set of table linens! When Sarah first moved to Australia from Britain, she was horrified by just how many creatures wanted to kill or harm her. These embroidery patterns are part of a larger body of work which were developed for her first solo show Drawing Threads in which she dealt with her (somewhat irrational) fears of "killer Australia." Sarah is happy to report that, after a year down under, she is still alive and kicking.

Tools and Materials

FLOSS:

■ 1 skein of DMC #310 (black)

FABRIC:

Recycled linens with pre-existing floral embroidery. Look in the back of your drawers, visit a charity shop or two, or rob your granny. Three different linens are required to complete the different designs.

ordinary sewing needle in a thin gauge

6–8-in (15.24–20.32-cm) embroidery hoop

fusible interfacing (a small amount to back the designs)

water-soluble pen

scissors

use of a photocopier and a light box or bright window

Stitches:

seed stitch (for wolf spider)

backstitch   French knots (for wolf spider)

Plan the Infestation

Start by photocopying the designs. The drawings should be to scale, but feel free to enlarge, reduce, or repeat the designs as you see fit. Place the design(s) onto a light source with the linen on top. Pick your placement carefully—the idea is that the insect

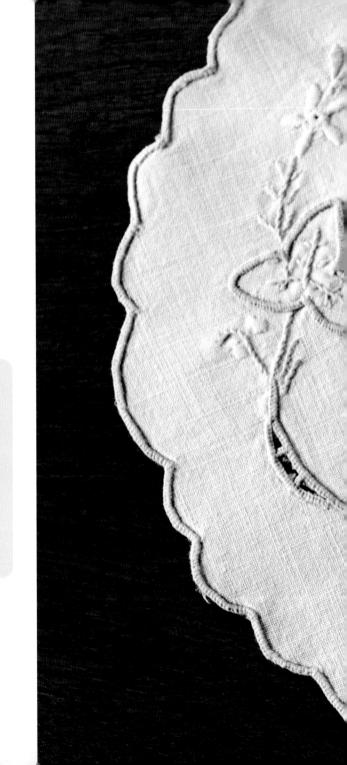

embroideries should be "hidden" amongst pre-existing traditional designs of the vintage linens.

Trace the design onto the linen with the water-soluble pen. Don't worry too much about little details like the hairs on the spider's legs. These can be added later and worked as much or as little as you like. Iron fusible interfacing to the back of the design to strengthen it while you sew. Make the interfacing patch larger than the design. You will trim off the excess when you're finished stitching.

Place the fabric into the embroidery hoop and stretch it taut. Split the thread into six separate strands and use one strand at a time to stitch. Thread the needle and tie a knot in the end. Trim the thread off just below the knot.

Begin to follow each design using a backstitch to create a continuous line. As the designs are based on line drawings, there is no fill stitch required. Move the embroidery hoop as needed to cover the whole design. Once the outline is complete, the design is finished.

NOTE: For the wolf spider (Fig. 7.7), add hairs with seed stitches and use two tiny French knots right next to each other for the eyes.

Lay a table with the embroidered linen and wait for the shocked and horrified cries of your dinner party guests!

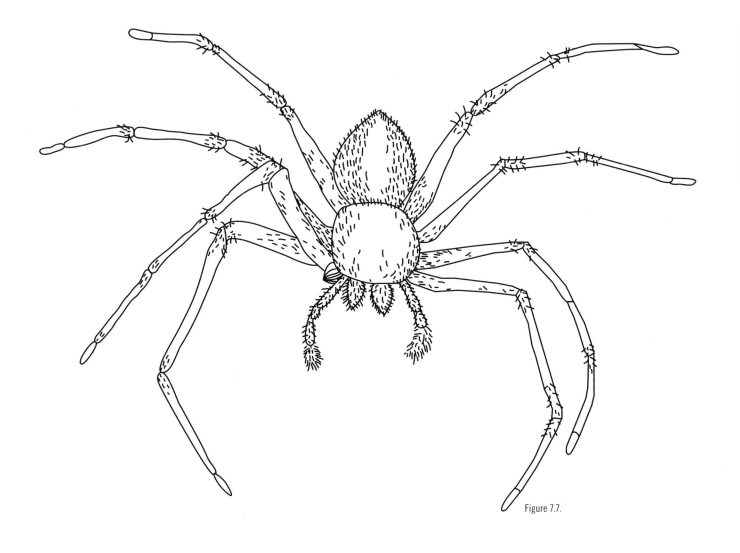

Figure 7.7.

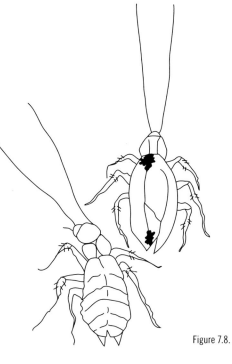

Figure 7.8.

Figure 7.9.

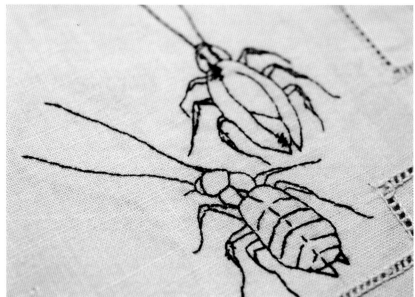

In 2006, Sarah graduated from Manchester Metropolitan University in the UK with a degree in embroidery. The following year, she set up her business, Guerilla Embroidery. Through the company, Sarah makes art, runs workshops, and produces works for clients such as Manchester Fashion Week and PlayStation. Her artwork has been published in several books and is included in art collections all over the world. Inspired by the colors and patterns of the natural world, Sarah works intuitively with fabrics to create her artworks, which are often finished with detailed hand embroideries taken directly from her drawings. Find Sarah's work online at **guerilla-embroidery.co.uk**.

Love Gun

NATALIE DRAZ

Love and war never seem so close as when you're dancing your heart out in a crowded nightclub. People who use campy pick-up lines over and over on new prospects inspired Natalie Draz to consider the act of dating as a hunting technique. This is how she got the idea for love guns—textile weapons embroidered with pick-up lines often heard while out on the town. The love gun, when used properly, is not only an aide-mémoire, it's a conversation starter for you and your target!

Tools and Materials

FLOSS:

9 skeins of DMC Light Effects Precious Metals E168 (Silver)

FABRIC:

0.25 yd (22.86 cm) of medium-weight cotton

6-in (15.24-cm) embroidery hoop

thin darning needle with a small eye (which will stand up to the pulling and tugging that the tangle-happy metal embroidery will require)

embroidery needle, size of your choice

thin polyester sewing thread

polyester sewing thread that matches fabric

polyester fill

carbon or transfer paper

pencil

marker

scissors

straight pins

sewing machine (optional)

Last, but not least, a pick-up line! While you can use any of them, asking your friends about the worst lines they've ever heard will provide both great lines and hilarious stories!

Stitches:

running stitch

Other skills:

hand sewing skills

sewing machine operation (optional)

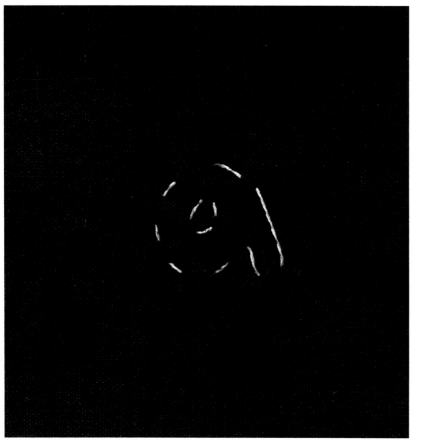

An example of how to outline the letters in running stitch

After choosing a pick-up line, use a thick felt pen to write it directly on the paper pattern pieces.

There are two methods that can be used to guide the stitches of your letters on the gun. The first is to directly transfer the letters with carbon paper or simply write them with a pencil or water-soluble pen. This method will leave some traces behind, especially on a light-colored cloth. The second method is to use a thin sewing thread in a contrasting color to baste the letters directly onto the cloth gun. After you are done with the embroidery work, you can remove the basting with a seam-ripper.

Stretch a square of fabric imprinted with the first gun transfer onto your embroidery hoop. Using embroidery thread, stitch around the gun outline in running stitch, covering the trace marks. If you choose to mark the phrase with basting thread rather than pencil or pen, stitch the outlines of the letters. Once the letters have been basted or transferred, use embroidery thread to outline the letters in running stitch.

Fill in the rest of the gun with embroidery thread in desired stitch pattern. Repeat this process on the second piece of fabric.

Once you've completed embroidering, cut out the guns from the fabric, leaving a 0.25-in (6.35-mm) seam allowance. Match up the two cloth guns, wrong-sides out. Pin the raw edges together. By hand or with a sewing machine, stitch around the seam allowance, following the embroidered edge. Leave a small 0.5-in (1.27-cm) opening on the gun's handle, which will allow you to turn the finished gun inside-out. Stuff with polyester fill and hand-sew together using matching thread.

Happy hunting!

Trigger Happy

For the outline of your gun, use the image provided (Fig. 7.10) or a gun image of your choosing. Use your computer or a photocopier to enlarge the outline to about 7 in (17.78 cm) long. Print out two gun outlines, making one in reverse so that you have two sides of the gun. Transfer the outlines onto two squares of fabric using the carbon paper transfer method (p. 110).

do you believe in love at first sight

or should I walk by again?

Figure 7.10. Love gun left and right templates. To make at the size of the example project, enlarge design 130 percent.

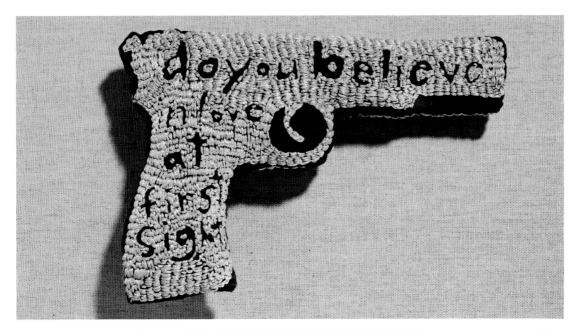

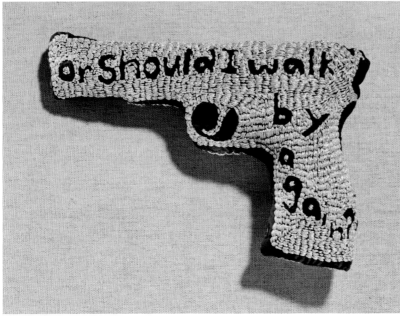

NATALIE DRAZ is a Toronto-based artist who works in a variety of disciplines including printmaking, textile art, and photography. She holds a degree in fine art and anthropology from the University of Toronto, but she tries to keep her pretentious scholarly voice in check. Subversive is her middle name, and she enjoys the irony of creating "women's work" that contrasts with controversial subject matter. Her pick-up lines are authentic and have been collected straight from those who have heard them or who used them. Part of proof Studio Gallery in Toronto, Natalie Draz encourages visitors to stop by and see where the love guns began. Find Natalie online at **nataliedraz. blogspot.com**.

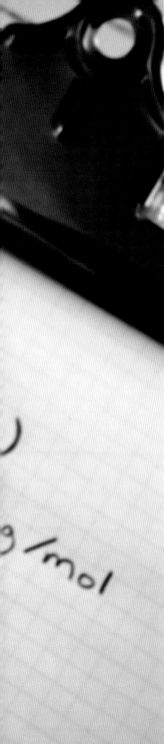

Oxytocin Notion

MALARIE BURGESS

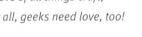

Molecules make up everyday life but are rarely seen in detail. This particular molecule is oxytocin, known as the hormone of love. Its stylized structure is intricate and complex—fitting for the chemistry of love—but the stitching will prove simple for a beginner. This project makes a great gift for geeky newlyweds or for the chemistry nerd in your life. It pulls together a love of all things craft, a love of all things science, and love itself, because, after all, geeks need love, too!

Tools and Materials

FLOSS:

■ 1 skein of DMC #310 (Black).

■ 1 skein of DMC #817 (Coral Red VK - DK)

FABRIC:

6 × 6-in (15.24 × 15.24-cm) square of cream colored felt (for the backing)

7 × 7-in (17.78 × 17.78-cm) square of natural colored, organic cotton-muslin

5-in (12.7-cm) embroidery hoop

embroidery needles, sizes 1 and 5

pencil

large fabric scissors

embroidery scissors

Stitches:

running stitch   backstitch

Make Your Molecule

Trace the molecule (from Fig. 7.11) directly onto the fabric using a pencil. Center the design on the fabric under a light source. Center fabric in the hoop and pull taut.

Lab Work

Using single strands of DMC #310, use a backstitch to trace the letters, working left to right. Once you reach the H on the bottom right, finish it by pulling the needle through to the back of the work. Flip the hoop over and weave the needle through the last three to five stitches to secure your work. Cut the thread.

Beginning with the top left part of the molecule, where the hexagon is, use a running stitch to follow the design pattern in DMC #817. If you are working with even-weave fabric, make your stitches two holes apart. If you are using a tighter weave, make your stitches shorter. Secure the thread below pre-existing stitches on the back of the work to finish.

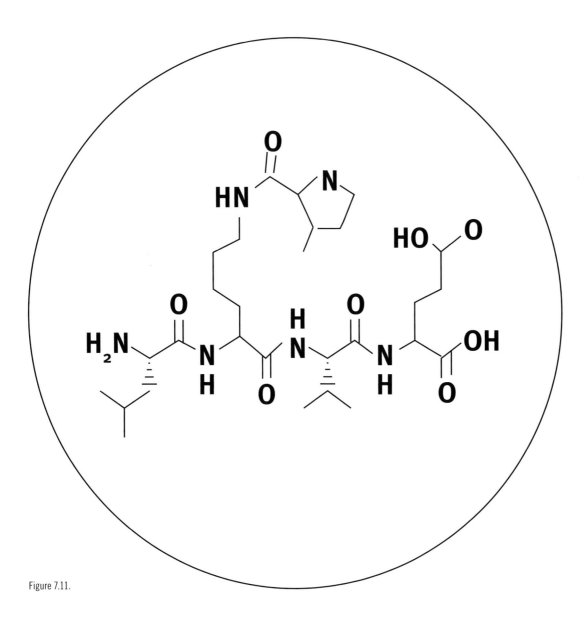

Figure 7.11.

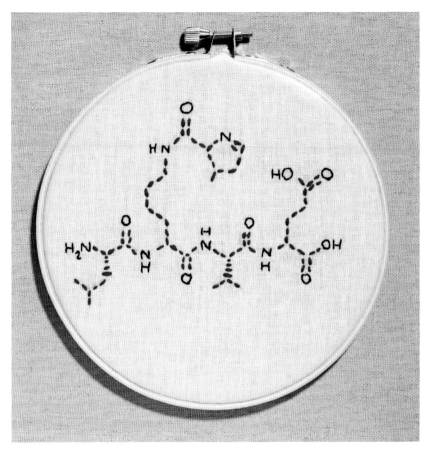

Born and raised in a small town in Maryland, **MALARIE BURGESS** lives in New York City with her awesome boyfriend and their beautiful cat. She has had a lifelong interest in the arts, and while her interests have shifted from music to theater to crafting, she enjoys all of it. Malarie started stitching with a sewing machine but found that hand-stitching was more enjoyable. She also creates mixed-media jewelry, using felt and vintage fabrics with metal pieces. She can be found online via her Etsy shop (**itsastitch.etsy.com**) and her blog (**itsastitch.tumblr.com**).

Finishing

Once you have completed the molecule, take a moment to lovingly admire your work. Then unscrew the hoop to remove the work.

Cut a 6 × 6-in (15.24 × 15.24-cm) piece of felt. Place this over the bottom hoop and lay your completed molecule on top. Push the top hoop over both pieces, making sure your molecule is placed where you want it. Once everything is in place, screw the hoop so that the pieces are snug. Trim off all extra fabric.

Your love molecule is now ready to hang or to give to the geek in your life!

Make Your Own Luck Wallet

SEWZINSKI (SARAH EDWARDS)

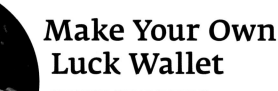

Have you ever spent a Saturday shopping at thrift stores, looking for hidden treasures like vintage fabric and embroidery floss? Some days you can't find anything but holiday sweaters and broken toys—but sometimes you luck out! Why not breathe new life into old leather goods and make something new and useful?

The Make Your Own Luck Wallet can hold the money and cards that you need to be prepared for your next thrifty hunt. No sewing machine is needed—only re-purposed goods, a little strength, and some simple embroidery skills to create a traveling lucky charm in which to stash your cash and find great things.

Tools and Materials

FLOSS:

- 1 skein of DMC #321 (Red)
- 1 skein of DMC #310 (Black)
- 1 skein of DMC #729 (Old Gold - MD)
- 1 skein of DMC #350 (Coral - MD)
- 1 skein of DMC #553 (Violet)
- 1 skein of DMC #333 (Blue Violet VY - DK)
- 1 skein of DMC #959 (Sea Green MD)
- 1 skein of DMC #3072 (Beaver Gray VY - LT)

MATERIAL:

13 × 5-in (33.02 × 12.7-cm) leather remnant. Use leather resourced from old skirts, jackets, purses, or upholstery scraps in a weight of 1.5 to 3.5 oz (43 to 99 g) leather, which should be thin and pliable enough to push a needle through. Leather goods often have a weight marked on them, so look for this when selecting a garment.

contrasting leather scraps (for button strap and appliqué designs)

13 × 5-in (33.02 × 12.7-cm) cotton fabric remnant

4-in (10.16-cm) embroidery hoop (a plastic hoop is recommended)

all-purpose leather needles (or any strong, sharp needles)

leather hole puncher, awl, or screw punch (for hole size ⅛ in/3 mm)

flexible stretchable fabric glue

Heat'n Bond Ultra Hold Iron-On Adhesive

Dritz heavy-duty metal snap

wax pencil or water-soluble ink pen

cardstock or cardboard to use for pattern

self-healing cutting mat (or hard surface you don't mind destroying, such as a stack of old magazines)

carbon transfer paper

scissors

ruler

iron

Stitches:

running stitch   backstitch

split stitch   straight stitch

NOTE: You can use any stitch you like. Mix it up and have fun with it!

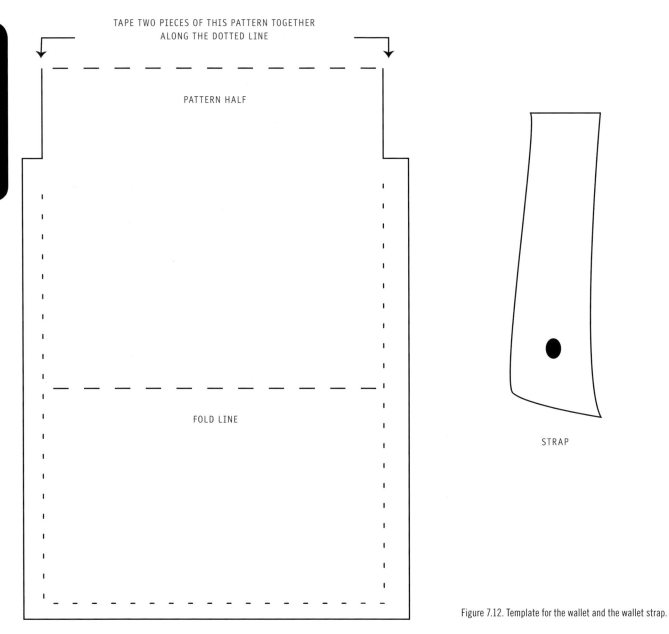

TAPE TWO PIECES OF THIS PATTERN TOGETHER
ALONG THE DOTTED LINE

PATTERN HALF

FOLD LINE

STRAP

Figure 7.12. Template for the wallet and the wallet strap.

Figure 7.13. Embroidery designs to decorate your wallet.

Crafty Construction

Trace each half of the wallet pattern (Fig. 7.12) onto a piece of card stock, so that you have two matching halves. Cut out the two pieces and tape the narrow ends together to make a complete wallet pattern. Trace the joined 12 × 4.25-in (30.48 × 10.8-cm) pattern onto the wrong side of the leather. (TIP: The wrong side feels like suede and looks unfinished.) Cut out the leather using the pattern.

Place the original paper pattern half over one piece of the leather with a sheet of carbon transfer paper in between. Using the guidelines on the pattern, mark where the holes should go on each end. You should now have a leather wallet pattern with twenty hole markings on each end, and a 2-in (5.08-cm) gap in the middle that has no hole markings. Place the leather onto the cutting surface, and punch out holes using the awl, screw punch, or leather punch.

A Lucky Charm

Fold each end of the wallet so that the first five holes on one side match up with the next five holes on the same end, and these ends are folded to make the structure of a billfold. Using a wax pencil line or water-soluble marker, mark the leather on the fold on each end of the wallet.

Fold the entire wallet in half over the center fold where the two pattern pieces were taped together. This mark will indicate where the center of the wallet will be. Make sure your embroidery stitches and appliqué stay inside the three fold lines (the flaps and the center fold) so that the embroidered imagery doesn't get cut off.

With the wallet flaps folded inside and the wallet folded in half, mark where the strap closure should be attached on the outside of the wallet. Using the holes on the sides as a guide, count three holes up from the folded edge, and mark the middle hole. This is where the closure will attach on the back exterior of the wallet. On the front of the folded wallet, make a mark in the middle, two holes

up from the fold. This will mark where the hole for the bottom of the snap closure will be placed.

Unfold the wallet and lay it flat, with the exterior facing up. Hand-sew the strap closure to the spot that you marked. Use backstitch and whip stitch to securely fasten it. Do not attach the snaps yet.

Make It Charming

With the leather wallet laying right-side up, place the carbon paper in between the embroidery design pattern (Fig 7.13) and the leather and trace the pattern, or draw your own design.

Place the plastic hoop around the design and pull the leather taut.

Begin to embroider by bringing the needle from the back of the leather and pushing it through to the front slowly. If you are not accustomed to embroidering on leather, it may take a while to get used to the angle and pressure needed; be patient and use caution. Don't turn your fingers into pincushions! The example project uses backstitch and straight stitch for the decorative elements of diamonds, starts, lightning bolts, and lucky horseshoes.

You can also embroider leather scraps and appliqué them onto the leather wallet with a running stitch to create more color and texture. Seed stitch and back stitch on top of the appliqué add further decorative elements.

Once you've finished embroidering the image, double knot the thread on the wrong side of the leather and trim any excess thread. The back of the project doesn't have to look tidy as it will be covered with the fabric lining; the surface should not be lumpy.

Line Your Pockets

Read the manufacturer's instructions on how to use the Heat'n Bond Ultra Hold Iron-On Adhesive. Trace the cardboard pattern onto the adhesive. Cut out the adhesive

shape and iron it onto the wrong side of the fabric using a dry heat setting. When it cools, cut out the adhesive-coated fabric piece and lay it over the inside of your wallet, with the right side of the fabric facing you.

Draw a stitch guideline around the fabric near the holes on the inside of the wallet, but don't cover them. The fabric should cover the messy inner side of the embroidery work, but not the holes for lacing the wallet together. Trim any excess fabric.

Remove the adhesive backing paper and, with the right side of the fabric facing outward, iron the fabric onto the interior of your wallet. Let it cool.

Stitch This Bad Boy Up!

The wallet should be sewn together inside-out (with the fabric lining on the outside), then turned right-side out.

Choose a color of embroidery floss that contrasts well with the color of the leather. Cut a 42-in (106.68-cm) length of floss. Thread the needle. Match up the five holes on each flap of the wallet and, starting at the bottom corner of one side, run the needle through each of the two lined-up holes three times before advancing up to the next set of holes. Repeat until you reach the top of the five-hole row.

Pull the floss through the top row of holes then stitch downward, going through each hole three more times before moving down to the next one. When you reach the bottom corner, knot the floss and tie it off. Trim off any excess floss hanging from the knot and secure with a spot of glue.

Repeat this process on the other three edges of the two wallet flaps. Once finished, you should have two pockets. Let the glue dry on your thread.

Make It Snappy

Turn the pockets right side out. Fold the wallet in half and double-check that the strap ends of the wallet are marked.

Insert a self-healing cutting mat or magazine corner inside the pocket and punch a hole for the snap closure. Then lay the cutting mat under the strap piece and punch a hole for the top piece of the snap closure. Attach the two snap pieces in the holes according to the manufacturer's directions.

Clean any residual marks left behind from the wax pencil or water-soluble marker by gently rubbing the marks with a cotton swab moistened with isopropyl alcohol.

You now possess a luck-making wallet—so go thrifting!

SARAH EDWARDS is an ex-furniture designer turned full-time indie crafter who picked up from her Iowa roots and transplanted herself to sunny Florida. Always designing, creating, and crafting, Sarah started her own business, sewZinski, in 2007. Inspired by her mother's love of sewing and needlework, Sarah decided to take a different approach to the craft of embroidery, applying it to re-purposed leather and fabric. Her embroidery expresses her love of pop culture, Asian and South American folk art, and nature. She loves collaborating with clients and engaging with other artists to bring her craft to a more personal level. Find Sarah online via her website (**sewZinski.com**), Flickr page (**flickr.com/photos/zinski**), and blog (**sewZinski.blogspot.com**).

Ransom-Note Pillow

ELLEN SCHINDERMAN

Ellen's Ransom-Note Pillow was inspired by the Nursery Crime novels of Jasper Fforde, whose novel The Big Over Easy involves a good egg in a hard-boiled town. Ellen wanted to embroider Humpty-Dumpty's ransom note: "Pay us or the egg gets it." Adjusting the ransom note project for this book, Ellen came up with a pattern involving individually embroidered letters. The biggest challenge in developing this project was finding a message that wasn't too dark or threatening—who wants a pillow that threatens someone you love?

Tools and Materials

FLOSS:

- 2 skeins of DMC #310 (Black)
- 2 skeins of DMC White
- 1 skein of DMC #646 (Beaver Gray - DK)
- 1 skein of DMC #307 (Lemon)
- 1 skein of DMC 666 (Red - Bright)

FABRIC:

- 1.5 yd (1.37 m) white cotton
- 0.5 yd (45.72 cm) gray cotton
- 0.3 yd (.330 cm) blue cotton
- 0.25 yd (22.86 cm) yellow cotton
- 1 yd (0.91 m) light-weight black corduroy
- 2 yd (1.82 m) black piping
- 18 × 18-in (45.72 × 45.72-cm) square pillow form
- 8 × 8-in (20.32 × 20.32-cm) Q-Snaps or an 8-in hoop
- iron-on transfer pen (Sulky brand recommended)

- sewing thread to match cottons
- straight pins
- cutting board
- scissors or rotary cutter
- tracing paper
- iron
- old pillowcase to cover a hard surface to iron on (not an ironing board); use one that you don't care about as the transfer ink may bleed through
- sewing machine
- sewing machine zipper foot for the piping

Stitches:

backstitch

satin stitch

Other skills:

appliqué

piping

basic sewing machine operation

Transfer Your Threat

Transfer the ransom note in this book (Fig 7.14) using the transfer pen method (p. 110), or make your own message—but make sure the letters are reversed (try reading them in a mirror, to be sure), so that they read properly once transferred.

Photocopy your ransom note and enlarge to fit the pillow. Make an iron-on transfer with the transfer pen and tracing paper. Trace the outlines of the letters. Cut the iron-on letters into pieces so that the letters in a word are not all transferred onto the same color of fabric.

On a hard surface (but not an ironing board as a soft surface will not allow for a firm transfer) covered with a clean pillowcase, use a hot, dry iron to transfer the letters onto pieces of the white, gray, blue, and yellow cotton. When transferring letters, space each one about 2.5 in (6.35 cm) apart on the fabric. Distribute the letters for variety so that they look as though they come from separate sources—this will give them a genuine "ransom-note" feel.

Hoop-up!

Stitch each piece of fabric that you have transferred the letters to by backstitching the outline of each letter and then satin stitching to fill. Vary floss colors as you go—this will also make them appear as though they were cut from different sources—but use predominantly black and white floss to emulate most printed material.

Cut the stitched letters apart from one another so that each is framed within a small rectangle of cloth. Leave at least a ⅛ to 0.5-in (3 mm to 1.27-cm) border of cloth around each letter. Using your sewing machine, zigzag the edge of each rectangle to prevent fraying.

Sew Your Pillow

Make the front and back of the pillow by cutting one piece of white cotton 18 × 18 in (45.72 × 45.72 cm) and one piece of black corduroy the same size. Machine stitch the edges of both pieces with a zigzag stitch.

For the front of the pillow, iron the white cotton and lay out the letters of your ransom note; don't worry if the letters overlap or if it looks crowded. Fold 0.5-in (1.27-cm) hems around the edge of each letter and steam press. You can use an ironing board for this part. Don't worry about straight squares—kidnappers don't! Pin the letters to the front of the

pillow one by one. Press each letter's edges, pin in place, press the next letter's edges, pin in place, and so on.

With a sewing machine or by hand, appliqué the letters to the front of the pillow using thread that matches the color of the fabric. Sew the letters systematically by fabric color so that you only have to change thread once for each color and not for each letter.

Pin the piping to the front of the pillow, then sew it in place using your sewing machine with a zipper foot.

With right sides together and wrong sides facing out, pin front (white cotton with letters) and back (black corduroy) of pillow together. Sew these pieces together by machine stitching around all four edges, leaving a 6-in (15.24-cm) opening on the bottom. Clip the corners carefully so you don't snip your stitching, and then press the seams open.

Flip the pillow inside out and insert the pillow form. Blind stitch the pillow closed. Clip loose threads and use a lint remover to remove excess thread or fuzz from the finished project.

Place your new pillow someplace threatening!

ELLEN SCHINDERMAN lives, works, and eats locally in Los Angeles. She uses fiber art as a way of seeing things anew through thread. The child of an antiques dealer, she has always been surrounded by the decorative and home arts, and it makes sense to her to combine artistic statements with beauty and tradition. As an artist and feminist, the reclaiming of needle and thread fascinates Ellen. Subverting the popular perception of what needlework is by stitching something transgressive tickles her to no end. Seeing unusual images or words on items of comfort and domesticity make people think twice about objects that they've taken for granted, and ask, "Do I really want to sleep with my head on a ransom note?" Ellen's blog, examples of her work, and her Etsy info can be found at **schindermania.com**.

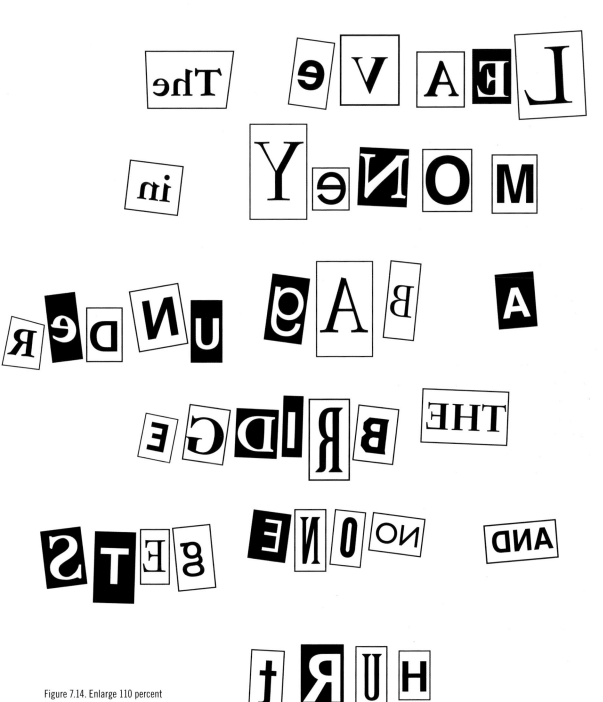

Figure 7.14. Enlarge 110 percent to fit example project size.

Hoopla: The Art of Unexpected Embroidery

Bosom Buddies

ALLISON TUNIS

These perky doilies were inspired by Allison Tunis's interest in feminist art, needlepoint, and humor. During her final year of university, her artwork came to be based on juxtaposing traditional needlepoint (a.k.a. "women's work") with stereotypical imagery that objectified women, thus bringing together the age-old archetypes of woman-as-housewife and woman-as-whore. These doilies came about from the desire to create something eye-pleasing and easy to understand while still making an intellectual statement. The doilies employ some rigorous color work—with thirty-five differently colored skeins—but they don't take a lot of time to make. They're fun and sassy, and they get their point across.

Tools and Materials

FLOSS:

1 skein of DMC White
1 skein of DMC #169 (Pigeon Gray)
1 skein of DMC #223 (Shell Pink - Med)
1 skein of DMC #225 (Shell Pink VY - LT)
1 skein of DMC #315 (Antique Mauve - DK)
1 skein of DMC #316 (Antique Mauve - Med)
1 skein of DMC #317 (Pewter Gray)
1 skein of DMC #318 (Steel Grey - LT)
1 skein of DMC #356 (Terracotta - Med)
1 skein of DMC #413 (Pewter Gray - DK)
1 skein of DMC #415 (Pearl Grey)
1 skein of DMC #451 (Shell Gray - DK)
1 skein of DMC #452 (Shell Gray Med)
1 skein of DMC #453 (Shell Gray - LT)
1 skein of DMC #535 (Gray VY - DK)
1 skein of DMC #640 (Beige Grey VY - DK)
1 skein of DMC #646 (Beaver Gray - DK)

1 skein of DMC #647 (Beaver Grey - Med)
1 skein of DMC #648 (Beaver Gray - LT)
1 skein of DMC #762 (Pearl Grey VY - LT)
1 skein of DMC #778 (Antique Mauve VY - LT)
1 skein of DMC #819 (Baby Pink Ultra VY - LT)
1 skein of DMC #822 (Brown Gray - LT)
1 skein of DMC #839 (Beige Brown - DK)
1 skein of DMC #840 (Beige Brown Med)
1 skein of DMC #841 (Beige Brown - LT)
1 skein of DMC #842 (Beige Brown VY - LT)
1 skein of DMC #844 (Beaver Gray Ultra - DK)
1 skein of DMC #3024 (Brown Gray VY - LT)
1 skein of DMC #3032 (Mocha Brown Med - DK)
1 skein of DMC #3033 (Mocha Brown - LT)
1 skein of DMC #3041 (Antique Violet - Med)
1 skein of DMC #3072 (Beaver Gray VY - LT)
1 skein of DMC #3726 (Antique Mauve MD - DK)

1 skein of DMC #3727 (Antique Mauve - LT)
1 skein of DMC #3740 (Antique Violet - DK)
1 skein of DMC #3743 (Antique Violet VY - LT)
1 skein of DMC #3772 (Flesh VY - DK)
1 skein of DMC #3781 (Mocha Brown - DK)
1 skein of DMC #3782 (Mocha Med Brown)
1 skein of DMC #3787 (Brown Gray)
1 skein of DMC #3790 (Beige Gray Ultra VY)
1 skein of DMC #3802 (Antique Mauve VY - DK)
1 skein of DMC #3858 (Rosewood - MD)
1 skein of DMC #3859 (Rosewood - LT)
1 skein of DMC #3860 (Cocoa Brown - MD)
1 skein of DMC #3861 (Cocoa Brown - LT)
1 skein of DMC #3862 (Mocha Beige - DK)
1 skein of DMC #3863 (Mocha Beige - MD)
1 skein of DMC #3864 (Mocha Beige - LT)

Tools and Materials continued on page 284

FABRIC:

2 round white doilies of the same diameter (easily found at thrift stores). The example project uses 5-in (12.7-cm) diameter doilies.

5 × 10-in (12.7 × 25.4-cm) 18-count white Aida cloth

4-in (10.16-cm) embroidery hoop

tapestry needle, size of your choice

masking tape

needlepoint scissors

sewing machine

sewing machine thread (or needle and thread)

scissors

Stitches:

basic counted cross-stitch

basic running stitch (hand or sewing machine)

PROJECT NOTES: These directions are for two finished doilies, each an appliqué of the cross-stitched design. The two doilies differ slightly; they make a pair but, as in real life, the breasts are not identical. The area stitched will measure approximately 2 in (5.08 cm) in diameter, and the doily itself will be approximately 6 in (15.24 cm) in diameter.

Preparation

Cut the Aida fabric into two 5 × 5-in (12.7 × 12.7-cm) squares. Edge each piece of fabric with masking tape to prevent fraying. Fold each square into quarters and mark the center point with a contrasting thread or pencil mark.

TIP: Separate your floss and use two strands of each color to stitch with.

Pierce the Nipples

Mark the center of the first pattern, and following the thread legend and accompanying diagrams (Fig. 7.15 and 7.16), start stitching from the center outward using a basic counted cross-stitch. Continue the stitching pattern until it is complete. Repeat this for the second pattern. Once the stitching is complete, trim fabric in circular shapes that will easily fit within the center of the doilies, leaving a 0.5-in (1.27-cm) fabric allowance around the stitched edges.

Sassy Sewing

Hem the edges by hand or machine stitch them with a basic running stitch. Trim any excess threads.

Sew the design into center of vintage doily using white thread on sewing machine or hand stitching. Straight stitch as close to hemmed edge as possible, following curve of your design. Trim any loose threads.

You now have two new breast friends!

ALLISON TUNIS holds a Bachelor of Fine Arts from the University of Alberta. During her studies, she focused on feminist and conceptual needlepoint, dealing mainly with self-image and body issues and the contrast between "women's work" and women's imagery. She strives to bring needlepoint into the new millennium, as well as into the arena of "Art" (with a capital A). Allison hopes to someday open her own needlepoint store and gallery in her hometown of Edmonton, Alberta. You can find Allison's work and patterns on Etsy at: **etsy.com/shop/capturedpassions**.

(FACING PAGE) LEFT TO RIGHT
Figure 7.15 and Figure 7.16

BOSOM BUDDIES

LEGEND:

- ● DMC #169 (Pigeon Gray)
- ○ DMC #315 (Antique Mauve - DK)
- ⊘ DMC #3072 (Beaver Gray VY - LT)
- ◖ DMC #3727 (Antique Mauve LT)
- ◀ DMC #3860 (Cocoa Brown - MD)
- ☾ DMC #3726 (Antique Mauve MD - DK)
- □ DMC #225 (Shell Pink VY - LT)
- ◪ DMC #762 (Pearl Grey VY - LT)
- ◆ DMC #839 (Beige Brown - DK)
- ◇ DMC #3858 (Rosewood - MD)
- ✚ DMC #778 (Antique Mauve VY - LT)
- ⬡ DMC #223 (Shell Pink Med)
- ✛ DMC #647 (Beaver Grey Med)

- ✖ DMC #317 (Pewter Gray)
- ▲ DMC #640 (Beige Grey VY - DK)
- ★ DMC #3863 (Mocha Beige - MD)
- ✴ DMC #3740 (Antique Violet- DK)
- ▲ DMC #316 (Antique Mauve Med)
- ▽ DMC #318 (Steel Grey - LT)
- ◣ DMC #3024 (Brown Gray VY - LT)
- ↓ DMC #415 (Pearl Grey)
- ← DMC #3032 (Mocha Brown Med - DK)
- ← DMC #648 (Beaver Gray - LT)
- ↗ DMC #535 (Gray VY - DK)
- ⅄ DMC #3861 (Cocoa Brown LT)
- ➤ DMC #844 (Beaver Gray Ultra - DK)

- ∧ DMC #3787 (Brown Gray)
- ⋎ DMC #356 (Terracotta Med)
- ◀ DMC #413 (Pewter Gray - DK)
- ► DMC #3864 (Mocha Beige LT)
- 2 DMC #451 (Shell Gray DK)
- 3 DMC #452 (Shell Gray Med)
- A DMC #842 (Beige Brown VY - LT)
- Z DMC #3041 (Antique Violet Med)
- ĸ DMC #3790 (Beige Gray Ultra VY)
- 8 DMC #3802 (Antique Mauve VY - DK)
- b DMC #3781 (Mocha Brown DK)
- r DMC #840 (Beige Brown Med)
- Σ DMC #3743 (Antique Violet VY - LT)

- ✔ DMC #841 (Beige Brown LT)
- ⸫ DMC #453 (Shell Gray LT)
- ◄◄ DMC #646 (Beaver Gray DK)
- ↰ DMC #3859 (Rosewood LT)
- ⊃ DMC #822 (Brown Gray LT)
- ⋈ DMC #3862 (Mocha Beige DK)
- 🔔 DMC #3772 (Flesh VY - DK)
- ↖ DMC #3782 (Mocha Med Brown)
- ⊟ DMC White
- ⊥ DMC #3033 (Mocha Brown LT)
- ⊏ DMC #819 (Baby Pink Ultra VY - LT)

Chug like a Champ

MARIE HORSTEAD

The 1950s illustration style on this pillow is misleading. A whimsical take on the traditional Victorian parlor pillow that often featured demure profiles of well-behaved young ladies, this one shows a woman guzzling down a beer like the guys do—"shotgun style." Pattern designer Marie Horstead was inspired by a warm summer night in Montreal with some girlfriends when, she says, "We had a case of cheap beers and ended up shotgunning them in the backyard. I took a photo of my girlfriends finishing off some PBR [Pabst Blue Ribbon]. This embroidery makes me laugh."

Tools and Materials

FLOSS:

- 3 skeins of DMC #310 (Black)
- 3 skeins of a floss that matches the fabric used to create the T-shirt appliqué
- 3 skeins of DMC #608 (Bright Orange), or another color of your choice, to create the hair
- 1 skein of DMC Light Effects Precious Metals E168 (Silver)
- blue, brown, or green floss to color the eye
- spool of red floss or sewing thread for the mouth and beer label

FABRIC:

- 8 × 8-in (20.32 × 20.32-cm) square piece of fabric to create the shirt. Recycled fabrics are encouraged.
- 1 yd (0.91 m) of white cotton, cut into two 11-in/27.94-cm) diameter circles. (Stitch your embroidery onto one of these circles)
- 33 × 3.5-in (83.82 × 8.89-cm) strip of patterned cotton (to create the mid-section of the pillow)

10-in (25.4-cm) hoop

embroidery needles, assorted sizes 5–10

white all-purpose sewing machine thread

basting thread in a contrasting color

Baby Lock Tear-Away Interfacing

fiberfill

carbon transfer paper

iron

sewing scissors

straight pins

pinking shears (optional)

hand-sewing needle and thread

sewing machine

scissors

Stitches:

seed stitch   running stitch   chain stitch

Skills required:

basic sewing machine skills

Figure 7.17. Enlarge by 140 percent before transferring.

Get Ready to Party

First trace the T-shirt shape onto tear-away interfacing and then transfer the full design (Fig. 7.17) onto the right side of one of the cotton circles using the carbon paper transfer method (p. 110). Lay interfacing on top of the circle of fabric; place the fabric square (that will be the T-shirt) underneath. Secure all three layers of material within the embroidery hoop.

Stitch Her Senseless

Stitch the shape of the body with a running stitch using DMC #310. Using floss that matches the fabric color of the T-shirt, trace the shape of the shirt with a backstitch, making sure that you stitch the top and second layers of fabric together. Carefully trim away the top layer to reveal the colored shirt fabric underneath. Trim close to the embroidery, but do not cut your stitches. The raw edges of the white cotton will fray slightly, which is the desired effect.

Fill in the hair with a chain stitch in the shape of the "bob" hairstyle. Use the metallic thread to color in the beer can with a running stitch. Red sewing thread or floss can be satin stitched to fill in the label of the beer can and the lips of the woman. Use a single stitch of blue, brown, or green thread to color her eyes. Gently tear the interfacing away from the embroidery.

Construct the Pillow

Fold the right sides of the patterned cotton piece in half lengthwise so that the piece measures 16.5 × 3.5-in (41.91 × 8.89-cm). Stitch the raw edges together to form a loop for the gusset of the pillow. Iron the seams so that the stitching lies flat.

With right sides together, pin the raw edges of the embroidered circle onto the cotton that will form the pillow gusset and hand-baste together. Leaving a 0.25-in (6.35-mm) seam allowance, machine or hand sew the raw edges together. Remove basting and iron the seams. With sharp scissors, clip around the curves to create some ease in the pillow. Repeat the pinning, basting, ironing, and clipping step for the back of the pillow, but leave a 4-in (10.16-cm) gap in the second seam. Once you've ironed and clipped all the seams, turn your masterpiece right side out. Stuff the pillow with fiberfill, then hand-sew the gap closed.

Your pillow is now complete. Toss it on the couch and invite your friends over for a few brews.

MARIE HORSTEAD got her start stitching at Capilano University in North Vancouver, British Columbia, and later took her off-the-cuff drawings to Concordia University in Montreal. She is inspired by the West Coast, her neighborhood cats, and summers on the beach. She now resides in East Vancouver where she enjoys blanketing, weaving, embroidering, and drinking beer.

Modern Cuckoo Clock

JOANNE ARNETT

Joanne Arnett loved the idea of cuckoo clocks but disliked their quaint and fussy appearance, so she distilled their elements to create an updated timepiece. To keep the black-and-white stitching fun, she cross-stitched the design. The flowers became more interesting, the fawn more cute, and the cuckoo more cheerful. This clock is more than a timepiece; it is the perfect mix of old and new, function and entertainment, kitsch and sophistication—which justifies the time spent making all of those tiny stitches!

Tools and Materials

FLOSS:

■ 5 skeins of DMC #310 (Black)

FABRIC:

15 × 18-in (38.1 × 45.72-cm) piece of white, 14-count Aida cloth

tapestry needle, size 24

quartz clock movement for 0.25-in (6.35-mm) thick clock face

small square of beeswax, found at most craft and natural food stores

sewing scissors

awl

illustration board, 11 × 17 in (27.94 × 43.18 cm) or larger

foam core board, 11 × 17 in (27.94 × 43.18 cm) or larger

electrical tape or Gorilla Tape

utility knife

pencil

highlighter

straight pins

self-healing board or surface for cutting

Stitches:

counted cross-stitch

stitches that you made! It's important to be able to see the pattern even after you've stitched a row in case you do need to go back and re-stitch. The highlighter's transparency will allow you to see the completed rows on your pattern diagram and let you backtrack if you make a mistake. Take your time, and continually refer to the pattern. Think, count twice, stitch once.

TIP: You may find that an embroidery hoop isn't necessary for cross-stitching on Aida cloth. The heavy cloth may be firm enough to maintain its shape without shifting. Also, waxed floss stays secure and retains its tension when stitched. As you work, roll the stitched fabric over itself and pin each side with a tapestry needle to keep the completed area out of the way. Clean, unpin, and roll as needed.

Divide floss into single strands. Pull individual strands of floss across the beeswax so that your thread creates a small groove in the surface of the hard wax. Next, pull each waxed thread between a folded paper towel or waste cloth placed under a hot iron. (Make sure your iron remains clean! If there is a lot of wax on your thread, you may need to use extra blotting materials.)

Stitch the Clock

Fold the Aida cloth in half and make the first stitch about 1.5 in (3.81 cm) from the top of the cloth. Begin stitching at the center top. Stitch half a cross in one direction all the way across a row, then stitch in the opposite direction across the row to complete each ×. Complete one row at a time, counting each stitch as you go.

When you have stitched the center of the clock face (the red cross on the pattern), tie a single strand of floss through the fabric to mark this point so you won't have to count spaces to find the center when it's time to mount the clockworks. Tie the thread in a bow, not a knot, so that it will be easy to remove later on.

PROJECT NOTES: This clock isn't difficult to make. If you can stitch an × on a piece of fabric, you can make it. Just remember that neatness counts, so take your time. To ensure that the stitched fabric can be mounted smoothly, the stitching needs to be as uniform as possible, so don't knot the floss!

Leave the ends of your floss loose when stitching. This will make it easy to remove floss from the needle and to easily remove stitches if you need to. To secure the floss when it runs out, pull the floss through a few stitches on the underside of the fabric.

When completing a row, mark it off your pattern with a highlighter. It's important to keep track of what's been stitched so you don't accidentally stitch crosses from a nearby row. If you make a mistake, you may not notice it for a few rows, and then you'll have to remove all of the

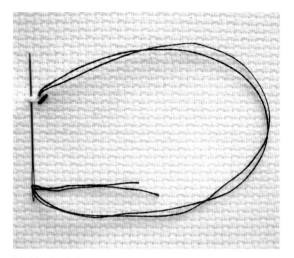

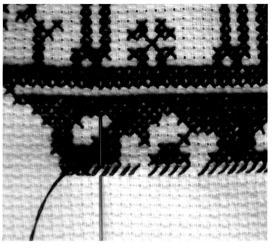

Stitching the clock.

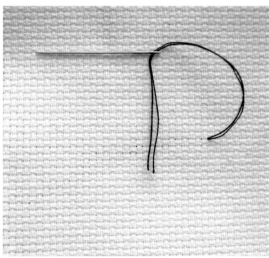

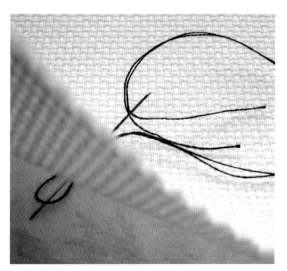

Threading your needle: to anchor thread without using a knot, double a single thread to obtain two strands of floss with a loop at one end. Thread the needle up from beneath the fabric for the first stitch. Pull the needle down through to complete the stitch, catching the loop when pulling the floss through the backside of the fabric.

Figure 7.18.

Once the final stitch is secure, unroll the fabric and press it flat with a layer of paper towel or cloth between the stitched clock face and the iron to absorb any remaining beeswax.

The Inner Workings

Push the awl through the marked center point of the clock face to make a small hole. Untie and remove the thread that marks the center point. Gently enlarge the hole with the awl until it is the correct diameter for the clockworks.

Mark a line on the Aida cloth with a pencil 1.5 in (3.81 cm) around the stitched design. Cut the fabric on this guideline.

Trace the outline of the clock pattern onto the illustration board and the foam core. Cut out the clock shape using a utility knife on a self-healing cutting surface.

Align the stitched fabric on the cut-out piece of illustration board. Secure the two pieces with a few small pieces of tape. Mark the hole for the clock hands with a pencil.

Remove the fabric from the illustration board. Using the awl, make an opening for the clock hands by gently pushing it through the illustration board. Test the diameter using the clockworks.

Place the illustration board on the foam core. Push the awl through the center hole to make opening for the clockworks in the foam core. If you need to make the hole larger than the width of the awl, gently use a pencil to continue widening the hole to the correct diameter.

Place illustration board securely on top of the foam core board, then wrap the embroidered fabric around both pieces. Hold the fabric in place with small strips of tape until correctly positioned, then secure it with larger pieces. On the bottom edge, carefully make the cuts required to free the fabric for wrapping but do not cut any closer than ⅛ in (3 mm) from the stitching.

JOANNE ARNETT started stitching five years ago to mend a broken heart. Her heart is now much better, and her embroidery keeps getting better and better too. When not working on crafty projects that involve cutting things into tiny pieces and adding glitter, she spends her time studying textiles and sewing garments. Her project researching and constructing corsets can be found at her blog bridgesonthebody.blogspot.com. Joanne lives on the banks of the Cuyahoga River in Ohio surrounded by fabric and books, and she anxiously awaits the return of fireflies each summer.

When the clock is wrapped, screw the clockworks through the hole in the foam core and assemble the hands according to the manufacturer's instructions. Place a battery in the clock, hang it on the wall, and enjoy checking to see what time it is.

Cuckoo!

Obsessive Beautification

AMANDA BOWLES

Mirror, mirror on the wall, who is the fairest of them all? Amanda Bowles describes her stitched illustration as follows:

"This project is Hollywood: It's the diet commercials you see every five minutes on television. It's the teenage girl living next door with an eating disorder. It's the mother of five who had surgery three times to try and rid herself of 'baby weight.' This project showcases the low self-esteem that seems to be ingrained into people from a young age. The idea of what makes a person desirable to others revolves around being young, slim, having perfect skin and hair, and perfect makeup. A person may go to great lengths to achieve these things, which, in the end, leave them nothing more than a shell. A soul is left forgotten—the true beauty that is not allowed to grow and shine. What happens when that shell starts to deteriorate?"

Stitch this project and ruminate on what true beauty means to you.

Tools and Materials

FLOSS:

- 1 skein of DMC #642 (Beige Gray - DK)
- 2 skeins of DMC #310 (Black)
- 1 skein of White
- 1 skein of DMC #744 (Yellow-Pale)
- 1 skein of DMC #743 (Yellow MD)
- 1 skein of DMC #740 (Tangerine)
- 1 skein of DMC #606 (Bright Orange-Red)
- 1 skein of DMC #776 (Pink - MD)
- 1 skein of DMC #712 (Cream)
- 1 skein of DMC #3782 (Mocha Brown - LT)
- 1 skein of DMC #3862 (Mocha Brown VY - DK)
- 1 skein of DMC #3325 (Baby Blue - LT)
- 1 skein of DMC #797 (Royal Blue)
- 1 skein of DMC #912 (Emerald Green - LT)

FABRIC:

The project example uses a "nude"-colored chemise made of thin cotton that was purchased second-hand.

embroidery needles, sizes 1–10

10-in (25.4-cm) embroidery hoop

scissors

Stitches:

backstitch   split stitch   brick stitch
satin stitch   French knots

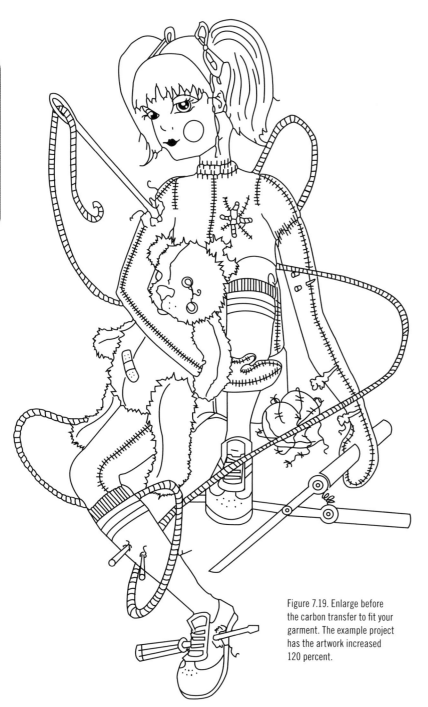

Figure 7.19. Enlarge before the carbon transfer to fit your garment. The example project has the artwork increased 120 percent.

Give Your Materials a Face-lift

Transfer Fig. 7.19 onto your prepared fabric surface using the carbon pencil transfer method (p. 110). Once the pattern has been traced, place the fabric into your embroidery hoop and pull fabric taut.

Fill in the Details

TIP: Complete the fill work before stitching the outlines of the patterns.

To achieve the "worn teddy" look, use DMC #3782 to create a rough brick stitch around the teddy bear's nose, ears, and arm. Use DMC #3010 in brick stitch to fill in the body. Make each section's stitched "fur" run a different way to add to the worn look. The lines denoting the bear's dotted seams can be backstitched in an upward motion using DMC #310. Outline the nose in satin stitches. Finish the teddy by making French knots in black for his eyes.

Outline the Band-Aid in a backstitch and fill with a satin stitch in DMC #776.

To stitch the hair of the doll, outline the image in backstitch. Use DMC #606 in a satin stitch to fill the bows. Make a French knot for the center of the bow. Use DMC #744 and DMC #740 to texture the hair in brick stitch. Fill remaining spaces with DMC #743 in brick stitch.

Use DMC #744 to satin stitch the large background "thread" that weaves around the doll's body. Use DMC #310 to couch the satin stitch diagonally.

Use DMC #606 to split stitch the heart, then stitch the seam of the heart with the same type of backstitch used to create the bear's seams, using DMC #310. Finish the heart with a backstitch outline and outline the thread surrounding it.

Each of the doll's socks has two blue stripes running across the top. To create the socks, begin stitching with white floss in a brick stitch near the ankle of each foot. Fill up to the first blue line. The center stripe and the top of

AMANDA BOWLES currently lives in Toronto's downtown core after many years of traveling far and wide, filing away all sorts of creative knowledge. She dropped out of high school at age fifteen, choosing to gallivant all over the country before fashion school called her name. At school, she realized that she hated the mindset of the fashion industry and chose to do humanitarian work instead. Finally, she returned to her crafty roots and started a clothing line focused on hats and accessories. For a few years, she has lived an interesting life as a designer and teacher of sex-ed, and manager of a large adult boutique, as well as continuing her never-ending crafty endeavors with comic books, zines, design projects, painting, vegan restraint kits, and all kinds of other interesting projects.

the socks will be satin stitched in white with a vertical satin stitch. Vertically satin stitch the remaining two stripes with DMC #797.

Using DMC #3325, fill the sides of the shoes with split stitch. The tongue of each shoe is a combination of both blues, stitched horizontally to create the appearance of laces. Use DMC #797 to fill the front of the shoe with a brick stitch. Outline the shoes and socks in DMC #310 with backstitch. The soles of the shoes are created with a few layers of backstitching. Create patterning on the tops of the socks with a widely spaced satin stitch.

Brick stitch DMC #797 to fill the doll's shorts with color.

Use DMC #642 for all the "pins and needles." Satin stitch the hedge-clipper blades, the screwdriver end, all the pins in the doll's leg, and the giant needle in her arm. Use DMC #912 to satin stitch the handles of the screwdriver and hedge clippers. Use French knots to create the bolts in the hedge clippers.

When the fill is complete, use DMC #310 to backstitch the outline of the face, body, bear, and the handles of the tools. Do not outline the thread surrounding the doll or any of the pins and needles.

To finish the doll's face, fill in the eye shadow and blush in the cheeks with DMC #776. Use a split stitch for the cheeks and a satin stitch for the eye shadow. Finally, finish the project by creating the "stuffing" coming out of the doll's body by making French knots in DMC #712.

Keep in mind that there is no such thing as "perfect" or "exactly the same" when creating a handicraft. As the subject matter of this piece suggests, imperfections make it your own!

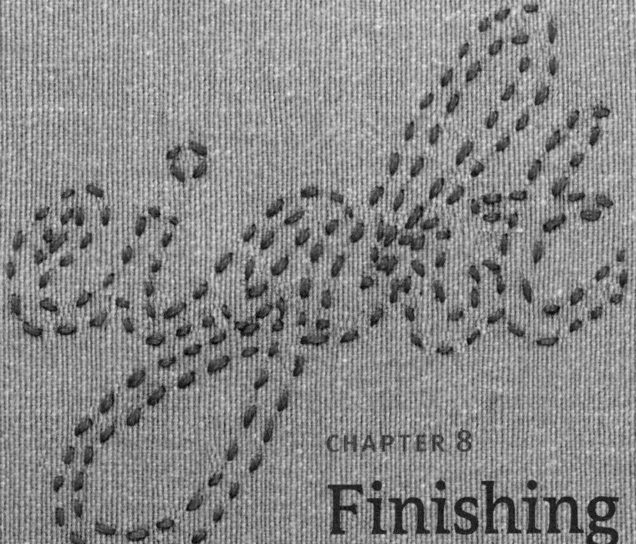

eight

CHAPTER 8

Finishing Techniques

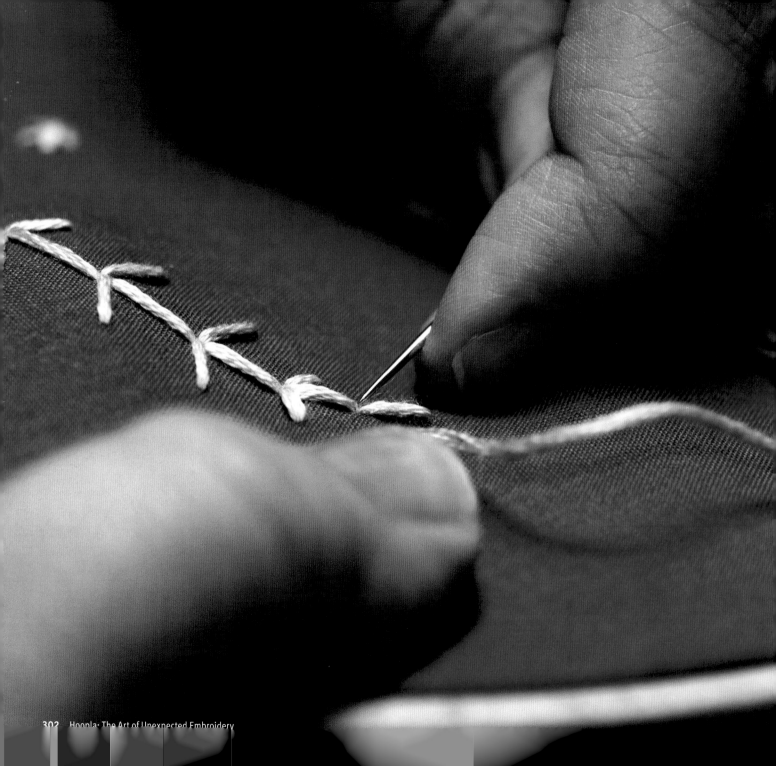

Once you've stitched your heart out, take some time to consider how to appropriately finish your embroidery. While cleaning, ironing, trimming, and framing may seem tedious, these techniques will make your work look polished and provide it with longevity. When you consider the level of care you took to pull each thread through your design, you'll want to make the time to display it properly.

Your Plan of Attack

Consider how your piece may need to be cleaned or pressed, and at what stage of the project these steps should occur. For most stitch-work designers, these steps occur at the very end of a project when the last stitch has been applied. For other works, this may be before special materials are added that may not take well to heat or water, such as feathers or sequins. Think about what sort of materials you are using and how they will react to cleaning. There are no firm rules, but knowing what will enhance your work is a big step in growing as an embroidery artist.

Of course, if you prefer your embroidery to be rough around the edges, leave it that way!

Sequins and beads should never make contact with an iron, as they could lose their color or melt under the heat. Feathers, fine netting, and organic material may disintegrate upon contact with water.

Keep It Clean

Even if you wash your hands every time you pick up your embroidery, it is inevitable that the oils from your fingers will transfer to the cloth. Fabric that contains body oils is susceptible to infestation by moths, carpet beetles, and other pesky creatures that like to munch on fabric. Wash your work before storing it.

When washing your stitching, be aware that not all embroidery floss is color safe. Before soaking a work, test a small swatch of your fabric and floss in cold water for two to five minutes to see if the color bleeds. Many floss companies will label their products "color safe," but if you are working with secondhand thread, test it. Likewise, certain buttons or beads may have excess paint particles, so give them a brief rinse before sewing them to the fabric.

Spin Cycle

Since stitch work is delicate, never put it in the washing machine—unless, or course, you desire tangled and fuzzy thread effects! If you do have to put embroidery work in a machine, it is advisable to clip all loose threads and wash the work in a mesh or muslin "delicates" bag.

Luckily, hand-washing fabric is easy—all you need is water, a gentle soap, and a plastic washtub or bucket. If you intend to hand-wash items often, consider earmarking one container to be used only for embroidery; it would be horrible to have your stitch-work stained by an unclean bin!

Different fabrics have inherent cleaning requirements. Before you wash, consider the fiber makeup of both your fabric and your thread. Washing is much easier when your fabric and floss are made of the same fiber. When in doubt, choose cold water to wash and rinse, as warm or hot water may shrink some fabrics and fade colors.

Fill a washtub with a thimbleful of a liquid hand-washing soap and cold water. Mix together until they look sudsy, and submerge your piece so that it lies as flat as possible in the tub. Leave the piece alone (do not agitate it, unless you're dealing with stains) for five to ten minutes. Drain the tub of water, leaving the embroidery piece inside. Refill the tub with cold water, allowing the water to soak into the piece for a few minutes to penetrate any leftover soap in the fabric. Repeat this two or three times until the water runs clear.

Drying

To dry, do not wring the water out by twisting your fabric, as this can cause wrinkles. Instead, gently hold your work by two corners to let excess water roll off. When it stops dripping, sandwich it between two clean towels and roll the towels up like a jellyroll, so that the excess water is pulled out by the absorbent towels. Remove the piece from the towels, and lay your piece flat to dry, away from heat and sunlight.

Trimming Loose Ends

Any tails of floss long enough to be seen outside the finished work (such as work that will be displayed in an embroidery hoop or used on something
functional like a pillowcase or T-shirt) should be trimmed. If it's in the way, trim it.

Pressing Issues

When ironing, remember you are using something that is extremely hot and potentially flammable. Never leave it unattended!

If you do not have room for an ironing board, you may be able to find a small table-top one in a department store. An ironing board is well worth owning, but, in a pinch, a clean cotton pillowcase wrapped around a small wooden board will work. Tack the pillowcase around

something soft to pad the surface (such as an old towel or some cotton batting) and ensure that the fabric is free of hair, dust, and dirt.

If your work is delicate, consider using a pressing cloth, which is simply a piece of clean scrap fabric that you lay over your finished work when ironing, in order to prevent touching the finished piece directly with the iron. A bit of unbleached muslin or a white dishtowel would work for this—just make sure that the fabric is light-weight and color-free.

Another factor to consider when ironing is fiber content. Untreated cotton and linen weaves always need to be ironed to look good. Permanent-press and synthetic fabrics sometimes iron well with a dry iron, but a steam iron will provide the moisture required to get them to lay flat. Untreated cottons, rayons, and silks must be slightly damp to iron properly. You will need to use a steam setting or a spray water bottle to moisten the fabric.

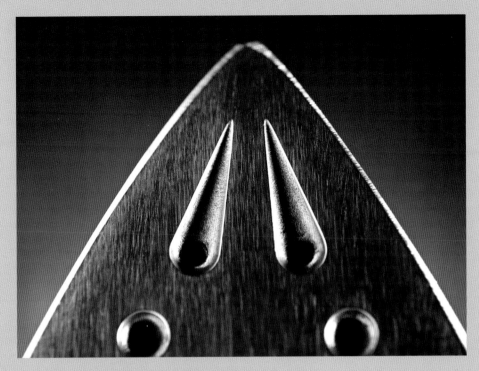

Display and Storage

Few of the projects in this book are displayed in a frame. Embroidery, needlepoint, and cross-stitch can be displayed in all kinds of ways. Hiding your work under glass doesn't necessarily provide the best artistic vantage point.

Brainstorm unique ways to hang your work. You can find inspiration all over the place. A trip to an art gallery can demonstrate ways to display your work, whether in hanging installations, snap frames, on pedestals, or on canvas stretcher bars. Picture frames can also be constructed out of unusual materials such as recycled wood, cast plaster, aluminum, or plexiglass. Visit an artists' supply store—they will have lots of ideas and can usually help you come up with something that is reasonable and beautiful.

Something as simple as a wooden embroidery hoop (as used in, for example, Oxytocin Notion on p. 267 and Against the Grain, p. 169) can look modern. Wooden hoops can be finished to your taste with stains, paints, shoe polish, varnish, or even glitter.

If you don't want to use a hoop or a frame, consider other sorts of hanging materials such as bulldog clips, wire coat hangers, bamboo dowels, or chains. If you are handy with woodworking materials, you can also consider building your own frames or stretchers out of balsa wood.

If you do choose to show your work under glass, make sure it doesn't compress the stitches; there should be some breathing room between your work and the glass frame so the fabric doesn't develop mildew.

However you choose to display your work, do it with pride. You took the time to make it, so make sure you take the time to show it off!

Most conventional irons will have different steam and pressing settings, but should conform to the international symbols for heat settings. These settings consist of three dots:

- One dot: cool setting of 248° F/120° C—best used for synthetics
- Two dots: warm setting of 320° F/160° C—best used for silks and wools
- Three dots: hot setting of 370° F/210° C—best for cottons and linens (most commonly used).

When using your iron on embroidery work, be sure to "press" rather than rub the iron over the fabric. When pressing, lift the iron up and down over the cloth in a light patting motion.

All Aflutter Necklace

KARYN FRASER

Karyn Fraser developed a whimsical project that is framed by the human face—an embroidered necklace. These soft, shiny feathers are stitched by hand and attached to satiny ribbons. Make one for yourself or several to give away to friends. This hand-stitched piece of wearable art will make recipients feel special. Karyn says, "Feathers are so varied and beautiful in nature; I couldn't help but think how organic an embroidered feather might seem."

Tools and Materials

FLOSS:

To create the gray feather:
1 skein each of

- DMC #535 (Ash Gray VY - LT)
- DMC #451 (Shell Gray - DK)
- DMC #3012 (Khaki Green - MD)
- DMC #3860 (Cocoa)

To create the gray-blue feather:
1 skein each of

- DMC #648 (Beaver Gray - LT)
- DMC #924 (Gray Green VY- DK)
- DMC #926 (Gray Green - LT)

To create the cream feather:
1 skein each of

- DMC #3866 (Mocha Brown - ULT VY LT)

- DMC #676 (Old Gold - LT)
- DMC #436 (Tan)
- DMC #758 (Terra Cotta VY - LT)

To create the orange feather:
1 skein of

- DMC #3826 (Golden Brown)
- DMC #152 (Tawny - DK)
- DMC #3866 (Mocha Brown ULT VY - LT)
- DMC #3864 (Mocha Beige - LT)

FABRIC:

15 × 18 in (38.1 × 45.72 cm) cotton even-weave 28-count gauge

5 × 9-in (12.7 × 22.86-cm) oval-shaped embroidery hoop

embroidery needle, size of your choice

1 yd (0.91 m) of 3/8-in (.95-cm) ribbon in a color that complements the floss colors

water-soluble fabric marker or transfer paper

masking tape for design transfer

scissors (appliqué scissors recommended)

fabric glue

flat-tipped paintbrush

Stitches:

satin stitch

Figure 8.1

Preparation

Begin by transferring the feather image (Fig. 8.1) onto fabric using a water-soluble fabric marker to trace the design. Outline the inner and outer lines of the feather, delineating the width of the surrounding border. It may help to tape the design and fabric to a light source.

If you are planning to stitch more than one feather, transfer as many as desired to the fabric, spacing them far enough apart to allow enough room to work each feather within the space of the embroidery hoop.

As in life, no two stitched feathers will be exactly alike. Experiment with color and proportion!

Stitching the Feather

Using all six strands of floss, begin to work in satin stitch where the feather meets the base of the quill, on the lower left side of the outside border. Each stitch should be worked close to the last to maintain an even edge. Continue to work down and around the border until the bottom of the opposite side is reached. Next, stitch the bottom portion of the quill. Once this is complete, run the needle, with the remaining thread, up and under these last stitches on the back of the piece to fill the middle quill portion. Continue working the quill portion back to the top of the feather. Tie off and trim excess thread.

Once the border has been completed, the body of the feather can be worked quickly. Change to a complementary floss color for the body. As with the border, work a satin stitch from left to right moving downward within the space. Use each color of floss until the desired effect is achieved. Change colors as needed, but remember to hide floss ends under the stitched work as much as you can.

Once complete, trim the feather from the fabric leaving a 0.5-in (1.27-cm) border around the finished stitching.

Finishing

To block the fabric and remove any remaining transfer marks from the feathers, submerge the finished piece in room temperature water for three to five minutes. Remove and gently press water from the feather with a towel. Once this has been done, carefully trim the fabric allowance from the embroidered piece. It will not be possible to trim this off entirely—and that's okay. The piece will be beautiful in its imperfection. Leave your finished work to dry flat.

The edges of the feather can be reinforced by applying a small amount of fabric glue with a paint brush to prevent fraying. As soon as the glue has dried, complete your necklace by adding a ribbon. Cut the ribbon in half (to make two 18-in/ 45.72-cm lengths). Turn the raw edge of the ribbon under twice so that it will be enclosed in the seam created when stitched to the feather. Press this folded edge down with an iron. Hand-sew each end of the feather to the folded ends of the ribbon. With a tiny running stitch, catch the back of the feather cloth to the folded ribbon. Be careful not to pull the thread through the embroidery stitches. Knot, then trim loose threads. Your ethereal necklace is now ready to float around your neck!

KARYN FRASER loves a challenge and has been known to search one out. She enjoys spending time with her husband and four children and is happiest watching a movie with her family—with their doors open to smell the rain. Inspired by her amazing grandmothers, Karyn is studying fashion and apparel design, and hopes to become a fiber and textile artist. She is looking forward to where her new education will take her; she finds fashion to be a fascinating subject, one in which her options are endless.

CHAPTER 9

Stitching Resources

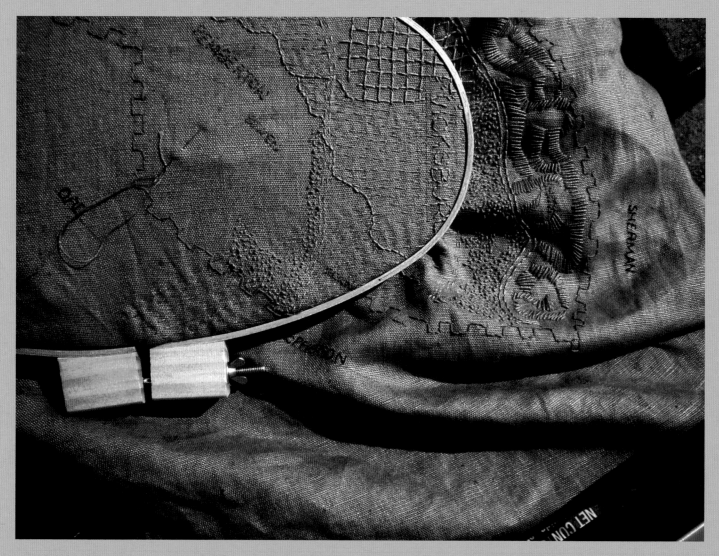

Annie Coggan Crawford's embroidery. Photo: Annie Coggan
Crawford/Caleb Crawford

N eedlework can be a meditative act that allows you to spend hours alone with your hoops and needles, but it doesn't have to be a solitary pursuit. There is a community of makers, both online and in the real world, who can provide you with camaraderie and inspiration.

Embroidery Blogs and Websites

Starting my blog was a freeing experience. I found a real community online. I knew other people who did fiber work, but not other men. You wouldn't be able to find this anywhere but on the Internet. It's a rare skill set. —AUBREY LONGLEY-COOK

I have found a wonderful needlepoint community online and have met many great friends. I have little difficulty finding other people who are willing to critique and share with one another in a way that simply doesn't exist in many other artistic fields. —CATE ANEVSKI

Blogs and websites may not seem like the most social experience to those who prefer their interactions in the offline world, but they can open a door to finding those who share your interests. Here are a few websites that feature embroidery work that is far from ordinary:

MR X STITCH (mrxstitch.com): "The Number One Contemporary Embroidery and Needlecraft Blog." This site is updated daily with extraordinary projects and thought-provoking articles.

FEELING STITCHY (feelingstitchy.com): A multi-author blog that focuses on embroidery interviews, tutorials, and crafty topics.

THE JEALOUS CURATOR (thejealouscurator.com/blog): An embroidery-friendly art blog with the tagline "I know that it's good when I'm left thinking damn, I wish I thought of that."

EMBROIDERY AS ART (embroideryasart.blogspot.com): Jenny Hart's curated blog of interesting embroidery projects.

RADICAL CROSS-STITCH (radicalcrossstitch.com): "Seriously Seditious Stitching." This website has free patterns, the Fabric of Resistance wiki, and inspiration for producing your own politically-minded patterns.

THE HAND EMBROIDERY NETWORK (handembroidery.ning.com): A social networking site with blogs, stitching swaps, forums, and photos.

FINE CELL WORK (finecellwork.co.uk): A UK-based organization dedicated to teaching prison inmates how to stitch and thereby provide them with a chance to earn money and the opportunity to rebuild their lives through craft and achievement.

STITCH OUT LOUD (stitchoutloud.blogspot.com): "Sending awesomeness and obscenities into the world one stitch at a time."

OPEN SOURCE EMBROIDERY (open-source-embroidery.org.uk): A fascinating project that connects needleworkers, knitters, and crocheters to the open source computer programming community.

TWENTY-FIRST CENTURY EMBROIDERY:
An Interview with Jamie Chalmers

Jamie Chalmers, otherwise known as Mr X Stitch, runs his eponymous blog, a must-read for anyone interested in contemporary embroidery and cross-stitch and featuring columns such as the Needle Exchange, Future Heirlooms, and Domestitchery. Jamie—along with collaborators including Beefranck, Penny Nickels, Arlee Barr, and Joetta Maue—is doing his best to "drag the world of embroidery into the twenty-first century." Jamie also co-hosts a podcast called Stitching n Junk, designs graffiti cross-stitch pattern kits, and still finds the time to create his own artwork.

Q: **How long have you been into needlework?**

A: I've been cross-stitching for about eight years. I have begun experimenting with other stitches, but I think that my heart will always remain with cross-stitch for its simplicity and structure. I tend to use normal floss and fabrics, although I do have a penchant for using glow-in-the-dark threads to embed hidden messages into white pieces.

My website has opened my eyes to a tremendous variety of methods and ideas, and I'm keen to try them. The only things that are holding me back are the laws of time and space, but once I can unlock extra hours in the day, I'm confident I shall explore many more techniques.

(FACING PAGE) Mr X Stitch, *Celebrity Misdemeanour 001*, 2009, floss on Aida cloth, 5 in (12.7 cm) in diameter. Photo: Jamie Chalmers

(ABOVE) Mr X Stitch, *D.I.S.C.O.!!*, 2009, floss on found vintage embroidery, 8 in (20.32 cm) in diameter. Photo: Jamie Chalmers. "We got there in the end, and our lovely Victorian friends are now shaking their booties at the funkiest disco in town."

(LEFT) Found vintage embroidery of a Victorian couple, artist and year unknown, 8 in (20.32 cm) in diameter. "Got this in a job lot of frames from a local charity shop. Wanted the frame but the stitchery is too good to be ditched." Photo: Jamie Chalmers

the history of embroidery and how it has been used as a social and political tool over the centuries.

Q: What would you say is the primary function of your work?

A: One of the main shortcomings of cross-stitch is that it is a purely decorative stitch, and although the stitches can be used to reinforce fabric, there's not a great deal of other function for it. Fortunately, there are plenty of other weapons in the embroidery arsenal that have greater functionality.

One particular thing that I do with my work is swap it with other stitchers. This has been a very rewarding experience, as I've not only gotten to know some terrific artists, I've also been able to develop a great collection of works from across the world. I plan on swapping pieces for as long as I am able.

Q: How did the Mr X Stitch website and community start?

A: I'd created three series of cross-stitch patterns and was selling them on Etsy. On honeymoon with my wife, I decided that I wanted to add extra value to the patterns and that a blog was a good tool to use, both for promotion and as a way of exploring my responses to the craft. As I began blogging, I started seeking out other stitchy artists and started writing posts about them. At the same time I began researching the secrets of successful blogs, like Cake Wrecks, and I started employing techniques like themed posts that were scheduled on specific days.

When I asked Beefranck to join me in the adventure, the site blossomed as we discovered new talent and new themes for posts, all laced with our own sense of humor. The other significant step in the process was establishing the Flickr group, the Phat Quarter, as this quickly became a place where both amateur stitchers and textile artists could share their work online. We continue to discover new talent there, as well as organizing swaps and competitions to keep things fun.

We have nine people who write for the site, providing a fantastic breadth of experience, knowledge, and talent. It is my hope that the site can develop into a great learning and

Q: Your work covers a wide range of subject matter, from pop culture quotes to graffiti-inspired stitch-work to Victorian-era people disco dancing. Where do you find your inspiration?

A: At the moment, all I know is that by the time I've finished one piece, an idea has usually come along for the next piece. One of my assets is my sense of humor, and I find that it is highly influential in many of my ideas...

An idea pops into my head, rolls around a while, and either gathers dust or momentum. If it's the latter I play around and see what I can concoct. I don't have much natural artistic ability, but I find that I can use computers to compensate for that. Once I've formed my idea, and bounced it off my closest stitchy friends for quality assurance, I choose my threads, and away I go.

Q: Is there anything about needlework that you don't like?

A: I don't like the way it's been marginalized and downgraded to a hobby by the mainstream craft industry. However, were that not the case, I wouldn't be Mr X Stitch! I'm very interested in

inspiration resource for students who wish to learn about textiles, embroidery, and similar topics, while maintaining the character that we've been able to instill throughout the content.

Q: You have lots of fun columns on your website such as Stitchgasm and NSFW (Not Safe for Work). Can you tell me more about these?

A: The first themed posts I began writing were Cutting (& Stitching) Edge posts, and after writing those, I decided that all our posts should be themed. A bolt of inspiration hit me one day when I coined the phrase "stitchgasm" for a piece of embroidery that makes you go "ooh!" and once Beefranck came on board, the ideas came quick and easy. I love a bit of alliteration and a smart bit of copywriting, so it's been fun coming up with the themes for posts.

NSFW Saturdays were created in response to an extreme reaction to some lesbian porn embroidery we featured. A couple of people were shocked by the piece, so we decided that, because it's important to feature these works to help the craft expand, we would showcase NSFW works in a controlled way, using safety pictures to protect the innocent. We believe that these kinds of works push the boundaries of the form, and, as a consequence, generate creative space for other people to explore. So we've stuck with it, but made it safe.

(ABOVE) Mr X Stitch, *Festevil*, 2009, floss on Aida cloth, 4 × 4 in (10.16 × 10.16 cm). Photo: Jamie Chalmers. "This is a poem I stitched on the last day at the Larmer Tree Festival. It was inspired by my experience there, but is no reflection on the festival itself. There's just something about festivals filled with posh people that irritates me a bit..."

(LEFT) Jamie Chalmers stitching at Roller Derby Practice, September 2010. Photo: Jamie Chalmers

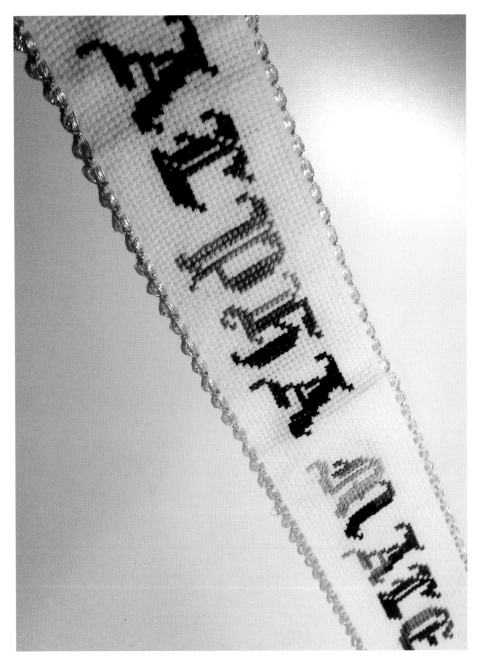

In response to NSFW Saturdays, we've also got Too Cute for Mr X Stitch Tuesdays, which feature the kind of stuff I'd never stitch because it's so darned cute. But it balances things out. I believe that fun is one element that has been somewhat drained out of the mainstream embroidery world, and so it's fortunate that we can lace this throughout the site. At the end of the day, if it ain't fun, it ain't worth it.

Q: **Can you tell me about your podcast?**

A: The podcast, Stitching n Junk, features interviews with a range of embroidery artists, as well as letters and voice-mails from our listeners. In many ways, it's an extension of the kind of conversations we've had online. Stitching n Junk is laced with humor, as you should expect by now, and one of the things I love about it is that we've had episodes that have discussed pre-industrialized textile manufactur-ers and farts within the same hour.

Q: **What sort of message do you hope that your work sends?**

A: People are always very gracious about my work, and I hope that my sense of humor and choice of subject matter compensate for my deficit of tech-niques. In general, I think that the

Mr X Stitch, *Alpha Male*, 2009, floss and metallic floss on Aida cloth sash, 6 × 2 in (15.24 × 5.08 cm). Photo: Jamie Chalmers

new stitchers that emerge are very supportive of one another, because they all enjoy the craft and understand the fundamental pleasures it gives. I continue to be amazed and inspired by new artists, and I hope that the work continues to raise the profile of embroidery out of the doldrums.

Find Jamie Chalmers online at **mrxstitch.com** or see more of his artwork on Flickr (**flickr.com/photos/mrxstitch/collections/72157617102014063/**)

(LEFT) Mr X Stitch, *Rock Out*, 2009, floss on Aida cloth, 5 in (12.7 cm) in diamater. Photo: Jamie Chalmers

(ABOVE) Jamie Chalmers stitching at the local skate shop, September 2010. Photo: Jamie Chalmers

Ray Materson, *Derek Jeter*, 2009, embroidery on cotton, 2.25 × 2.75 in (5.72 × 6.99 cm). Photo: Ray Materson

(NEXT PAGE) Liz Kueneke, *The Urban Fabric—El Tejido Urbano* (Quito, Ecuador). Photo: Liz Kueneke

Make It Social

Prefer to make friends in the offline world? Reserve September 3rd for International Stitch in Public Day! Needleworkers of all sorts are encouraged to bring their craft out into the public sphere. In past years, stitchers have made their crafts at work, on planes, on trains, at sports games, in coffee shops, and even in shopping malls.

I've done a great deal of embroidery while traveling: sitting at bus stops, on ferries, at family gatherings, and concerts. Embroidering has been a great way to meet people. I'm pretty certain they wouldn't have talked to me without the invitational embroidery hoop in my hands.
—SARAH HAXBY

Like sports? The National Needle Arts Association in America has teamed up to create Stitch N' Pitch with the Major and Minor Baseball Leagues. More than 150 of these needlepoint, knitting, and cross-stitch-friendly events take place throughout North America each year (stitchnpitch.com).

Make your own group: while the term "stitch and bitch" has been widely used by groups of knitters in the last decade, there's no reason why you can't claim the term for an embroidery group. Find a local café or restaurant that is willing to host your friends for an hour or two. Stitching in groups can be rewarding; you can show off your work, teach each other tricks, and make progress on your current project.

Around the World in Eighty Stitches

Jet-setting? Why not visit one of these vast needlework collections?

ALL-RUSSIA MUSEUM OF DECORATIVE AND FOLK ART
(Moscow, Russia): **vmdpni.ru** (in Russian), **all-moscow.ru/culture/ museum/decprikl/decprik.en.html** (in English)

With more than 40,000 pieces of folk art, this museum's collection includes embroideries by craftswomen from many parts of the Russian Federation.

DAS DEUTSCHE STICKMUSTER MUSEUM (The Sampler Museum)
(Celle, Germany):
celle.de/index.phtml?La=1&ffsn=false&object=txl342.17503.1&sub=0
(in German)

The only museum in the world that has embroidered samplers almost 400 years old.

THE MUSEUM OF KOREAN EMBROIDERY (Seoul, South Korea):
bojagii.com (in Korean), visitkorea.or.kr/enu/SI/SI_EN_3_1_1_1.jsp?cid=268147 (in English)

This museum is dedicated to the history of embroidery and embellishment in South Korea. Holdings include over 3,000 items pertaining to embroidery and stitching; many pieces are embroidered with traditional Korean motifs and Buddhist designs.

MUSEUM OF RUSHNYK (Pereiaslav-Khmelnytskyi, Ukraine): hutsul.museum/eng/collection/fabrics (in English)

Part of the National Museum of Hutsulshchyna and Pokuttya Folk Art, this gallery is devoted to the ceremonial rushnyk (Ukrainian: рушник), a traditional East Slavic towel, highly decorated with ornamental patterns and embroideries.

THE NATIONAL HANDICRAFTS AND HANDLOOMS MUSEUM (New Delhi, India): nationalcraftsmuseum.nic.in (in English)

One of the largest craft museums in India, its collection is rich with the history of Indian embroideries. Some of its prized holdings include handkerchiefs and shawls from Chamba—a region known for its rare brocade—embroidered Baluchari saris, and elaborate Kutch embroidery.

THE TEXTILE MUSEUM (Washington DC, US): textilemuseum.org

This museum's holdings span 5,000 years; items in the collection date from 3,000 BCE to the present. Textiles in the collection come from cultures around the globe, including India, Southeast and Central Asia, Persia, Turkey, and Greece, among others. Notably, the museum holds four decades of embroideries from the Ottoman Empire.

THE TEXTILE MUSEUM OF CANADA (Toronto, Ontario, Canada):
textilemuseum.ca

Canada's textile museum is dedicated to collecting textiles up to 2,000 years old and to examining how textiles will change in the future. The museum produces exhibitions that illuminate contemporary life. Can't make it to the museum in person? They also have an excellent online database of their holdings where you can search textiles in a multitude of ways, from fiber composition to technique, and a fun social-media site, called the Social Fabric (**textilemuseum.ca/socialfabric**), where you can interact with others and discuss textiles through video and online commentary.

THE VICTORIA & ALBERT MUSEUM (London, England): vam.ac.uk/collections/textiles/index.html

One of the world's greatest museums for art and design, the Victoria & Albert holds many specimens of embroidery to feast your eyes on. The museum archives contain the design work of many European embroidery luminaries, including William Morris & Co., Ramah Judah, embroiderer and knitter, and Francis Johnston, a needlework pattern designer. The V & A also has excellent website resources devoted to historical and contemporary embroidery.

During my recent trips to India, Eastern Europe, and Japan, I was mesmerized by seeing their traditional ornate, time-consuming, and meticulous works. I'm now inspired to heighten my craftsmanship to the next level with my artistic creativity. —TAKASHI IWASAKI

Flossy Flicks

Some days, stitching just doesn't go well—you prick your fingers and your threads become tangled. When this happens, consider taking a break with a movie where embroidery has a cameo:

La Bohème (1926). In a twist on the original story of Puccini's classic opera, Mimi, a poor waif living in Paris in the 1830s, is caught in a love triangle between poor Rodolphe, a playwright, and wealthy Count Paul, who tries to use Mimi's embroidery to get close to her.

The Heiress (1949). The well-bred daughter of a wealthy surgeon refuses to be a socialite, preferring to hole up in her room with her embroidery work.

Les Brodeuses / Sequins / A Common Thread (2004). Seventeen-year-old Claire discovers that she is pregnant and chooses to give birth anonymously. During her pregnancy, she is taken under the wing of Madame Mélikian, a haute couture embroiderer.

The Curse of the Golden Flower / Man cheng jin dai huang jin jia (2006). This Chinese battle-epic, set in the later Tang Dynasty, is a visual feast. An empress embroiders 10,000 golden chrysanthemums for her army of resistance to wear.

Bright Star (2009). A drama based on the ill-fated romance between poet John Keats and seamstress/embroiderer Fanny Brawne. Fanny's handiwork is seen throughout this beautiful film.

By the Book

From feminist histories of embroidery to practical advice, here is a short selection of embroidery books to curl up with on a rainy day:

Don't know anyone who can help you with an embroidery technique? Mary Kay Davis's *The Needlework Doctor: How to Solve Every Kind of Needlework Problem* (1983) should be able to help you fix what ails you.

Left-handed? If traditional instructions do not make sense to you, try *The Left-Handed Embroiderer's Companion: A Step-by-Step Stitch Dictionary* (2010) by Yvette Stanton.

Want to learn more embroidery techniques and play with some fun patterns? Jenny Hart's *Embroidered Effects: Projects and Patterns to Inspire Your Stitching* (2009) has some great ideas for stitch combinations.

Want to know more about how the history of embroidery has shaped the lives of women? Rozsika Parker's *The Subversive Stitch: Embroidery and the Making of the Feminine* (1984, new edition 2010) will cover all you need to know.

Have to say something off-color through your stitch work? Pick up Julie Jackson's crabby cross-stitch classic *Subversive Cross-stitch: 35 Designs for Your Surly Side* (2006).

Need an informative guide on how to use unusual materials in your stitch work? *Creative Recycling in Embroidery* (2006) by Val Holmes includes topics on recycling fabric and fiber waste, and how to use plastics, woods, metals, and images to create embroidery.

Need to escape? Amanda Lee has written a mystery series about an embroidery shop called the Seven Year Stitch. Titles in the series include *The Quick and the Thread* (2010) and *Stitch Me Deadly* (2011).

Want to examine how something as ubiquitous as a vegetable can inspire beautiful stitch work? Françoise Tellier-Loumagne's stunning photographic book *The Art of Embroidery: Inspirational Stitches, Textures, and Surfaces* (2006) will make you consider how intricate stitched designs can develop from the most mundane things.

Some of the best embroidery technique books are out of print, but you may be able to find them at your local library or for sale in thrift shops. Keep your eyes open for new resources!

The following magazines will keep you up-to-date on stitching:

Embroidery (**embroidery.embroiderersguild.com**)

Cross-stitcher (**crossstitchermagazine.co.uk**)

needle (an online magazine) (**needlemagazine.com**)

Natural Graffiti

ANDREA DRAJEWICZ

Living in the city, it's easy to forget that nature is all around us. We rush from house to car to office and back again, walking concrete paths and breathing machine-conditioned air. These embroidery pieces, designed to be installed in urban environments, draw attention to the natural world hiding among our human-built places: a mother bird tending her eggs in a nest tucked in a ventilation shaft, a spider patiently waiting in its dew-dotted web in the crook of a street sign. These serve as reminders that nature is still always present—even in the most urban environments—and tickle a sense of wonder. Brighten up someone's day with one of these crafty delights.

Tools and Materials

FLOSS FOR NEST ONE:

- 1 skein of DMC #869 (Hazelnut Brown - VY DK)
- 1 skein of DMC #422 (Hazelnut Brow - LT)
- 1 skein of DMC #433 (Brown - MED)
- 1 skein of DMC #779 (Brown)
- 1 skein of DMC #610 (Drab Brown - DK)
- 1 skein of DMC #371 (Mustard)
- 1 skein of DMC #400 (Mahogany - DK)
- 1 skein of DMC #413 (Pewter Gray - DK)
- 1 skein of DMC #632 (Desert Sand - ULT VY DK)

FLOSS FOR NEST TWO:

- 1 skein of DMC #898 (Coffee Brown VY - DK)
- 1 skein DMC #647 (Beaver Gray - MED)
- 2 skeins DMC #632 (Desert Sand ULT VY - DK)
- 1 skein of DMC #779 (Brown)

- 1 skein of DMC #611 (Drab Brown)
- 1 skein of DMC #413 (Pewter Gray - DK)

FLOSS FOR SPIDER'S WEB:

- 1 skein DMC White
- 1 skein DMC Light Effects E5200 (white)
- 1 skein DMC Light Effects Precious Metals E168 (Silver)
- 1 skein DMC 632 (Desert Sand ULT VY - DK)
- 1 skein DMC 413 (Pewter Gray - DK)

FABRIC:

8 × 8-in (20.32 × 20.32-cm) light gray linen even-weave. One piece required for each nest project; three pieces to complete all three.

5-in (12.7-cm) embroidery hoop

blunt-tip cross-stitch needle, size of your choosing

jute twine

small twigs and branches (approximately 10–12 in/25.4–30.48 cm long and less than 0.5 in/1.27 cm in diameter)

scissors

EXTRA MATERIALS FOR THE NESTS:

small feathers (collected from nature or purchased from a craft store)

metallic or metallic-looking beads in various sizes (for Nest One)

38-gauge needle-felting needle

block of foam for a needle-felting surface

small bits of wool fleece in turquoise (for Nest One) or pale green (for Nest Two)

small pine cones (for Nest Two)

EXTRA MATERIALS FOR THE WEB:

beading needle (the eye of the needle should be no wider than its shaft to allow the threaded needle to pass easily through the seed beads)

24 light-blue and clear seed beads

24 light-blue glass beads in various sizes

Tools and Materials continued on page 326

Skills required:

NEST ONE:

web stitch

split stitch

couching

backstitch

needle felting

French knots

NEST TWO:

weaving stitch (a.k.a. Queen Anne stitch)

couching

backstitch

French knots

needle felting

SPIDER'S WEB:

couching

backstitch

Pekinese stitch

web stitch

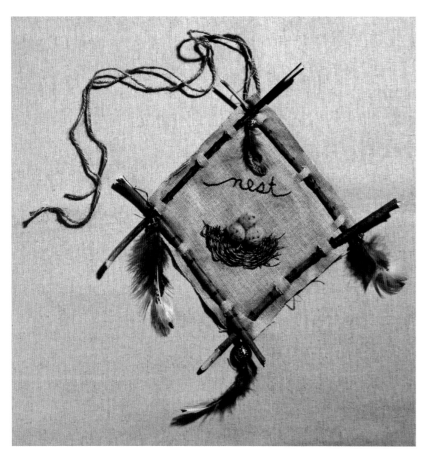

Incubation (for all three projects)

Line up the pattern(s) (Figs. 9.1, 9.2, and 9.3) with the edges of the fabric, keeping in mind that you will be working on the diagonal. Using the carbon paper transfer method (p. 110), transfer the design(s) onto fabric. Place the prepared fabric piece within the embroidery hoop, stretched taut.

DIAGRAM NOTE: The dashed lines in Fig. 9.1 mark the patterns' cutting lines and are not to be stitched. Once the embroidery is complete, cut tabs following these lines in order to insert the branches that will support the finished piece.

Stitching Nest One

Using six strands DMC #869, stitch the outline framework for the nest. Cut 7–12 in (17.78–30.48 cm) lengths of DMC #422, DMC #433, DMC #779, DMC #610, DMC #371, and DMC #400. With one strand of each color, create a multi-colored floss of six strands on your needle. Working from left to right across the framework, weave over and under the framework. Stitch loosely, being careful not to pull the thread tight enough to distort the framework. If the tension of your stitching is too tight, tack the framework down in a few places.

Once you've completed working left to right, begin to work right to left, weaving over the framework thread where you previously went under and vice-versa.

After completing several rows of stitching, add in four short rows; pass over the first three or five strands of the framework before turning back. This will help to fill in the right side of the nest. Then stitch two more rows, stitch over to the left side, and once again add in four short rows, passing over the last three or five strands of the framework before turning back. This will help fill in the left side of the nest.

Continue stitching in this fashion, alternating several full rows of stitching with short rows of stitching on both the left and right sides as needed until the framework has been filled in to your satisfaction.

As you approach the end of the length of thread, simply leave the ends loose and hanging on the front of the work. Start the next strand by weaving it under existing stitching, leaving an inch or so of the end hanging loose in front of the work.

Stitching Nest Two

With four strands of DMC #898 and two strands DMC #647 held together (totaling six strands on the needle), stitch the base framework that you will weave your stitchwork through.

With one strand each of DMC #647 and #632 and two strands each of DMC #779 and #898 held together (totaling six strands on the needle), begin to weave over and under the framework in a woven stitch pattern, working left to right. Stitch loosely, being careful not to draw the thread so tightly it distorts the framework.

Once you've worked from left to right, work from right to left, weaving over the framework thread where you previously went under and vice-versa. Use the tip of your needle to snug each row up against the previously completed row to ensure solid coverage and to allow the woven stitch to fill in the nest shape. Several short rows of woven stitch can also be used fill in the nest shape.

With six strands of DMC #413, backstitch the word "nest" on both Nests One and Two. Remove the embroidery from the hoop. Press the fabric to remove any creases left by the hoop.

Hatch the Eggs

To create the egg, take a small piece of fleece and roll it between your palms until it starts to form a loose ball. Manipulate it with your fingers until it starts to approximate a loose egg-shape. Using a felting needle, poke the ball until the felt becomes dense. Make two or three eggs to fit your nest.

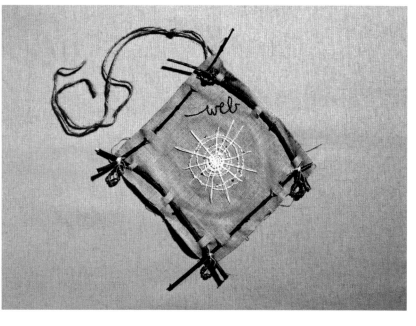

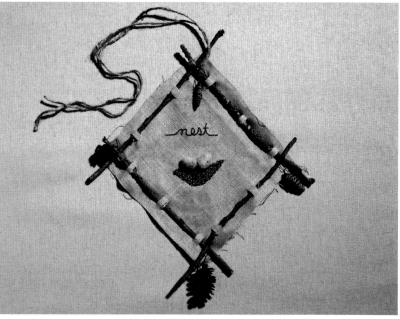

To create speckling on the eggs, use two strands of floss (DMC #632 for Nest One, DMC #611 for Nest Two) to create French knots on the surface of each egg. When completing a knot, angle your needle so that it emerges on another point on the egg's surface where you can create another knot. Once the egg is speckled, simply draw your remaining thread through to the back of the egg and leave a long tail to secure the egg to the nest. Repeat this process on the other egg(s). Secure the eggs in the nest with a few stitches.

Stitch the Web

Using three strands of DMC White, two strands of DMC Light Effects E5200, and one strand of DMC Light Effects E168 held together (totaling six strands on the needle), stitch the framework for the web. Begin the web somewhat loosely for approximately 0.75 in (1.9 cm) around the center of the framework.

TIP: As the cotton thread and the Light Effects thread stretch differently, it may be easier to stitch with shorter lengths of thread than you are accustomed to. Readjust the position of the threads on the needle frequently to keep them from twisting.

Continue creating the web design by stitching between the spokes of the web with backstitches of varying length.

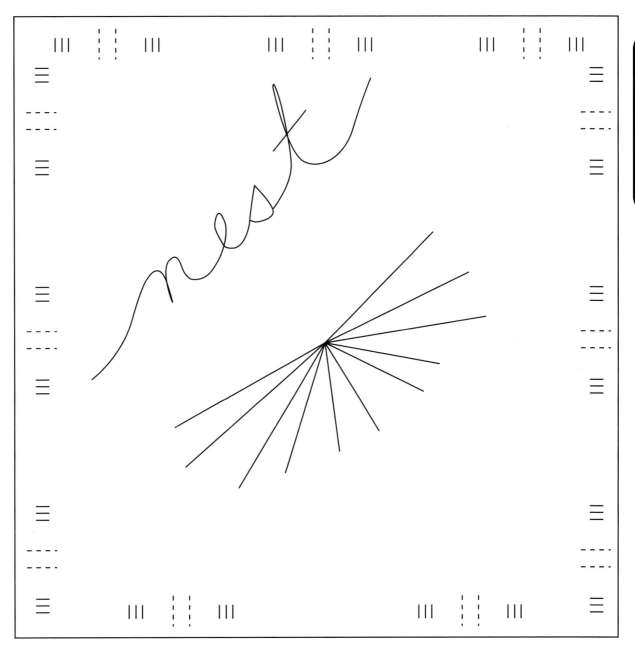

Figure 9.1. Nest One. Copy at 100 percent of size.

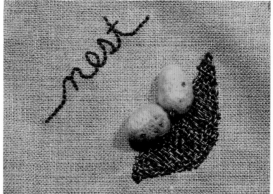

Place some stitches over the spokes of the web and others under the spokes. With one strand DMC Light Effects E168, make three to five loops of Pekinese stitch through the backstitches, where indicated by the pattern. With a beading needle and one strand DMC White, sew several light blue seed bead "dewdrops" onto the web.

With six strands DMC #413, backstitch the word "web."

Finishing

With each project, fold the fabric along one edge 0.75 in (1.9 cm) from the selvedge. The cutting lines, as indicated by each pattern piece, should be centered over the fold. Cut the slits marked on the fold, adjusting to fit your branches. Take care not to cut through your stitch work or cut too close to the edge of the fabric. Repeat this step on the other sides of the fabric.

Gently feed a branch through the tabs on one side of the fabric until it is nicely positioned on the branch. Repeat on each of the four sides, overlapping the branches at the corners. Using a modified couching stitch and two strands DMC #632, secure the branches to the fabric with several couching stitches placed side by side on either side of each tab.

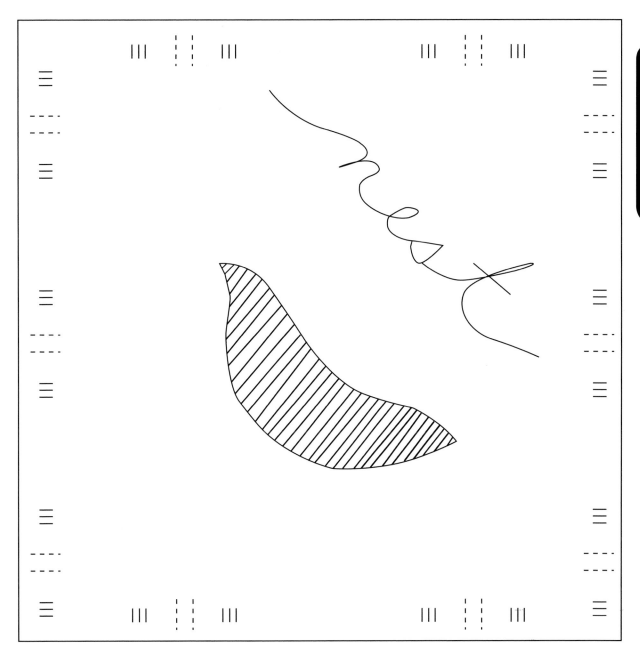

Figure 9.2. Nest Two. Copy at 100 percent of size.

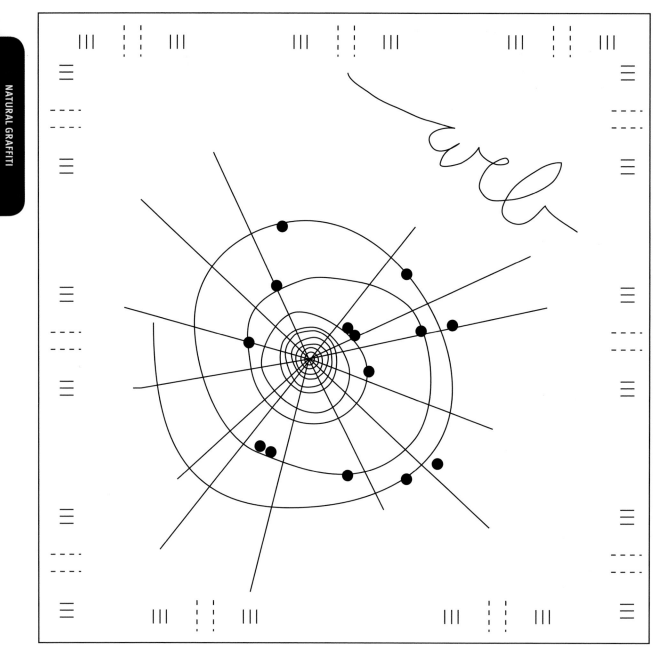

Figure 9.3. Spider's Web. Copy at 100 percent of size.

Embellish Nest One

Using two strands DMC #632, create a slipknot in the center of the length of thread and knot it around the base of a feather. Slide a bead over the thread and up onto the base of the feather. Wrap the tails of the thread several times around the corner point where two branches cross each other, making sure that the feather and beads are free to dangle. Fasten off securely. Repeat this process on each of the remaining three corners.

Embellish Nest Two

Using two strands DMC #632, create a slipknot in the center of the length of thread and knot it around the base of a pinecone. Wrap the tails of the thread several times around the corner point where two branches cross each other, making sure that the pinecone is free to dangle. Fasten off securely. Repeat this process on each of the remaining three corners.

Embellish the Web

Using two strands DMC White, feed twenty-four clear seed beads onto the thread. Bring the tail of the thread back through the first bead to form a teardrop-shaped loop. Wrap the tails of the thread several times around the point where two branches cross each other, making sure that the beaded dewdrop is free to dangle. Fasten securely. Repeat this process on the opposite corner. Repeat again, this time using twenty-four light blue seed beads, and fasten to the bottom corner. Use two strands of DMC White and a mix of small and medium beads to create three slightly larger teardrop shapes and fasten them in the same way.

Using two strands of DMC White and a mix of small and medium beads, create one last string of beads. Wrap these around the top-most corner where the branches overlap, and tie it securely.

Hang the Nests and Web

Fasten a length of twine to the back of each piece, close to the top, so that you can hang it from a tree, lamppost, street sign, or other urban object. Spread some nature— and some embroidered anarchy!

Growing up with artist parents, **ANDREA DRAJEWICZ** learned to embrace her creativity from an early age. Andrea is a writer, mother, and crafter who firmly believes that everyone should find passion in what they do. Her interests include technical and creative writing, reading books, small-scale vegetable gardening, and creating handicrafts of all kinds: knitting, crochet, embroidery, sewing, needle felting, and embellished scrapbooking. Most of all, she loves sharing the many joys of learning, playing, and crafting with her children and friends in the hope of igniting an appreciation of the world and finding joy in things great and small.

Read more about Andrea's creative adventures online at **kidsbyhand.wordpress. com** and **joyfulwriter.wordpress.com**.

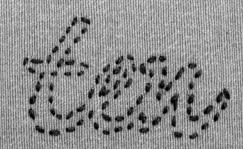

CHAPTER 10

Without
Reservation

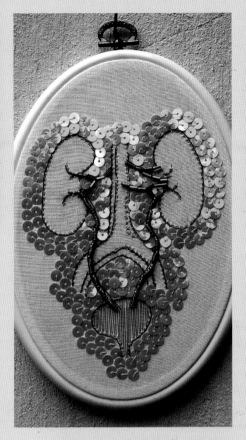

(FACING PAGE) Richard Saja, *Miniatures*, 2010.
Photo Richard Saja

(TOP TO BOTTOM, LEFT TO RIGHT) Penny Nickels,
Fetish Triptych: Cronus, Graeae, and Phorcydes, 2010,
hand embroidered on velvet, with seeds, elk canine,
and sea urchin, 4 in (10.16 cm) in diameter. Photo:
The Hopeso Group

Claire Platt, Kidneys, 2007, cloth, floss, beads,
sequins, 7 × 5 in (17.78 × 12.7 cm). Photo:
Claire Platt

Ulrika Erdes, *Public Embroidery: Cross-stitched Seat*,
2007, embroidery floss on upholstery, 7 × 7 in
(17.78 × 17.78 cm). Photo: Ulrika Erdes

Alexandra Walters, *Caw! Caw!*, 2010, hand-spun
and commercial wool thread on a linen background,
11 × 16 in (27.94 × 40.64 cm). Photo: Alexandra
Walters

Rosa Martyn, *Trickling Down My Leg*, 2010, from
Scarlet Work, embroidery thread liberty print fabric,
15 × 5 in (38.1 × 12.7 cm)
Photo: Rosa Martyn

The embroidery artists who conclude
this book are rule-breakers. Whether
speaking out against societal norms, stitching
what ails them, creating graffiti with floss, or
cheekily subverting traditional textiles, they
each create thought-provoking work. Let their
opinions inspire you to use embroidery
as a potent means of communication.

MEET ME IN THE DAYROOM:
An Interview with Alexandra Walters

Alexandra Walters is an artist, nurse, mother, and military wife living in Oklahoma. Through her jaw-dropping work, Alexandra has embroidered her experiences of being a military wife and her personal experiences with her body image and mental health. Known for her courage in tackling personal subject matter, her art-therapy blog Meet Me in the Dayroom has resonated with readers and stitchers alike.

Q: **When did you start to embroider?**

A: I don't have any memory of not embroidering, but I didn't make the switch to art until April 2008. I was experiencing a lot of illness and depression. I decided that the care I was getting was not enough; I had to find a form of rehab that I could impose upon myself. When I first started the art-therapy blog, it was called Self-Inflicted Art Therapy. I embroidered my own perceptions of my body. I started doing anatomical structures, a brain, and nerve cells. I had anxiety, so I embroidered sickly blue lungs and, instead of showing the fully-inflated alveoli, they had these dashed lines indicating sketchy structures.

Q: **Why does so much of your embroidery work feature military themes?**

A: I participated in a stitch-a-long[1] to "stitch a famous Oklahoman," and the only famous person I was interested in was Clarence Tinker, for whom our military base is named. The portrait got me thinking about old portraits of family members who had a tremendous effect on our lives, even though we never met them. The military is thought of as a family, so I wanted to create an ancestor-worship of sorts.

Q: **You have created a series of portraits, including many self-portraits, and a portrait of Mikhail Kalashnikov, the inventor of the AK-47.**

---

1 A stitch-a-long is a voluntary group of embroiderers or sewers who create either the same project or a series of projects with the same theme at the same time and report on their progress to one another.

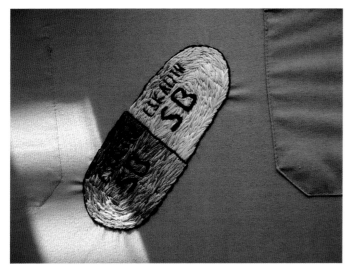

(TOP) Alexandra Walters, *Prozac, Flash*, 2008, from the series *The Promise of Pills*, cotton and silver thread, 14 × 10 in (35.56 × 25.4 cm). Photo: Alexandra Walters

(BOTTOM) Alexandra Walters, *Lithium*, 2008, embroidery thread on a re-purposed scrub smock: embroidery 11 × 14 in (27.94 × 35.65 cm), scrub smock: 25 × 25 in (63.5 × 63.5 cm). Photo: Alexandra Walters

I was experiencing a lot of illness and depression. I decided that the care I was getting was not enough; I had to find a form of rehab that I could impose upon myself.

A: I became obsessed with interpreting the human face through thread. I liked experimenting with how much expression I could get out of a face. I thought that if I could look at my face as a series of shapes, then I could see myself objectively and be more accepting of my own face. It was cathartic. My portrait of Mikhail Kalashnikov was my interpretation of ancestors who created things whose impact on modern life they couldn't possibly have comprehended.

Q: **You also worked some stars into a portrait (*Sandy 007*) that are reminiscent of quilting stars, and I believe those were influenced by traditional Afghani quilt making. Is that correct?**

A I like to read about different ethnic types of embroidery, and I was startled at how much Afghanistan's geometric embroidery looks like quilting patterns. When I was thinking of [my husband's commander] Sandra Finan's time in Afghanistan, I thought it would be perfect for her. Two hundred years ago Afghani women were making quilts; now the women are making this embroidery, and there are women running this masculine military complex. [The stars] serendipitously tie those three vastly different groups together.

It is important to me to strip off all of the insignia on the military portraits. I didn't want to focus on rank—I wanted to make them human. As Sandy's was the only female portrait, I wanted to add little bit of rank with stars or medals or banners to even the playing field. I didn't want her beauty to take away from her achievements.

Alexandra Walters, *Absence Makes the Heart Grow Fonder* (self-portrait, cropped), 2010, linen, hand-spun and dyed yarn, commercial crewel wool, hand-spun buffalo down, re-purposed airman battle uniform (ABU), pixelated camouflage material, 11 × 14 in (27.94 × 35.56 cm). Photo: Alexandra Walters

Alexandra Walters, *Waiting Room*, 2010, hand embroidery, cotton and linen floss, scrub smock from the Army hospital where Alexandra was born, 25 × 25 in (63.5 × 63.5 cm). Photo: Alexandra Walters. "This shirt used to be a deep burgundy, but it has seen countless surgeries, births, and deaths."

Alexandra Walters, *Norman Schwartzkopf*, 2010, cotton, silk, and linen threads on a cotton background, 11 × 16 in (27.94 × 40.64 cm). "Embroidered portrait of Norman Schwartzkopf, the military leader who first sent my husband to war in the 1990s." Photo: Alexandra Walters

Q: **How do you plan your portraits?**

A: I start with a picture in my head. When I did the series of pills, a lot of people didn't realize they were fiber art. This didn't upset me—it was really flattering—but I decided from that point on that I would never do anything that did not have something explicitly "embroidery" about it. I don't want to lose touch with the medium. I always reserve part of the composition to mark it with a special stitch that could only be done with fiber, not paint or any other medium.

I like that it's a slow process. I like showing off the fact that I have sub-clinical obsessive-compulsive disorder. I like that people can tell that I am obsessively persistent, that I spent hours with this thing and that it was part of my life for a long time.

Q: **Do you have a favorite type of embroidery stitch?**

A: I really like my "Alex" stitch. It's just a straight stitch, but there's no parallel orientation. It's piled up on top of each other, and criss-crossed at places and clumped up together.

Q: **Do you have a favorite piece of your work?**

A: I am fond of my weapons—which are probably the most controversial of my artworks. People on the Internet got very upset with these, and I got nasty comments about being some sort of gun-loving American. The controversy was such a shock to me.

Q: **What do you want people to take away from your work?**

A: I'd like people to notice my technique and accuracy. From looking at a tiny thumbnail [of the work], you can recognize which model gun I used on those tea towels.

Everybody's very supportive of [America's] troops in the Iraq war, but there's not a lot of recognition for the families and wives who are alone. I thought there was something poignant about using this art on household textiles, but it kind of got lost in the controversy. I don't condone violence; I was trying to be a lot more expository—"This is a gun, this is a dish

towel," you know? I'm not trying to promote gun control. I'm not trying to promote gun ownership, but I did find out a lot about other people from what they thought of my work.

Q: **If you were trying to convince someone else to take up embroidery, how would you convince them?**

A: I have a little quote that I used to put on my blog when people had problems that said something like identify your problem and name it and stitch it and stab it with a needle a few thousand times, then get over it.

Find more of Alexandra's work online at **meetmeinthedayroom.wordpress.com**.

I don't condone violence; I was trying to be a lot more expository—"This is a gun, this is a dish towel," you know? I'm not trying to promote gun control. I'm not trying to promote gun ownership, but I did find out a lot about other people from what they thought of my work.

(FACING PAGE) Alexandra Walters, *Sandy 007*, 2010, floss and fabric, 11 × 16 in (27.94 × 40.64 cm). "Portrait of my husband's commander when I first became a military bride. I met her on my wedding day, and she is as much a part of my life as a distant relative." Photo: Alexandra Walters

Alexandra Walters, *Caw! Caw!*, 2010, hand-spun and commercial wool thread on a linen background, 11 × 16 in (27.94 × 40.64 cm). Photo: Alexandra Walters

(THIS PAGE) Alexandra Walters, *M9*, 2009, hand-spun and dyed wool, Martha Stewart tea towel, 10 × 7 in (25.4 × 17.78 cm). Photo: Alexandra Walters

Alexandra Walters, *Portrait of Mikhail Kalashnikov, Inventor of the AK-47*, 2010, cotton, linen, and silk floss on re-purposed US Air Force "dress blues" uniform shirt, mounted to painting canvas, 14 × 11 (35.56 × 27.94 cm). Part of a series on the military as "one big happy extended family." Photo: Alexandra Walters

UNUSUAL EMBELLISHMENT:
An Interview with Claire Platt

Claire Platt lives in London, England where she teaches art and textiles. Although both of her great grandmothers were needleworkers, Claire learned to stitch from old needlecraft books and online videos. Her embroidery work uses luxe materials to create beautiful and strange anatomical pieces.

Q: **What sort of work do you do?**

A: I tend to be drawn toward scientific and technical-looking drawings. My biggest body of embroidery work encompasses various anatomical pieces, and I use unusual colors, metallic threads, beads, and sequins to draw the viewer in and then surprise them with the subject matter.

What makes my work unusual is using anatomical subject matter, or, to put it a little more bluntly, I'm "that girl who makes embroidered vaginas."

Q: **What is the biggest challenge with the sort of embroidery work that you do?**

A: With my anatomical pieces, I think it was the scale of |creating the collection of seventy-five pieces. It was a huge learning curve as I developed my skills and style while making the pieces.

The other challenge was the collection's installation. Each piece is hung individually within the space, and though it may look somewhat random, it's a long process to get the right colors, organs, hoop sizes, etc. in just the right place!

Q: **Where do you get your inspiration for your embroidery work?**

A: I adore the textile archives at the Victoria & Albert Museum, contemporary textile artists, visiting exhibitions, technical drawings, miscellaneous sewing bits and pieces I've collected, antique markets, and old knitting books. I like to collect bits and pieces from different places and keep them in my studio because I know that eventually they will provide some kind of input to my practice.

I keep a sketchbook that I filled with drawings, magazine cuttings, pieces of fabric—almost like a scrapbook. Once I've

Claire Platt, *Heart*, 2007, cloth, floss, beads, sequins,
6 in (15.24 cm) in diameter. Photo: Claire Platt

pulled out a particular theme, I'll make a defined set of drawings. Normally, I work on several pieces at once as there are a few different stages to complete. First I copy the drawings to fabric. I then stitch the outline of the drawing and wash each piece to remove the fabric marker. Meanwhile, I select the colors, and I lay them out next to the appropriate embroidery. I always work sequins first, then beads, then plain stitch work. While I'm working on the pieces, I'll play around with how to hang them on a spare wall in my studio. When a group of embroideries is finished, I try to pick a favorite, and this inspires the next set of drawings and embroideries!

Q: **What sort of message do you hope that your work sends out into the world?**

A: I hope that it might inspire someone to consider different mediums when it comes to making their own work. I've mostly had really positive feedback, although I do get the occasional remark that the work is disgusting, crude, and unsettling. Everyone's different!

Find more of Claire's work online at **claireplatt.com**.

(FACING PAGE) Claire Platt, *Kidneys*, 2007, cloth, floss, beads, sequins, 7 × 5 in (17.78 × 12.7 cm). Photo: Claire Platt

(THIS PAGE) Claire Platt, *Vagina*, 2007, cloth, floss, beads, 7 × 5 in (17.78 × 12.7 cm). Photo: Claire Platt

Claire Platt, *Golden Child*, 2007,
cloth, floss, metallic thread, beads,
sequins, 6 × 6 in (15.24 × 15.24 cm).
Photo: Claire Platt

Claire Platt, *Mammary Gland*, 2007, cloth, floss, beads, sequins, 6 in (15.24 cm) in diameter. Photo: Claire Platt

EMBROIDERED CONTRADICTIONS:
An Interview with Laura Splan

Laura Splan is a mixed-media artist based in Brooklyn, New York. Her conceptual artwork, which often incorporates intricate machine embroideries, subverts domestic and scientific subject matter. By mixing traditional symbols of femininity with biomedical and anatomical imagery, her work combines the seemingly comforting with the unsettling.

Q: **Many of your pieces of artwork involve machine embroidery. What drew you to this craft as a way to express your art?**

A: The use of computerized machine embroidery allows the work to resonate within a conceptual framework beyond the traditional realm of "craft." Much of my work explores traditional artifacts, materials, techniques, and aesthetics through a postmodern lens. The technological and digital processes are at odds with the seemingly traditional hand-crafted objects. This tension is echoed by the materiality of the objects themselves—biomedical imagery is used as embroidery motif; the detritus of a modern beauty regimen is used as fabric. The work can be at once emotional and scientific, personal and technological, familiar and strange, seductive and repulsive, low-tech and high-tech.

Q: **Tell me about the *Doilies* project.**

A: *Doilies* is a series of five sculptures each about eight inches (twenty centimeters) in diameter. Each doily is based on the structure of a different corona virus. Beginning with a digital image of a cross-section of the virus, I create a design. The design is imported into computerized embroidery software, and the stitches are created and manipulated for angle, density, and other stitch attributes. The digital embroidery files are output on a computerized embroidery machine onto water-soluble fabric. Once the machine embroidery is completed, the water-soluble stabilizer is dissolved in water, leaving the embroidered doily as a free-standing sculpture.

The lace doily has traditionally referenced design motifs from nature. These decorative objects would be heirlooms, handed down from one generation to the next. My work explores the "domestication" of microbial and biomedical

Laura Splan, *Doilies (HIV)*, 2004, free-standing computerized machine-embroidered lace mounted on velvet, 8.5 × 8.5 in (21.59 × 21.59 cm). Photo: Laura Splan

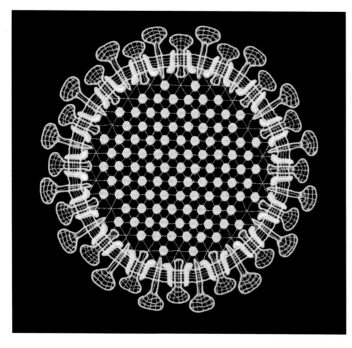 

imagery. Recent events, epidemics, and commercial products have brought this imagery into our living rooms, kitchens, and bathrooms. Bio-terrorism, SARS, and antibacterial products alike have all heightened our awareness of the microbial world. *Doilies* serves as a metaphor for the way we have adapted our lives to these now everyday concerns.

Q: **Please tell us a bit about your works *Handkerchief* and *Fan*. What inspired these pieces?**

A: *Handkerchief* is embellished with a design based on the anatomy of a human tear duct. Lacrimal glands and nasolacrimal ducts appear as a decorative border on the delicate handkerchief constructed out of water-soluble facial peel. The sculpture is a joke of sorts on the conflict of the functional and the decorative. The fragile material debunks its ability to effectively function as a handkerchief. Tears would simply dissolve the handkerchief, leaving one with the stitched

The sculpture is a joke of sorts on the conflict of the functional and the decorative. The fragile material debunks its ability to effectively function as a handkerchief. Tears would simply dissolve the handkerchief, leaving one with the stitched threads of the embroidery that depict the structures of the body from which the tears have come.

(LEFT TO RIGHT) Laura Splan, *Doilies (SARS)*, 2004, free-standing computerized machine-embroidered lace mounted on velvet 8.5 × 8.5 (21.59 × 21.59 cm). Photo: Laura Splan

Laura Splan, *Doilies (Herpes)*, 2004, free-standing computerized machine-embroidered lace mounted on velvet, 16.75 × 16.75 in (42.55 × 42.55 cm). Photo: Laura Splan

(FACING PAGE) Laura Splan, detail of *Handkerchief (Anatomy of Tears)*, 2009, machine embroidery with thread on cosmetic facial peel, 8.5 × 8.5 in (21.59 × 21.59 cm). Photo: Laura Splan

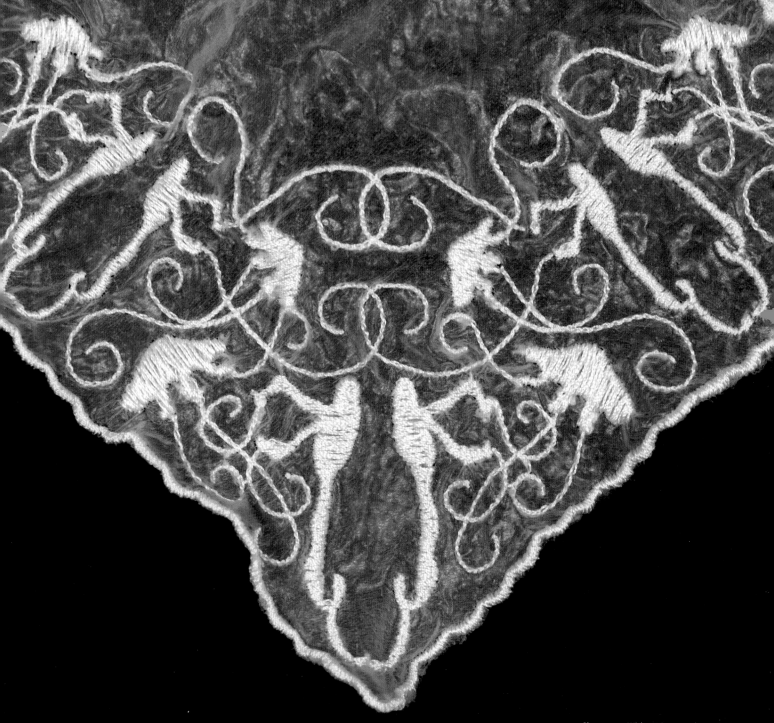

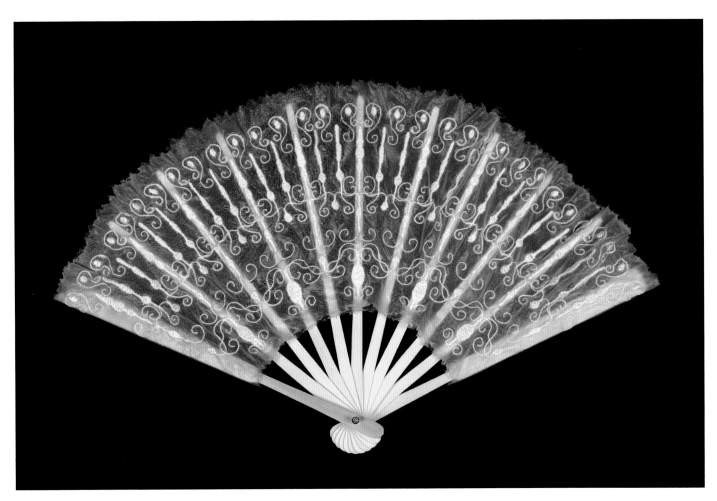

Laura Splan, *Fan (Anatomy of the Gaze)*, 2009, machine embroidery with thread on cosmetic facial peel, bamboo, mixed media, 9 × 15 × 1 in (22.86 × 38.1 × 2.54 cm). Photo: Laura Splan

threads of the embroidery that depict the structures of the body from which the tears have come.

Fan is modeled on a traditional bridal fan. The embroidery motif is based on the anatomy of the human retina. Rods, cones, and cells populate the radial structure of the hand fan. In the Victorian era, fans and parasols were used to communicate flirtatious messages from women to their suitors. Twirling the fan in the left hand meant "We are being watched" and a fan in the left hand in front of the face meant "I am desirous of your acquaintance." This method of communication functioned within a paradigm in which the woman was in a passive position, expressing

desire through the subtle movements of a fashion accessory. The social function of the fan was dependent upon the male gaze and placed [the man] in a position of dominance. While the fan and its language have fallen out of fashion, women today have inherited or learned a subtle language of the body that caters to the male gaze.

Q: **Do you have a favorite piece among your work that involves embroidery?**

A: *Subcutaneous* is a series of hand-embroidered sculptures on facial peel. One of the sculptures in the series has an embroidered quotation from Albert Einstein: "A perfection of means and confusion of aims seems to be our main problem." This quote resonates with me.

Find more of Laura Splan's work online at **laurasplan.com.**

Laura Splan, detail of *Fan (Anatomy of the Gaze).*
Photo: Laura Splan

(THIS PAGE) Laura Splan. *Subcutaneous*, 2009, hand embroidery with thread on cosmetic facial peel, wood embroidery hoops, mixed media, hoop diameters 6–7 in (15.24–17.78 cm). Photo: Laura Splan

(FACING PAGE) Laura Splan, *Trousseau*, 2009, machine and hand embroidery with thread on cosmetic facial peel, mixed media, dimensions variable. Photo: Laura Splan

PUBLIC EMBROIDERY:
An Interview with Ulrika Erdes

Ulrika Erdes is a university student studying fine arts in Gothenburg, Sweden. With an interest in performance art, Ulrika stages "public embroideries," applying her needle and thread to upholstery in public places such as trains or buses. Hoping to spread her philosophy and practice, she also provides kits and gives workshops to those who are interested in stitching their own community interventions.

Q: **How did Public Embroideries come about?**

A: Four years ago, I was living in Malmö, a city in the southern part of Sweden. I was walking up the stairs to my flat, and I thought, what if someone had embroidered the seats on the bus? That would be cool; if I saw that, I would be happy! Then I just thought, okay, I'll do that.

Q: **What was the first thing that you stitched publicly?**

A: It was a heart on a train. They have little foldable trays to |put your lunch or your computer on. So I stitched the heart [on the fabric] behind this tray—and I was very nervous.

Q: **Did you get caught?**

A: No, I've never been caught. But one time, as I was stepping onto a bus, the bus driver just smiled at me and said, "Oh, hello. No embroideries today, okay?" I've done it on trains

(FACING PAGE) Ulrika Erdes, *Public Embroidery: Cross-stitched Seat*, 2007, embroidery floss on upholstery, 7 × 7 in (17.78 × 17.78 cm). Photo: Ulrika Erdes

(LEFT) Ulrika Erdes, *Public Embroidery: Cross-stitched Heart on Seat*, 2006, embroidery floss on upholstery, 7 × 7 in (17.78 × 17.78 cm). Photo: Ulrika Erdes

(RIGHT) Ulrika Erdes, *Public Embroidery: Cross-stitched Bird on Seat*, 2007, embroidery floss on upholstery, 7 × 7 in (17.78 × 17.78 cm). Photo: Ulrika Erdes

The basic idea is to spread a positive feeling, to give people a smile on their lips. There are more profound ideas about the public sphere as well: Who owns it, and who can decide what you can and you can't do there?

that travel between distant places; I've done it on buses that stay in the city. I've done it on many different types of vehicles.

Q: **Do you freeform the shape? How do you decide what it's going to look like?**

A: When I decided to start embroidering, I made a small sampler book. When you're cross-stitching, you have motifs to follow, so I made short words, two types of hearts, and some simple stuff that I brought along so I had a sketch to follow. It's totally free-hand on the seat, so it's a bit difficult to make it perfect when the bus is bumping.

Q: **What do you hope that people will take away from your public embroideries?**

A: The basic idea is to spread a positive feeling, to give people a smile on their lips. There are more profound ideas about the public sphere as well: Who owns it, and who can decide what you can and you can't do there?

I also have a feministic view—the public sphere is traditionally a very male-dominated idea, and the private sphere is where the female is supposed to be. Embroidery is a very female thing to do. It's nice and gentle. When you bring this traditionally feminine craft out into a rough and public space, it's a clash, which I find very interesting.

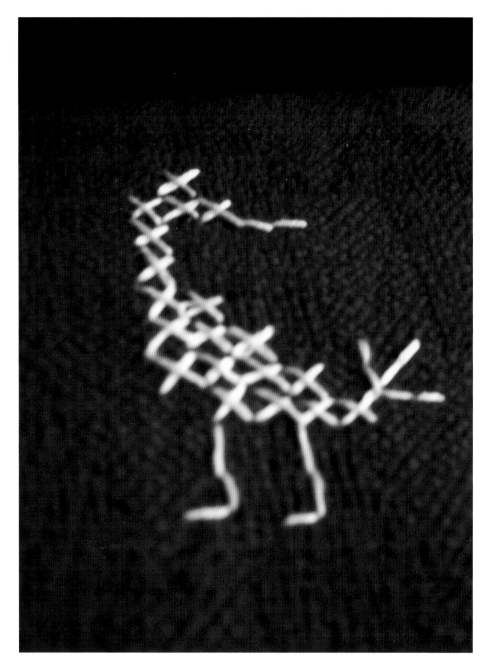

(PREVIOUS PAGE) Ulrika Erdes, *Public Embroidery: Cross-stitched Bird on Seat*, 2007, embroidery floss on upholstery, 7 × 7 in (17.78 × 17.78 cm). Photo: Ulrika Erdes

(LEFT) Ulrika Erdes, *Public Embroidery: Cross-stitched Seat*, 2007, embroidery floss on upholstery, 7 × 7 in (17.78 × 17.78 cm). Photo: Ulrika Erdes

(RIGHT) Ulrika Erdes, *Public Embroidery: Cross-stitched Heart on Seat*, 2007, embroidery floss on upholstery, 7 × 7 in (17.78 × 17.78 cm). Photo: Ulrika Erdes

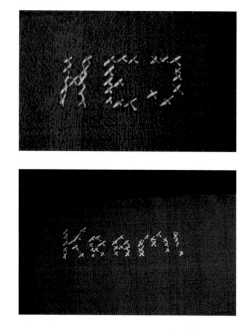

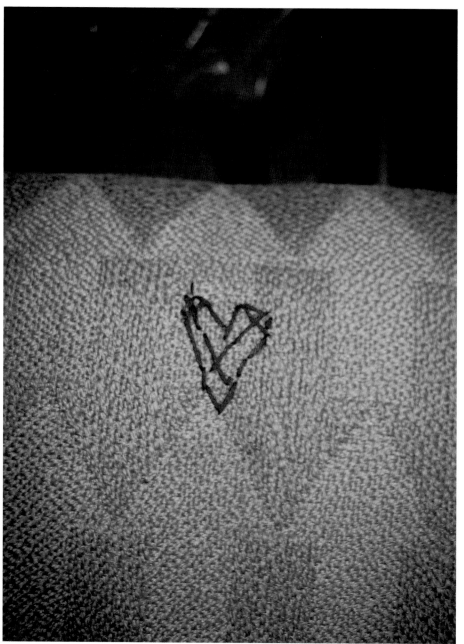

(ABOVE)Ulrika Erdes, *Public Embroidery: Cross-stitched Hello on Seat*, 2007, embroidery floss on upholstery, 7 × 7 in (17.78 × 17.78 cm). Photo: Ulrika Erdes

Ulrika Erdes, *Public Embroidery: Cross-stitched Hug on Seat*, 2007, embroidery floss on upholstery, 7 × 7 in (17.78 × 17.78 cm). Photo: Ulrika Erdes

(RIGHT) Ulrika Erdes, *Public Embroidery: Cross-stitched Heart on Seat*, 2007, embroidery floss on upholstery, 7 × 7 in (17.78 × 17.78 cm). Photo: Ulrika Erdes

(NEXT PAGE) Ulrika Erdes, *Public Embroidery: Cross-stitched Bird on Seat*, 2007, embroidery floss on upholstery, 7 × 7 in (17.78 × 17.78 cm). Photo: Ulrika Erdes

Public embroidery is associated with street art, where most street artists work anonymously, but to me, it's been important be open about the fact that I'm the one who's been doing it. It's a way of showing that I believe in it. It's important to respect the public sphere—it's a common living room. We have to tend to it and take care of it. If I'm open to saying, "It's me who is doing this," then we can have a talk about these issues.

Q: **There must be some legal risk involved with being transparent about your actions.**

A: Absolutely—you have to take responsibility for your actions. The reactions have been very diverse. In one part of Sweden, I had an exhibition at the Kalmar Museum of Art, and the transit company was so happy because they thought that it made the journey a better experience for passengers.

But where I lived in Malmö, it was the complete opposite. One company threatened to report me to the police, and they took away all my embroideries. I think it's very interesting that the approach can be so different in places so close to each other.

To learn more about Ulrika's work, find her online at **ulrikaerdes.se/public_embroidery.html**.

REBEL TOILE:
An Interview with Richard Saja

A former art director, Richard Saja lives with his ninety-eight-year-old aunt and a disagreeable Siamese cat in Jackson Heights, Queens, New York. Richard transforms traditional French toile with embroidery to create shocking, modern embroidered pieces. Well known as a mentor and friend to many modern embroidery artists, Richard sells his embellished work through his company Historically Inaccurate Decorative Arts.

Q: **How long have you been embroidering?**

A: About ten years ago, a friend and I decided to start a small design business. We debuted a collection of ten different cushion styles, including one hand-embroidered toile cushion design, at the International Gift Show. At the first couple of shows, my hand-embroidered pillow garnered an amazing amount of press attention, including the *New York Times* and *I.D. magazine*. When we split up the business, I took our tagline as my company's name, Historically Inaccurate Decorative Arts, and concentrated solely on hand-embellished work.

Q: **How did you become inspired to embellish toile?**

A: While I was developing the original collection of cushions, I remember waking one morning thinking about toile figures with Maori tattoos embroidered onto their faces. I liked the idea and purchased the toile print I use to this day in the garment district of New York City. I'm about to run out of the print—and would love to know where I can get more. It was apparently discontinued in the 1980s.

Most toiles aren't really of a scale large enough to successfully embroider intricate tattoos onto faces, so I revised the concept to encompass any sort of embroidered contextual embellishment and the toile & tats line was born. The originals were remarkably crude and graffiti-like compared to the work I do now, but, being completely self-taught, that's to be expected, I suppose.

Q: **Some of the embellishments that you've added on toile include putting fur on humans, making figures into clowns, turning gentlewomen into chickens, and men into monsters. How do you decide how to transform your subject matter?**

Richard Saja, *The Morning After.* 2008, embroidery floss,
toile, 20 in × 20 in (50.8 × 50.8 cm). Photo: Richard Saja

Richard Saja, *Burning for You Too*, 2010, embroidery floss,
toile, 20 × 20 in (50.8 cm × 50.8 cm). Photo: Richard Saja

Richard Saja, *Green Man*, 2010, embroidery floss, toile, 20 × 20 in (50.8 cm × 50.8 cm). Photo: Richard Saja

(ABOVE) Richard Saja, detail of *Just This Once*, 2009, Photo: Richard Saja

(FACING PAGE) Richard Saja, *Just This Once*, 2009, embroidery floss, toile, 23 in (58.42 cm) diameter. Photo: Richard Saja

I've also made a very conscious effort to resist any allegiance with one movement or another: art, craft, design, interiors, etc. I travel between all of these worlds adapting and perfecting my work and am not interested in anyone else's agenda

A: I work very much in the moment and don't ever premeditate imagery. I sometimes have to decline commissions where the client requests specific themes. It's not interesting to me to work that way.

Q: **You've also done some experimentation with glow-in-the-dark thread. Tell me about this work.**

A: As a child, I was mesmerized by glow-in-the-dark anything...especially if something secret happened once the lights were turned off. While researching machine embroidery, I discovered that a large commercial house had developed a line of glowing threads that I combined myself in order to embroider with. It's tricky keeping all the strands together, but the result is really something. Whenever I arrive with a concept that uses a glowing element, I attempt to capture that child-like surprise and delight in discovering that the object has another gift that is revealed only after the lights are turned off.

Q: **You seem to have a fascination with animal/human hybrids.**

A: Remember the children dressed in animal skins from the Disney version of *Peter Pan*, the *Lost Boys*? They had a profound affect on me as a child; I wanted to grow up and be one—the skunk or the rabbit or the fox. It's difficult to articulate how or why this

(FACING PAGE) Richard Saja, *Detail of The Masked Dance*,
2007, embroidery floss, toile, 20 × 20 in (50.8 × 50.8 cm).
Photo: Richard Saja

(ABOVE) Richard Saja, *Miniatures*, 2010, embroidery floss, toile,
cotton floss on a cotton print toile, 2.75 × 2 in (6.99 × 5.08
cm). Part of a series of sixteen embroideries done as a Richard
Saja/Opening Ceremony/Keds collaboration. Photo: Richard Saja

preoccupation has come to be. Whatever the case, I've been exploring it my entire life and never tire of the theme. It's somehow related to sexuality and nature and the subconscious, but that's as far as my understanding of it has gotten thus far.

Q: **Why embroidery?**

A: I have no real talent as a painter or draftsman, but embroidery allows me to work with color and imagery. The historic-textile aspect of the work also greatly appeals to me as I feel like I can perhaps foster a newfound appreciation for something that's been around for hundreds of years and is so seemingly antithetical to prevailing trends and styles.

Q: **Is there anything about embroidery that you don't like?**

A: If you're referring to its technical aspects, no. If you mean the embroidery "world," yes: I wish people would make original work rather than simply embroider celebrities. I don't find that at all interesting, regardless of the technical finesse that may have gone into a piece. I've also made a very conscious effort to resist any allegiance with one movement or another: art, craft, design, interiors, etc. I travel between all of these worlds adapting and perfecting my work and am not interested in anyone else's agenda. The group mentality only

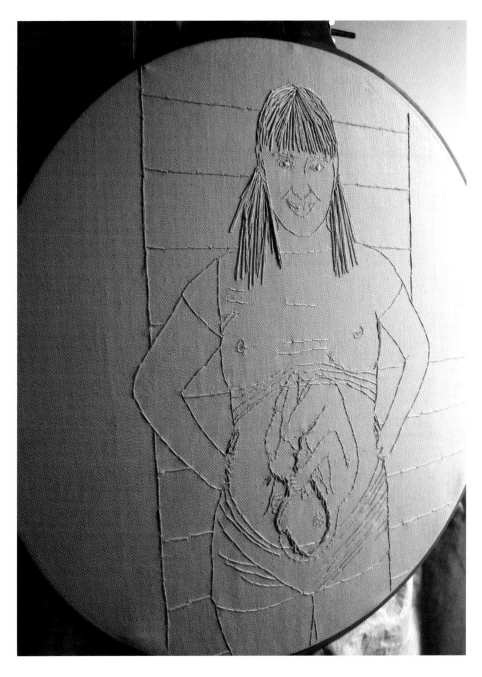

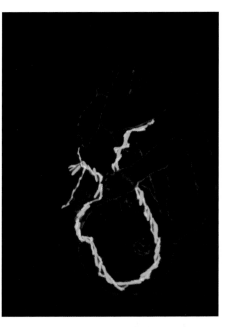

(FACING PAGE) Richard Saja, *Miniatures*, 2010. Photo: Richard Saja

(THIS PAGE) Richard Saja, *Glow Baby Glow*, 2009, cotton, rayon, and glow-in-the-dark floss on linen, 22 in (55.88 cm) in diameter. Photo: Richard Saja

(ABOVE) Richard Saja, detail of *Glow Baby Glow*, 2009. Photo: Richard Saja

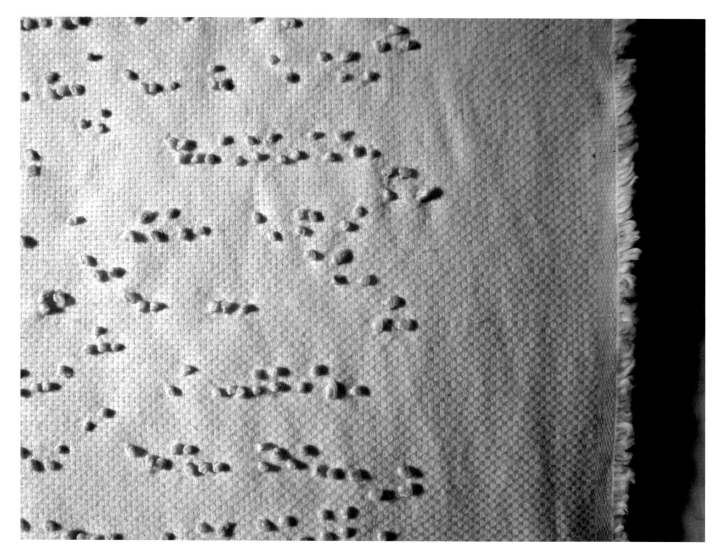

Richard Saja, detail of *The Great Milky Way*, 2009,
glow-in-the-dark embroidery floss on linen, 10 ft × 8 in
(3.04 m × 20.32 cm), 2009. Photo: Richard Saja

seems to foster antipathy for the others, and that seems counter-productive to the respect the work deserves.

Q: **Do you believe that your gender or social class has any bearing on your attraction to and involvement with needlework?**

A: No. Needlework is something that I fell into—the culmination of a lifetime's worth of education, both art-school and academic. I gave a lecture last year at the American Craft Council, and the moderator was so hung up on the fact that I was a man embroidering that she seemed unable to see anything past that, barely addressing the themes of my work at all. I felt that she had a completely outmoded way of thinking and had gotten stuck in a rut promulgating an issue that's now become irrelevant. There's nothing particularly masculine or feminine about my work or embroidery, and I resent being pigeonholed because of someone else's intellectual torpor.

Q: **Do you have a favorite piece among your work?**

A: *The City of Lost Angels*, a work where a message of Milton's is embroidered in braille, is perhaps my personal favorite. The passage from Milton's *Paradise Lost* has always been dear to me, appealing to my "wearied hope" stance on life.[2] I know the passage by heart and embroidered it in the tiniest of French knots vertically and in glow-in-the-dark thread on a black silk moiré so that the passage appears to be a city seen from afar. When the lights go out, the city's unearthly glow is like something seen in a dream or a distant memory.

Richard Saja at work. Photo: Richard Saja

To find out more about Richard Saja's work visit his blog at **historically-inaccurate.blogspot.com**.

---

2   "...our final hope/Is flat despair: we must exasperate/ Th' Almighty Victor to spend all his rage,/And that must end us, that must be our cure,/To be no more; sad cure; for who would lose,/Though full of pain, this intellectual being,/Those thoughts that wander through Eternity,/ To perish rather, swallowd up and lost/In the wide womb of uncreated night,/Devoid of sense and motion?"—John Milton, *Paradise Lost*, online at gutenberg.org/ebooks/20

SUBVERTING THE TRADITIONAL:
An Interview with Rosa Martyn

Rosa Martyn is a feminist and crafter living in London, England. Brought up by a radical left-wing mother, she was not taught how to do crafts but fell into a love affair with embroidery at age sixteen. Rosa attended art school for a year, where her "bloody-minded nature, rebellion, and feminism" slowly seeped into her stitch, before she went to study embroidery formally at the Royal School of Needlework (RSN), one of the last institutions dedicated to the practice and restoration of fine embroidery.

Q: **What attracted you to study embroidery formally?**

A: I interviewed for a textile design course and realized that it wasn't for me. Oddly, I came across the embroidery program on the last night you could possibly apply, and I thought, that sounds ridiculous, I'll apply for that. Then it turned out that the course leader is one of my favorite embroiderers, James Hunting. When I went for the interview, I fell in love with the place. It's the only place you can learn proper embroidery techniques in England, and possibly the world.

Q: **What sorts of projects do you do at the Royal School of Needlework?**

A: Our first project was woolen needlepoint, like "tapestry" cushions. We then studied Jacobean crewelwork. Then we went into silk shading, which is embroidered photo realism and is

horrible to learn how to do. My classmates were moaning about it incessantly. But one day it clicked, and we can now embroider flowers that look like flowers. We also did gold work with metal thread and traditional blackwork.

We also had a business unit on kit-making so we could learn how to actually make money out of this little craft we're learning. We're going to be doing stumpwork and whitework. There are a lot of techniques in embroidery to learn, and we get all the contextual aspects of it as well.

Q: **For your studies, you created a video performance piece called Scarlet Work which used embroidery. Can you tell me more about this piece?**

A: It was a blackwork project, but we could base it on any color we liked, provided it was monotone. I started thinking about red and the notion of blood. I asked women for the story of their first period. I then created a repeating uterus pattern that included quotes from these women and their stories. I applied the pieces onto a water-soluble fabric and dissolved it onto my leg while video taping it. It got some odd responses, but most of my classmates were supportive.

Q: **Can you tell me about the London Craftivist Collective that you belong to?**

A: We meet once a month to craft with one another and to plan campaigns. We've done work around conflict in Sudan, and, during the British election [in 2010], we wanted to tackle voter apathy. We make patterns encouraging people to vote because it's the only chance you have to get your voice across, so you might as well utilize it. The craft isn't always embroidery; as a collective, we all bring whatever we can do, and we teach each other. I am the stitcher of the group, so I make the patterns. I did a few recently, encouraging people to give blood. We're mainly known for mini protest banners that we put little backstitch letters on, encouraging people to be green, or non-violent—whatever seems necessary and topical. Because we're a collective, we've got people from all different areas of

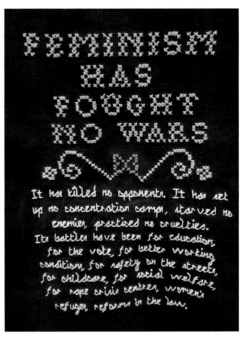

(ABOVE) Rosa Martyn, Craftivism collective work with a quote from Dale Spender, 2010, embroidery floss on a military jacket, 8 × 6 in (20.32 × 15.24 cm). Photo: Rosa Martyn

(PREVIOUS PAGE) Rosa Martyn, Craftivism collective work with a quote from the character Meldrick Lewis of the television show *Homicide: Life on the Street*, 2010, embroidery thread, cotton, 6 × 5 in (15.24 × 12.7 cm). Part of the Campaign against Conflict, hung in Kingston town center, in the UK. Photo: Rosa Martyn

Hoopla: The Art of Unexpected Embroidery

In the world at large, men are always taken more seriously than women. Non-stitchers believe that, because we're women, we're born with the knowledge of stitch in our ovaries or something ridiculous.

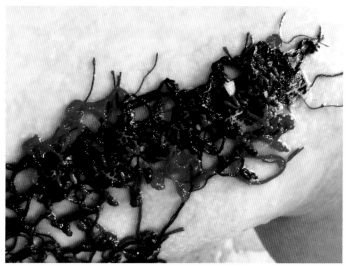

(FACING PAGE) Rosa Martyn, *Trickling Down My Leg*, 2010, from Scarlet Work, embroidery thread, liberty print fabric, 15 × 5 in (38.1 × 12.7 cm) Photo: Rosa Martyn

(TOP) Rosa Martyn, *Don't Tell Dad*, 2010, from Scarlet Work, embroidery thread, liberty print fabric, 15 × 5 in (38.1 × 12.7 cm). Photo: Rosa Martyn

(BOTTOM) Rosa Martyn, *It Means You Are Normal*, 2010, from Scarlet Work, embroidery thread, liberty print fabric, 15 × 5 in (38.1 × 12.7 cm). Photo: Rosa Martyn

VOTE!

IT IS YOUR RIGHT,
YOUR VOICE,
AND YOUR LIFE.

Love from The Craftivist Collective xo

www.craftivistcollective.com

Bad politicians are given power by good people who don't vote.

Love from the Craftivist Collective xo

www.craftivist-collective.com

(TOP) "Patterns brought to you for free, by the craftivist collective. Because we care!" (2010). Photo: Rosa Martyn

(BOTTOM) "Patterns brought to you for free, by the craftivist collective. Because we care!" (2010). Pattern released for public use and protest by the London Craftivist Collective. Photo: Rosa Martyn

the world and backgrounds, and everyone's coming for different reasons. It's just nice to share.

Q: **The idea of making your patterns available to the public is a really beautiful way to pass along your concerns and share them with others.**

A: With cross-stitch, there's so much free software for pattern building, and they're really easy to make. I don't see why anyone charges for them! With little things like that, you might as well just share it. There were a lot of people that probably weren't into it until they found a free pattern and stitched it.

Q: **I'm curious about your obsession with bulls.**

A: Kirstie Macleod, an established artist, asked everybody in my degree program to stitch something from their childhood onto the bodice of a dress that she was to wear during a performance art piece. I was inspired by the book *Ferdinand the Bull*, and I decided I would stitch a pair of bulls charging at one another across the breasts.

I know they're male, but their tiny little hooves support the entire huge weight of their body, and unless they see red, they're completely docile creatures. I just started thinking about them as a very feminine powerful symbol. When I started stitching the bulls, it was during a hard time for me.

When I showed them to Kirstie, she said that she couldn't believe that anybody had stitched them by hand because they were done so well. It raised my confidence, so I decided to use the bulls again every so often, out of gratitude. One day I was down at the RSN studio, where people restore old tapestries, and the head of the studio said, "I just found this, and I knew you liked bulls, so I pulled it out." The piece that she showed me had been stitched in the 1980s for some military reason, and it had just been lying in the box, completely ignored ever since. It was a little black bull that looked exactly like the bulls that I'd stitched. Even the stitching was exactly the same and in the same direction. It was just incredible. I remember bursting into fits of giggles as soon as I saw it.

Q: **Do you believe your social class has any bearing on your attraction to needlework?**

A: I'd say my class does allow for me to do it, because I can afford it. It's an actual possibility for me and it's not just a pipe dream. But I don't think that there's a difference between the genders in wanting to do embroidery. I find this whole "manbroidery" business patronizing. Why do they need a special term because they're men doing embroidery? It's still embroidery.

In the world at large, men are always taken more seriously than women. Non-stitchers believe that, because we're women, we're born with the knowledge of stitch in our ovaries or something ridiculous. I learned the craft just as any man would have to. I've put in just as much effort. People will say, "Wait, he's a man, but he's doing embroidery? He must be doing it for a real reason, as opposed to girls, who just do it 'cause they all love it."

Rosa Martyn poses with one of her stitched activist armbands. Photo: Nicola Jarvis

Q: **What sort of message do you hope that your work sends out to the world?**

A: I hope it empowers women. I want women, young and old, who see it to be relieved of their intrinsic female self-doubt, even if just for a split second. As women, we're constantly being told by advertising and the like that we're just not good enough—and the little rare moments where we do feel good enough, capable, confident, and strong are worth holding on to. It seems like an impossible job, but I'd say it's a cause worth fighting for.

Find Rosa online **mylittlestitches.wordpress.com.**

Bite the Hand That Feeds You

ROSA MARTYN

Inspired by Rosa Martyn's feminine bulls? Try creating one yourself using both cross-stitch and free-hand embroidery techniques.

This project fights against the traditional constraints of gender. A bull, typically a masculine symbol of strength, is used here to represent the hidden strength in females. It fights off the flowers it has been taught to cover itself in. The design is applied to the back of an army jacket, a garment often worn at public protests. This project embodies a fight against the rules the media have given us to live by, a call to arms to cast away those absurd notions, and be whoever you choose to be.

Tools and Materials

FLOSS:

1 skein of DMC #894 (Rose Pink)

1 skein of DMC #892 (Petunia Pink)

1 skein of DMC #746 (Vanilla)

1 skein of DMC #726 (Mimosa Yellow)

1 skein of DMC #741 (Tangerine Orange)

1 skein of DMC #3609 (Light Pink Plum)

1 skein of DMC #3837 (Deep Violet)

1 skein of DMC #907 (Granny Smith Green)

1 skein of DMC #905 (Parrot Green)

1 skein of DMC #310 (Black)

FABRIC:

A medium-weight canvas jacket (the example jacket was purchased from an army supply store)

14 × 7-in (35.56 × 17.78-cm) 14-count Aida cloth

14 × 7-in (35.56 × 17.78-cm) piece of vanishing canvas

embroidery needle, size 10

chenille needle, size 22

14-in (35.56-cm) embroidery hoop

waste thread for basting

white chalk or tailors' pencil

scissors

Skills required:

counted cross-stitch

backstitch

running stitch

Running with the Bulls

Begin by folding the Aida cloth tightly into quarters to make four creases. Lay the cloth on the back of the pressed jacket, right side up. Using a needle and regular sewing thread in a large running stitch, tack the Aida cloth onto the part of the jacket where you wish the design to appear.

Center the jacket and Aida cloth in the embroidery hoop. If you cannot fit the entire design within the hoop, you can shift it later in the process. Begin stitching at a central point of the grid pattern, at the lowest-hanging petal of the daisy on the right-hand side, and at the central point of the Aida cloth where the creases meet.

Cut a length of the DMC #746 (Vanilla) 7–12 in (17.78–30.48 cm), and separate out two strands with which to thread your needle. Make a knot in the tail of the floss.

Cross-stitch through both the jacket and the Aida: begin stitching from the top, so that knot rests on the top of the design. The cross-stitching underneath the jacket will catch the thread and you will be able to cut the knot off when finishing your work.

Continue with the design, cross-stitching the floral-design grid using two strands each of the appropriate colors, as denoted in the pattern legend. When you get to the end of the thread, weave it (with the needle) in and out of the previous stitches on the back of the work. This, along with tying the knots on top, will prevent the wrong side from being too bumpy and uncomfortable to wear.

When the floral design is complete, remove the Aida. (TIP: Wetting the Aida will make removal easier.) Carefully cut the spare Aida around the design, leaving 0.5 in (1.27 cm) around the flowers. Make a few snips amidst the flowers to ease removal. Using tweezers, gently tease out the Aida one thread at a time. Remove vertical threads first, so you can easily pull out the horizontal threads in one swift motion. This will take a long time, but the result of perfect crosses atop a fabric background will be worth it.

On the wrong side of the jacket, draw the outline of the bull design in chalk or tailor's pencil (this outline is represented by the thick black line on the pattern). Draw lightly so that if you make a mistake you can brush it off, and can brush it away easily from the finalized design. If you are using a vanishing pen in a contrasting color, you can be a bit bolder.

Cut a length 7–12 in (17.78–30.48) of DMC #310 (Black) and thread the needle with three strands of the floss. Backstitch along the outline. Begin stitching with a knot at the back of the work, and backstitch around the entire outline.

Once the outline is complete, use the chalk to write a phrase (such as "Bite the Hand That Feeds You") onto the jacket. Use your own placement, color, and handwriting style. Backstitch over the lines using the same method that was used to outline the bull. Finish by securing your floss, clipping any loose threads, and brushing off any remaining chalk or lint from the jacket.

Wear your jacket with pride to places both political and peaceful!

BITE THE HAND
THAT FEEDS YOU.

Figure 10.1. Enlarge 170 percent
to achieve the size of the example
project.

MAKING ART ALL DAY LONG:
An Interview with Penny Nickels

A fourth-generation artist, Penny Nickels lives in Portland, Oregon, with her husband, Johnny Murder. Nick-named the "Bonnie and Clyde of Embroidery," the couple, who are both artists and art critics, work all day—from sun rise until sunset—creating art. Penny's background in print-making translates well into embroidery; she creates highly detailed and visually arresting stitchwork.

Q: **What attracted you to embroidery?**

A: I was trained as a printmaker in intaglio and etching. After college, it's hard to do that kind of work when you don't have access to a studio. I did a lot of relief printmaking and realized that it would translate easily into embroidery. The skill set is similar—it's all implied lines that work well with embroidery. My first pieces were a couple of prints that I had turned into embroidery patterns. Pretty much all of my embroidery work is based in printmaking.

Q: **I can really see how your printing background crosses over to your embroidery work.**

A: When I was researching blackwork, I came across an article that explained that intaglio became prominent during the height of blackwork in the UK. A lot of the early blackwork patterns were taken directly from etchings, which was an art form that worked

(THIS PAGE) Penny Nickels, *You Are Cordially Invited*, 2010, hand embroidery on cotton, 7 × 10 in (17.78 × 25.5 cm). Design is based on The Ossuary by Matthäus Merian. Variations of the original design have been done by too many artists to list here, but arguably the most recognizable versions were by Emmanuel Büchel, Hans Holbein the Younger, Jacques-Antony Chovin, and Hieronymus Hess. Photo: The Hopeso Group

(FACING PAGE) Penny Nickels, *Hypaepa Commemorative Stamp*, 2009, hand embroidery on cotton, 7 × 8 in (17.78 × 20.32 cm). Photo: The Hopeso Group

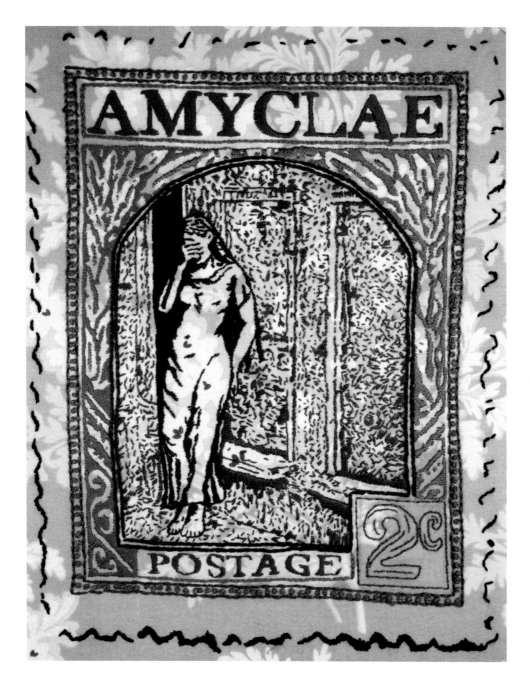

well when produced and printed as patterns. There were stitches that were actually used to create print-making marks. When I discovered this, I thought, "Oh my god, I'm not alone!"

I use a lot of satin stitch and French knots. French knots remind me of mezzotint marks, which use a tool called a rocker to make tiny little dots that fill with ink to create really dark blacks. These stitches are my favorite because they remind me of printmaking marks.

Q: **You work in many art forms. What do you find challenging about embroidery?**

A: It can be extremely time-consuming and exacting work, but I love process art, which is why I also love printmaking and why I hate painting. Painting is too immediate for me. I'm committed to the time that embroidery takes. It doesn't bother me that it sometimes takes a hundred hours to accomplish a piece.

I like to use things that aren't typically found in embroidery in a contemporary sense, such as seeds. Even though you can find these materials in Asian and African embroidery, you don't often see them in the American works. I like that kind of texture and referencing to original work. Sometimes I dye my own fabric and spin my own floss.

I feel that embroidery is really dynamic. My husband John says that it is like working in two-and-a-half dimensions—you are not quite doing three dimensions, it's more like a bas-relief. It gives pieces a lot of movement.

Q: **Can you tell me what motivated your website This Is Handmade?**

A: I started the site because I would get inquiries from buyers wanting huge pieces for only $100. I can look at the pieces of other artists and tell that a project has taken forty to fifty hours, but it's being sold for thirty dollars. I have to care about my body and the toll that my work takes on me. I need to charge a living wage.

(FACING PAGE) Penny Nickels, *Electra in Amyclae Commemorative Stamp*, part of the series *Curl Up With a Good Book, The Ladies of the Oresteia*, 2010, hand embroidery on cotton, 9 × 12 in (22.86 × 30.48 cm). Photo: The Hopeso Group

(THIS PAGE) Penny Nickels, *Clytemnestra and the House of Atreus Commemorative Stamp*, part of the series *Curl Up With a Good Book, The Ladies of the Oresteia*, 2010, hand embroidery on cotton, 9 × 12 in (22.86 × 30.48 cm). Photo: The Hopeso Group

Right now, I'm working on a quilt based on a play by Aeschylus as a reference to bedtime stories. The theme of Orestria is an exploration of the domestic space gone wrong. I liked using the idea of quilt, which is a domestic object that often invites one to read in bed, as the canvas for a series of embroideries on these themes. If you were to create this work as a painting in a gallery, you could probably charge whatever you wanted, but for some reason, the second it becomes "practical," [i.e., a quilt] it is devalued. I've had some interesting exchanges when people ask me to make them things—they throw out these ridiculously low numbers because they don't know the amount of time it takes to make a piece. We live in a throw-away society. You can look at This Is Handmade and see that five minutes, or seven minutes, or eight minutes of working on something accomplishes practically nothing.

Q: **Do you think that some of the lack of perceived monetary value for handmade work has come from the fact that traditionally embroidery is seen as "women's work"?**

A: I think it comes from people's previous experience of handmade goods. Most of the time, handmade items are given as gifts; until fairly recently, they were not purchased. "I have a quilt that my

(FACING PAGE) Penny Nickels, *Iphigenia in Aulis Commemorative Stamp*, 2010, part of a quilted work in progress, *The Ladies of the Oresteia*, hand embroidery on cotton, 9 × 12 in (22.86 × 30.48 cm). Photo: The Hopeso Group

(THIS PAGE) Penny Nickels, *Cassandra in Troy Commemorative Stamp*, part of the series *Curl Up With a Good Book*, *The Ladies of the Oresteia*, 2010, hand embroidery on cotton, 9 × 12 in (22.86 × 30.48 cm). Photo: The Hopeso Group

grandmother made me," or "I have a scarf my mom made me." They don't have any sort of monetary value attached to them—there is no reference for it.

Artists aren't rock stars or sports figures. It is hard enough to pick someone off the street and ask them to name five famous artists, let alone five famous fiber artists. Most people don't have any references—they don't know about it. The tradition of textile art in fine arts is there, but it occupies a tiny space, and it mostly gets viewed through a crafting lens.

Q: **Where do you get your inspiration for your embroidery work?**

A: Most of it is profoundly personal to me. I've always been interested in story-telling and how that has influenced the way that I feel about the world at large. A lot of my work deals with myths that I feel are still valuable today. When you take myths out of the mindset of academia and thousands of years of history, the stories are current. It is interesting to see that these stories are always the same and continually happening.

Q: **You've said that you liked subjects that are morally gray.**

A: I think that as I've gotten older, my sense of ethics and morals are a lot grayer than they were when I was younger. I like these mythical characters because there is something honest about them. Nobody is completely good or bad. Good people are capable of doing terrible things. Most people are kind of mediocre and have some shining moments. I don't see the need to gloss over that and demonize or sanctify them. All the shades of gray make them interesting.

Q: **Is there anything else that you'd like to tell me about embroidery?**

A: I'm always surprised that people who are accomplished stitchers use commercial patterns. There's nothing that you can do in painting, sculpture, or song writing that hasn't been done. If you have an interesting idea, you may be the first person to create it with embroidery. I can't think of another art form where that is a possibility. It's a lot of work, but it is rewarding. It's kind of a magic trick when it is done.

(FACING PAGE) Penny Nickels, *Seed Stitch: Imaginary Swatches Series*, 2009, hand embroidery with hand-spun silk and commercial floss on hand-dyed silk, husks, and seeds, 6.5 in (16.51 cm) in diameter. Photo: The Hopeso Group

Find Penny Nickels online via her website (**donkeywolf.blogspot.com**) or watch her collections of real-time crafting videos at This is Handmade (**thisishandmade.tumblr.com**).

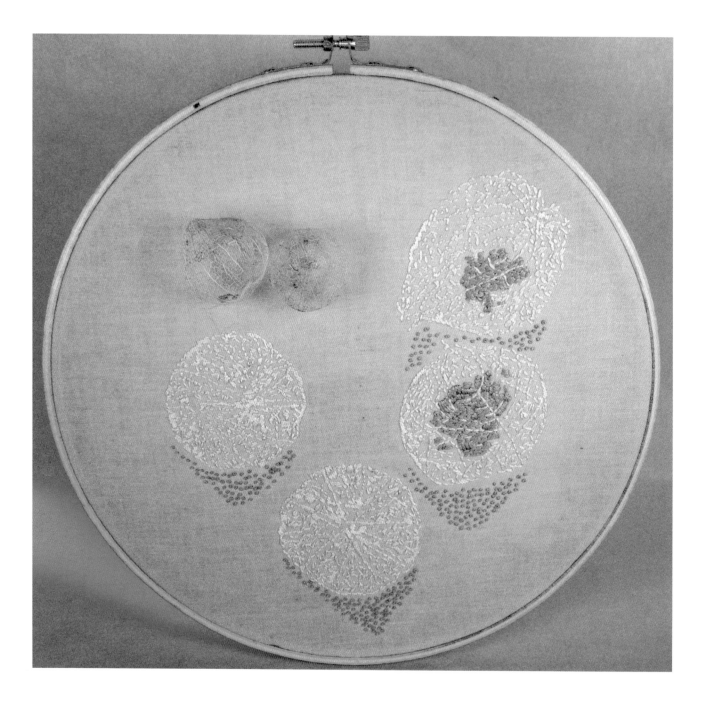

Penny Nickels, *Fetish Triptych: Cronus, Graeae, and Phorcydes*, 2010, hand embroidered on velvet, with seeds, elk canine, and sea urchin, 4 in (10.16 cm) in diameter. Photo: The Hopeso Group

I'm always surprised that people who are accomplished stitchers use commercial patterns. There's nothing that you can do in painting, sculpture, or song writing that hasn't been done. If you have an interesting idea, you may be the first person to create it with embroidery. I can't think of another art form where that is a possibility. It's a lot of work, but it is rewarding. It's kind of a magic trick when it is done.

Index

Embroidery projects listed in **bold** typeface.

Leanne Prain

Crafty since childhood, Leanne Prain has a passion for stitch work, knitting, surface design, and sewing. In 2009, she co-authored the subversive knit graffiti book *Yarn Bombing: The Art of Crochet and Knit Graffiti* with Mandy Moore.

Leanne holds a Master of Publishing degree from Simon Fraser University and a BFA in creative writing and art history from the University of British Columbia. She lives in Vancouver, BC. Leanne can be found online at **leanneprain.com** and on her textile-themed blogs **yarnbombing.com** and **unexpectedembroidery.com**.

Jeff Christenson

Jeff Christenson is a food and object photographer, and can't recall how he got mixed up in the dangerous world of craft. He is based in Vancouver, BC, and has helped to document the work of many of the city's talented crafters.

Jeff was the main contributor of images for *Yarn Bombing: The Art of Crochet and Knit Graffiti*, and his craft photos have been published in news and magazine articles worldwide.